The En.

Frontiers of Narrative

Series Editor
David Herman, Ohio State University

THE
EMERGENCE
OF MIND

Representations of Consciousness
in Narrative Discourse in English

Edited by David Herman

UNIVERSITY OF NEBRASKA PRESS | LINCOLN AND LONDON

All rights reserved
Manufactured in the
United States of America
∞

Publication of this volume was assisted
by the Department of English and the
College of Arts and Sciences at
Ohio State University.

Library of Congress
Cataloging-in-Publication Data
The emergence of mind:
representations of consciousness
in narrative discourse in English /
edited by David Herman.
    p.   cm. — (Frontiers of narrative)
Includes bibliographical
references and index.
ISBN 978-0-8032-1117-9
(pbk.: alk. paper)
1. English literature—
    History and criticism.
2. Consciousness in literature.
I. Herman, David, 1962–
PR149.C665E64 2011
820.9'353—dc22
2010030151

Set in Iowan Old Style
by Kim Essman.
Designed by R. W. Boeche.

Contents

Part IV: Remodeling the Mind in
Modernist and Postmodernist Narrative

Acknowledgments

As noted in the introduction, this volume is the first of its kind: namely, a collection of new essays by specialists in different literary periods who examine trends in the representation of consciousness in English-language narrative discourse from around 700 to the present. Because of the chronological organization of the book, with each chapter focusing on only part of the time span encompassed by the volume as a whole, the project has truly been a team effort, requiring unusually close coordination among the contributors. Indeed, given its collaborative (and cumulative) nature, *The Emergence of Mind* can be viewed less as an edited collection of discrete essays than a book-length study with a single, focal concern coauthored by nine people. I have learned so much from working with the contributors, and I thank them all for their deep learning, patient collegiality, and shared commitment to—and belief in the importance of—this project.

Furthermore, it has been a privilege to work on the volume in the context of the Frontiers of Narrative series, another genuinely collaborative endeavor. I would like to take this opportunity to thank some of the many people (currently or formerly) at the University of Nebraska Press who have made the series and hence the present book possible. My sincere thanks go to Terra Chapek, MJ Devaney, Tish Fobben, Acacia Gentrup, Heather Lundine, Courtney Ochsner, Ladette Randolph, Kristen Elias Rowley, Sara Springsteen, and Rhonda Winchell. I would like to single out Kristen Elias Rowley for her tireless, proactive assistance with series-related matters over the past several years, as well as her all-around professionalism and dedication to making books in the series the best they can possibly be. I am also grateful to the two external reviewers for their invaluable comments and suggestions for revision, and to copy editor Monica Phillips for her careful, productive work on the manuscript.

My work on this volume was supported in part by a research fellowship from the American Council of Learned Societies and a supplemental external fellowship subsidy awarded by the College of the Arts and Humanities at Ohio State University. I am grateful to both institutions for affording me the time needed to complete this study.

Finally, I thank Susan Moss not only for her loving support of all my endeavors, narratological and other, but also for discovering Anna Shipstone's "Blue Lady," used as cover art for the volume.

Introduction

DAVID HERMAN

What This Book Is About,
Who It Is For, and What It Aims to Do

In her foundational 1978 study of strategies for representing consciousness in narrative fiction, *Transparent Minds*, Dorrit Cohn
begins her analysis by underscoring what she takes to be "the
singular power possessed by the novelist: creator of beings whose
inner lives he can reveal at will" (4). As Cohn's study demonstrates, however, the power in question manifests itself through
a multiplicity of methods for evoking fictional minds, which can
of course be as richly various, as strikingly memorable, as minds
encountered outside the domain of fiction. From Chaucer's Par-
doner to Eliot's Edward Casaubon, from Behn's Oroonoko to
Woolf's Clarissa Dalloway: the multifarious perceptions, inferences, memories, attitudes, and emotions of such characters are
in some cases as vividly familiar to us readers as those of the
living, breathing individuals we know from our own day-to-day
experiences in the world at large. Equally diverse are the investigative frameworks that have been developed to study such fictional minds, their operations and qualities, and the narrative
means used to portray them. *The Emergence of Mind* aims to provide new perspectives on the strategies used to represent minds
in stories and to suggest the variety of analytic approaches that
can help illuminate those methods of mind creation. More than
this, the volume is the first of its kind: a collection of new essays by specialists in different literary periods who, using a range
of research tools, examine trends in the representation of consciousness in English-language narrative discourse from 700 to
the present.[1] Taken together, these nine essays thus trace commonalities and contrasts in the presentation of consciousness
over virtually the entire time span during which narrative dis-

course in English has been written and read. In doing so, the book's chapters collectively outline new directions for studying fictional minds—not only across different epochs of English-language narrative, but also (by extension) vis-à-vis the world's many narrative traditions.

The volume seeks to promote genuine dialogue among scholars of narrative, on the one hand, and researchers in the many disciplines concerned with the nature and functioning of the mind, on the other hand, while also benefiting specialists and students working within various subfields (or historical periods) of English-language literature. Target audiences thus include not just narratologists, philosophers of mind, linguists, psychologists, and anthropologists, but also researchers concerned with different literary periods who share an interest in the power of narrative to figure the mind in all its complexity, as it perceives, assesses, remembers, and imagines situations and events. Each contributor uses several case studies from his or her focal period to examine techniques for presenting fictional consciousnesses; in addition to novels, these case studies encompass verse narratives (Lockett, Fludernik, Hart, Bradburn, and Vallins), romance tales in prose (Hart and Zunshine), allegory (Bradburn), hagiography (Fludernik), children's narrative (Zunshine), and hypothetical narrative vignettes used in the service of philosophical treatises (Zunshine). Yet the volume delimits its focal object more narrowly than this initial characterization would suggest, because all the chapters discuss narratives that originated from what are now Great Britain and Ireland. By focusing on methods of mind portrayal as they evolved in a geographically localized area of narrative practice, the contributors can point to critical junctures in the history of consciousness representation within a particular narrative tradition—while also suggesting how other developmental trajectories might be traced in other such traditions.

Thus, in addition to the variety of the methods used to explore representations of fictional minds, the historical or diachronic focus of the volume makes it relevant for several (overlapping) fields of study. Literary historians and theorists of the novel, for example, can use the volume as a kind of source book, given that each chapter features detailed case studies in discussing techniques for mind presentation that were more or less dominant in a given period. Further, the chapters cumulatively provide a basis for investigating the dividing line between "narrative universals" (Hogan 2005)—in this instance, constraints on consciousness representation built into narrative as a discourse genre—and variable, period-specific techniques for representing minds. At the same time, the volume's diachronic profile will make the book useful for historians of the English language and specialists in such fields as historical pragmatics (Jucker 2008), and also for cultural and intellectual historians who use developments in the literary domain as a window onto changes and innovations in the wider sociocultural context.[2]

In the realm of narrative studies, fictional minds and the strategies used to present them have become a prominent concern, thanks to a number of convergent research initiatives.[3] Relevant work includes not only Cohn's (1978) groundbreaking analysis, which attempts to map categories of speech presentation on to the representation of characters' mental processes, but also other pioneering studies of the linguistic texture of speech and thought representation, conducted by scholars such as Brian McHale (1978), F. K. Stanzel (1984 [1979]), Geoffrey Leech and Michael Short (2007 [1981], 255–81), Ann Banfield (1982), Michael Toolan (2001 [1988], 116–42), and Monika Fludernik (1993, 1996, 2003).[4] Another important strand of work focuses on the thought-worlds or "subworlds" of fictional characters, as analyzed by Marie-Laure Ryan (1991) and Paul Werth (1999), among others. At issue are the embedded worlds in which, in the context of a larger storyworld evoked by a fictional narrative as a whole, characters make plans, deliberate among possible choices, and imagine wished-for states of affairs. Still more recently, scholars of story have begun to draw explicitly on ideas from psychology, philosophy, linguistics, and other fields clustered under the umbrella discipline of the cognitive sciences to explore aspects of fictional minds. Pertinent here is Alan Palmer's (2004) rethinking of Cohn's "speech-category approach" via research on what Palmer terms the social mind in action. Pertinent, too, are some of the contributions assembled in Herman (2003a); Patrick Colm Hogan's (2003, 2005) reanalysis of the surface structure of fictional plots in terms of deep structures of emotion; George Butte's (2004) use of Merleau-Ponty's ideas to examine moments of "deep intersubjectivity," or characters' multilayered attributions of mental states to one another; Lisa Zunshine's (2006) discussion of similar phenomena from perspectives afforded by work in cognitive and evolutionary psychology rather than phenomenology; and several of the evolutionary-psychological and other studies included in Abbott (2001).[5]

Yet with some exceptions (e.g., Cohn 1978; Fludernik 1996; Palmer 2004, 240–44; Stanzel 1984 [1979]), rather than studying the evolution of the system of mind-revealing techniques over time most of the existing work on consciousness representation aims to give a snapshot of the possibilities for representing minds in narrative at a given moment in the history of the system's development. Thus, while building on previous scholarship in this area, the present volume seeks to extend the earlier studies by developing an approach grounded in the historicity of narrative forms and the mutability of their representational functions. Collectively, the chapters of this book throw new light on the history of the interface between narrative and mind over the past thirteen centuries; they do so by using case studies to examine changes in the way English-language narrative discourse has cued readers to build storyworlds that are more or less densely populated with fictional minds.[6]

Getting Down to Details:
How Storyworlds Are Populated with Minds

To get an initial sense of the variety of discourse strategies that can be used to evoke fictional minds in narrative texts, consider this short passage from chapter 2 of George Eliot's 1872 novel, *Middlemarch*, where Dorothea Brooke's sister, Celia, negatively evaluates her sister's expressed (and, as it turns out, ill-fated) preference for Edward Casaubon over Sir James Chettam as a potential spouse:

[1] *Celia thought privately, "Dorothea quite despises Sir James Chettam; I believe she would not accept him." [2] Celia felt that this was a pity. [3] She had never been deceived as to the object of the baronet's [Sir James Chettam's] interest. [4] Sometimes, indeed, she had reflected that Dodo would perhaps not make a husband happy who had not her way of looking at things; and stifled in the depths of her heart was the feeling that her sister was too religious for family comfort. [5] Notions and scruples were like spilt needles, making one afraid of treading, or sitting down, or even eating.* (Eliot 1910 [1872], 25)

How does one go about parsing these five sentences so as to make sense of Celia's mind—to construe her take on and responses to situations and events in the storyworld that she inhabits, along with the other characters who populate that fictional world? Or, to put the matter another way, how do readers use discourse cues of the sort provided by Eliot to build storyworlds that contain more or less richly detailed—and appreciably distinctive—fictional minds?

For her part, Cohn (1978) influentially drew on theories of speech representation as the basis for her account of how readers interpret minds like Celia Brooke's. Just as narratives can use direct discourse, indirect discourse, and free indirect discourse to present the utterances of characters, fictional texts can use what Cohn calls quoted monologue, psychonarration, and narrated monologue to represent the processes and states of characters' minds. Subsequent theorists, seeking to underscore even more clearly the assumed analogy between modes of speech and thought representation, and thereby consolidating what Palmer (2004) terms the speech-category approach to fictional minds, have renamed Cohn's three modes as direct thought, indirect thought, and free indirect thought, respectively. Thus, in the passage from *Middlemarch*, sentence 1 exemplifies direct thought (by analogy with direct speech, as in *Celia said, "Dorothea quite despises Sir James Chettam"*); sentences 2 and 3 are examples of indirect thought (by analogy with indirect speech: *Celia said that this was a pity*); and sentence 5 arguably exemplifies free indirect thought (by analogy with free indirect speech: *Celia said that her sister was too religious for family comfort. Notions and scruples were like spilt needles).* In sentence 5, although Eliot continues to use past-tense verbs, these can be read as "backshifted" from the present tense that would have been used in a direct thought quotation (along the lines of *Celia thought, "notions and scruples are like spilt needles"*). At the same time, the evaluative appraisal expressed through the simile, as well as the use of terms like "notions" and "scruples" rather than "convictions" or "beliefs" for the tenor of that comparison, can be assumed to reflect Celia's own tacit construal of the situation. Granted, the impersonal pronoun "one" makes the sentence read like a general maxim or gnomic sentiment; but given the larger context, that sentiment, rather than floating free from the particulars of this fictional world, can be anchored in Celia's vantage point on events.[7] Meanwhile, sentence 4 can be viewed as a hybrid construction, combining aspects of indirect and free indirect thought. Although the sentence is largely a third-person report of Celia's act of reflection and of the contents or result of that act, in the first clause the use of the nickname or term of endearment "Dodo" (for Dorothea) colors the report with Celia's subjectivity. Then, in the second clause of sentence 4, the mention of a feeling stifled in the depths of Celia's heart returns the sentence to the mode of indirect thought, or perhaps the mode that Leech and Short (2007 [1981]) call "narrative report of thought act," which in comparison with indirect thought is less closely tied to or indicative of a particular subjectivity or quality of mind.[8]

As should already be evident, Cohn's study and work related to or taking inspiration from it afford a powerful investigative lens for studying representations of consciousness in narrative. This research suggests how even a single passage from just one text can present readers with multiple species of discourse cues, each prompting interpreters to draw, with more or less latitude, particular sorts of inferences about fictional minds. In the years since Cohn developed her pioneering approach, however, commentators concerned with the representation of consciousness in stories have factored in other kinds of discourse cues and other contexts for interpreting them, with some of those theorists also proposing, more broadly, new ways to frame the study of fictional minds. The chapters of this volume reflect some of the major innovations in the field, and to provide further context for the project I turn now to an overview of two main areas of interest within this domain of inquiry—areas concerned with distinct but interrelated questions. For the first area, the key question is: what is the best way to study the structure of fictional minds and to characterize their functioning? For example, if analysts seek to go beyond the speech-category approach set out by Cohn and others, what tools should they use to describe and explain mind-evoking features of a passage like the one taken from *Middlemarch*? For the second area of interest, the key question is: what trend lines can be discerned in the development of narrative strategies for representing the states and activities of fictional consciousnesses? For instance, how do Eliot's methods of presenting minds compare with the methods used in earlier and later texts, and what broader patterns in the history of consciousness representation do those commonalities and contrasts reveal?

The Structure of Fictional Minds

As indicated at the outset, Cohn (1978) characterizes narrative fiction as sui generis because of its power to reveal the contents of minds. Here Cohn builds on Käte Hamburger's *The Logic of Literature* (1957), which likewise argued that "the representation of characters' inner lives is simultaneously the touchstone that sets fiction apart from reality and builds the semblance (*Schein*) of another, non-real reality" (Cohn 1978, 7). Hamburger, as Cohn also discusses in her later (1999) attempt to identify "signposts of fictionality" (formal features that set fictional narratives apart from nonfictional ones), held that certain language patterns are unique to fiction, such as verbs of consciousness in third-person contexts, interior monologues, and temporal and spatial adverbs referring to the characters' here and now, and on that basis suggested that "narrative fiction is the only literary genre, as well as the only kind of narrative, in which the unspoken thoughts, feelings, perceptions of a person other than the speaker can be portrayed" (Cohn 1978, 7–8; see also Banfield 1982, 65–108, 141–

80; Gorman 2005, 166–67). Or in Hamburger's own words: "epic fiction [i.e., third-person or heterodiegetic fictional narration] is the sole instance where third-person figures can be spoken of not, or not only[,] as objects, but also as subjects, where the subjectivity of a third-person figure *qua* that of a third-person can be portrayed" (1993 [1957], 122).

Yet recent developments in the philosophy of mind, cognitive and evolutionary psychology, and related fields call into question the claim that readers' experiences of fictional minds are different in kind from their experiences of the minds they encounter outside the domain of narrative fiction—a claim that I will refer to in what follows as the "Exceptionality Thesis." Of particular importance here is work on the competencies and practices bound up with what has come to be called folk psychology, or people's everyday understanding of how thinking works, the rough-and-ready heuristics to which they resort in thinking about thinking itself. We use these heuristics to impute motives or goals to others, to evaluate the bases of our own conduct, and to make predictions about future reactions to events. In short, folk-psychological rules of thumb are what people use to characterize their own and others' reasons for acting in the ways that they do.[9] Although the nature and origins of humans' folk-psychological practices are matters of lively dispute, that dispute itself provides grounds for questioning the Exceptionality Thesis—that is, the purportedly unique capacity of fictional narratives to represent the "I-originarity" of another as a subject, in Hamburger's parlance. Drawing on this recent work in the sciences of mind, I question the supposed Exceptionality of fictional minds by highlighting the Cartesian dualism that underlies arguments such as Cohn's and Hamburger's—and also later scholarship building on their arguments.

Dualism of the Cartesian kind informs two related assumptions underpinning the arguments at issue: first, that because the mind is "inside" and the world "outside," in contexts of everyday interaction others' minds remain sealed off from me in a separate, interior domain; and second, that this sealed-off-ness of actual minds means that it is only in fictional contexts that I can gain direct access to the subjectivity of another. As I discuss in my chapter in this volume, however, a variety of post-Cartesian frameworks for research, moving away from older geographies of the mental as an interior, immaterial domain, suggest the extent to which minds are inextricably embedded in contexts for action and interaction, and arise from the interplay between intelligent agents and the broader social and material environments that they must negotiate. In turn, if minds are not closed-off, inner spaces but rather lodged in and partly constituted by the social and material structures that scaffold people's encounters with the world, then access to the I-originarity of another is no longer uniquely enabled by engagement with fictional narratives. A binarized model that makes fictional minds external and accessible and actual minds internal and hidden gives way to a scalar or gradualist model, according to which minds of all sorts can be more or less directly encountered or experienced—depending on the circumstances.

Let me clarify here that my quarrel is not with the claim developed by Hamburger and then Cohn that certain language patterns, or collocations of discourse features, are unique to or distinctive of narrative fiction.[10] Thus I am not disputing what a reviewer of this volume called "the distinctiveness of literary modes of articulation and representation." What I am disputing, rather, is the further inference, based on this initial claim about fiction-specific techniques, that only fictional narratives can give us direct, "inside" views of characters' minds, and that fictional minds are therefore sui generis, or different in kind from everyday minds. In the subsections that follow, I dispute this further inference by arguing on the one hand that (whatever their distinctive repertoire of representational techniques) fictional narratives do not provide wholly direct or immediate views of others' minds, and on the other hand that experiencing someone else's I-originarity is not limited to the domain of fiction. In a further disagreement with the reviewer whom I just mentioned, I deny that in making these arguments I am surreptitiously changing the subject from matters of technique to matters of theme when it comes to the study of narrative representations of mind. Instead, my focus is on how narratively organized discourse prompts interpreters to populate storyworlds with minds, a process that encompasses both the "what" and the "how" of mind representations.

To be sure, it is a basic convention of fictional discourse that in distanced, third-person narration reports about what is happening in a storyworld are "authenticated" in a way that reports given by characters, including characterized first-person narrators, are not (Doležel 1998, 145–68). Thus, in the passage from *Middlemarch* quoted previously, the structure of the narrative authenticates the narrator's report of what Celia is thinking, but not (or at least not to the same degree) Celia's own inferences about Dorothea's beliefs and attitudes—inferences that remain anchored in a particular character's vantage point on the storyworld. As Doležel (1998) puts it, "a general rule defines the character of the dyadic authentication function [i.e., the way authentication works in narratives that alternate between the discourse of a third-person narrator and the direct speech of fictional individuals]: entities introduced in the discourse of the anonymous third-person narrator are *eo ipso* authenticated as fictional facts, while those introduced in the discourse of fictional persons are not" (148). Nonetheless, it is important to disentangle issues of authentication, in this case the manner in which fictional narratives can stipulate as true a character's mental contents and dispositions, from issues of accessibility, or the strategies that interpreters use to make sense of those stipulated contents and dispositions, not to mention other, non- or less fully authenticated mind-contents. And as I go on to discuss, the procedures used to engage with the minds evoked in fictional narratives necessarily piggyback on those used to interpret minds encountered in other contexts (and vice versa).

At the same time, the post-Cartesian frameworks for inquiry that I also describe in more detail below can be used to resist the dichotomization of fictional and actual minds from another direction. These frameworks suggest how in contexts of everyday interaction another's I-originarity is not locked away inaccessibly in some inner recess of the self, but rather spread out across the elements of a given social encounter and situated within that encounter's spatial environment and temporal flow. From this perspective, it is not the case that third-person fictional narration is unique in providing access to another's subjectivity. Rather, in any communicative encounter, I can experience another's I-originarity by engaging with the propositional content of that person's utterances as well as his or her facial expressions, bodily orientation, gestures, and so forth—and also with the way our encounter is situated within a broader material and social context. As P. F. Strawson (1959) argued some fifty years ago, part of the *meaning* of the concept of person is having a constellation of interlinked mental and material predicates (e.g., "doesn't feel well" and "is lying down with a flushed appearance"); hence the very idea of person entails that mental states and dispositions will be self-ascribable in one's own case and other-ascribable in the case of others.

Thus, to preview the two subsections that follow: from one direction, dichotomous treatments of fictional and actual minds can be questioned via research suggesting that readers' knowledge of fictional minds is mediated by the same kinds of reasoning protocols—namely, reasoning about people's *reasons for acting*—that mediate encounters with everyday minds. In this sense, fictional minds are accessible but not transparent. A second argument, trending in the opposite direction, can also be grounded in recent work in the sciences of mind. Now the claim is that, contrary to the assumptions of Exceptionality, people do in fact experience others' minds, encountering the I-originarity of others in everyday settings as well as fictional narratives. Everyday minds are not transparent, but they are accessible. Though these two arguments follow divergent paths, their force is ultimately the same: they provide a basis for disputing the Exceptionality Thesis, as developed by theorists like Hamburger and Cohn, and extended in more recent work on modes of fictional narration that are taken to be "anti-mimetic," or to challenge real-world understandings of (for example) the nature of consciousness (Mäkelä 2006; Richardson 2006; Alber, Iversen, Nielsen, and Richardson 2010).[11]

Positively, these two arguments against Exceptionality suggest the need not to flatten out historical or stylistic variation in methods for presenting and experiencing fictional minds, or to ignore what the reviewer called "the distinctiveness of literary modes of articulation and representation," but rather to develop a unified picture of mind representations of all sorts, fictional and other. By connecting consciousness representation in narrative with other discourses of mind, a unified picture of this sort can prevent the cordoning off of fictional discourse as an anomalous case, incapable of illuminating the nature of conscious experience more broadly.[12] Again, in working to develop counterarguments to Exceptionality I am not trying to deny the difference between fictional and other kinds of representations; indeed, according to a number of specialists on children's cognitive development, acquiring the ability engage in symbolic, fictionalizing play and to recognize its distinctiveness from nonfictional representations of the world is a crucial growth point in the ontogeny of human intelligence (see, e.g., Boyd 2009, 177–87; Harris 1991; Hobson 2002, 76–78, 110–22; Leslie 1987; Tooby and Cosmides 2001, 14–15). Yet acknowledging (the cognitive benefits of) the ontological divide between fiction and nonfiction is consistent with hypothesizing that the same protocols for engaging with minds cut across this divide. In outlining that hypothesis, my aim is to underscore the importance of bringing to bear on fictional narratives the full battery of tools being developed in mind-oriented research and, conversely, the broad relevance of research on narrative representations of consciousness for disciplines such as psychology and the philosophy of mind, among others.

Two Accounts of Folk Psychology; or, the Mediation of Fictional Minds

As noted by Slors and Macdonald (2008), one of the cornerstones of recent research on folk psychology is Premack and Woodruff's 1978 article "Does the Chimpanzee Have a Theory of Mind?" which characterized attributions of mental states as analogous to the positing of unobservable entities in the construction and refinement of scientific theories.[13] The two accounts of folk psychology that have been dominant within the philosophy of mind and related fields over the past several decades took shape against the backdrop of two presuppositions supporting Premack and Woodruff's argument: namely, (1) that to detect intentionality in others' behavior is to have some knowledge of the other's mind, and (2) that in order to acquire such knowledge one needs to have some sort of theory (Slors and Macdonald 2008, 154). According to one of the dominant accounts, which accepts both presuppositions 1 and 2, folk psychology is a kind of low-level theory; it is based on a set of rules or explanatory principles similar in kind to those associated with scientific theories but targeted specifically at propositional attitudes such as *believing X* and motivational attitudes such as *desiring Y*. This account is standardly called "theory theory," with some variants emphasizing how the theory at issue is an innate endowment, bestowed upon humans in the form of an inherited Theory of Mind module, and others stressing the way children use a trial-and-error procedure to build up and refine a theory of the minds of others—just as scientists (dis)confirm theories about the structure of the world on the basis of observational data. According to the second account, which denies presupposition 2 but at least on some versions accepts presupposition 1 (Slors and Macdonald 2008, 156), folk psychology is a simulative ability—that is, an ability to project oneself imaginatively into scenarios involving others. By running off-line a simulation of what one would do in similar circumstances, one can explain or predict what another has done or will do in the target scenario. This second account of folk-psychological practices and abilities is standardly called "simulation theory."[14]

In turn, to characterize the assumptions and inferences that readers make about the minds of characters in fictional worlds, story analysts have developed both theory- and simulation-based accounts of the mind-reading practices that, according to the first argument for the non-Exceptionality of fictional minds, are required for such narrative engagements. This research, by mapping aspects of theory theory (e.g., Zunshine 2006 and this volume) as well as simulation theory (e.g., Currie 2004, 176–88) on to the heuristics used by interpreters to make sense of characters' actions in storyworlds such as *Middlemarch*, suggests that the same basic folk-psychological competencies and practices cut across the fiction/nonfiction divide (for additional discussion, see Herman 2008, 249–52; Palmer 2004, 143–47). In other words, folk-psychological heuristics, whether described in terms of theory or of simulation, are no less necessary a support for authors, characters, and readers than they are for participants in everyday communicative exchanges.

A theory-based account of the passage from *Middlemarch*, for example, would develop the assumption that narrative understanding requires explaining behaviors via unseen, hypothesized mental states. Eliot's narration could be read as attributing a variety of mental states to Celia, which involve, in turn, further attributions by Celia that are designed to explain Dorothea's overt behaviors.[15] From this perspective, Celia interprets Dorothea's earlier conduct (during her conversation with Sir James Chettam) by hypothesizing that Dorothea despises Chettam; Celia then uses that hypothesized aversion to predict, in turn, that Dorothea would reject any proposal of marriage by Chettam. The passage also prompts readers to attribute to Celia, first, the recognition that Chettam is interested in Dorothea, even though Dorothea herself, who thinks that Chettam favors Celia, is "deceived as to the object of the baronet's interest"; and, second, the belief that Dorothea is too inflexible to accommodate others with perspectives different than her own. At another level, readers' construals of Celia's behavior can be described in terms of attributions of the same general kind, whereby Celia can be assumed to want her sister to thrive in marriage but also believe (fear) that Dorothea holds potential suitors to too strict a standard.

For its part, a simulation-based account of Eliot's text would likewise focus on the relation between interpreting the passage and the problem of knowing other minds (cf. Slors and Macdonald's first presupposition), but would posit a different mechanism to account for how the knowledge of minds comes about (cf. the second presupposition). Specifically, the simulationist would argue that Celia makes sense of Dorothea's reasons for acting by using her own mind to model her sister's conduct and the beliefs and desires that might account for it—just as, at another level, readers rely on comparable simulation routines to make sense of Celia's responses to Dorothea's conduct.[16]

The Second Argument against Exceptionality; or, the Accessibility of Everyday Minds

The theory- and simulation-based accounts thus dispute the Exceptionality Thesis by suggesting that making sense of fictional minds requires readers to use the same sorts of heuristics that they rely on to interpret others' minds in the world at large. Recently, however, analysts have called into question both theory- and simulation-based models of folk psychology, pointing up the need for new approaches to studying the interfaces between narrative and mind. This work brings us to the second argument against the Exceptionality Thesis. The second argument disputes the claim that only narrative fiction affords direct experiences of others' minds and that in all other contexts in interacting with others we must at best "theorize about an unseen belief" or "mind-read" (Gallagher 2005, 212).

Both theory theory and simulation theory are premised on the assumption that another's (and possibly also one's own) mind cannot be directly known or experienced, but rather must be theorized about or modeled via simulation routines. By contrast, philosophers such as Gallagher (2005) and Zahavi (2007) have drawn on the work of phenomenologists like Merleau-Ponty, Gurwitsch, and Scheler, as well as on Wittgenstein and other commentators, to reject the assumption that it is impossible for humans directly to *"experience* other minded creatures" (Zahavi 2007, 30; see also Butte 2004). As Zahavi puts it, "affective and emotional states are not simply qualities of subjective experience, rather they are given *in* expressive phenomena, i.e., they are expressed in bodily gestures and actions, and they thereby become visible to others" (30). Hence, under "normal circumstances, we understand each other well enough through our shared engagement in this common world, and it is only if this pragmatic understanding for some reason breaks down, for instance if the other behaves in an unexpected and puzzling way, that other options kick in and take over, be it inferential reasoning or some kind of simulation" (38). Along similar lines, Hobson (2002), focusing on children's psychological development, argues that "infants perceive and respond to people's bodies [in contrast with objects that are not person-like] in very special ways"; specifically, infants appear to "apprehend feelings *through* the bodily expressions of others" (243). Extrapolating from the developmental process to the more general business of making sense of the minds of others, Hobson draws on Wittgenstein's ideas (see also Strawson 1959) to suggest that "we have a kind of direct route into the minds of others. We do not perceive a smile as an upturned configuration of the mouth and by an intellectual process decide that this configuration means the person is happy" (244).

At the same time, work questioning theory- and simulation-based approaches takes issue with the privileging of third-person over second-person contexts in research on folk psychology, which has led to the assumption that making sense of others' minds is a detached or "spectatorial" affair (cf. Hutto 2008, 1–21).[17] As developmental research going back to Vygotsky (1978) suggests, crucially formative experiences for children are direct, second-person encounters with caregivers (cf. Hobson 2002, 2007)—these encounters being ontogenetically prior to third-person contexts like those often discussed in formal studies of folk psychology. And Gallagher (2005) argues that subsequent deployments of folk-psychological abilities follow suit, contending that "only when second-person pragmatic interactions or our evaluative attempts to understand break down do we resort to the more specialized practices of third-person explanation and prediction" (Gallagher 2005, 213).[18]

Consider the structure of the passage from *Middlemarch* in light of these arguments for the accessibility of everyday minds. Prima facie it appears that Celia's assessment of Dorothea's reasons for acting does involve detached or spectatorial attributions of mental states, as she considers her sister's conduct toward

Sir James Chettam. Recall, however, that Celia is not distanced from but rather closely involved in the situation, insofar as she is party to Chettam's visit with the Brookes and insofar, too, as Dorothea mistakenly thinks that Celia is the object of Chettam's romantic regard. Recall, further, that Celia's assessment derives both from her conversation with Dorothea immediately prior to the scene at issue and also from a much longer history of direct, face-to-face interactions with her sibling. These interactions inform Celia's understanding of Dorothea's attitude toward Chettam specifically, her more general diagnosis of Dorothea's lack of tolerance for divergent perspectives (and its bearing on Dorothea's prospects for marriage), and her analysis of the role of religion in Dorothea's life vis-à-vis her family. In portraying how these characters draw on a variety of contextual and interactional resources to make sense of one another's minds, Eliot's text models methods of folk-psychological reasoning that do not centrally involve theorizing about or simulating invisible, internal mental states. Instead, the emphasis is on how minds are lodged in the structure of social interactions. The passage thus accords with research suggesting that the I-originarity of others is accessible across various types of encounters and that such accessibility therefore cannot serve as a criterion for distinctively fictional minds.

Indeed, Celia's intimate familiarity with Dorothea's life course, and the manner in which she undoubtedly draws on her familiarity with that larger context to assess probable reasons for her sister's actions, points to the plausibility of another way of characterizing the relationship between narrative discourse and folk psychology. This other perspective inverts the approach used by analysts who argue that folk-psychological competencies are needed for people to be able to make sense of stories, and instead suggests that storytelling practices are at the root of folk psychology itself (Bruner 1990; Hutto 2008; Herman 2009b). On this account, Celia is engaged in story-based procedures for action modeling; that is, Celia uses her own evolving sense of Dorothea's life story to construct a model of how the actions Dorothea performs are situated in time and (social) space, and of how they emerge from and impinge upon the larger pattern of actions that constitutes her life course. Accordingly, it is not that folk-psychological abilities support the construction and interpretation of a story of self or other; instead, the construction of the story facilitates reasoning about one's own and others' mental states, in fictional as well as real-world scenarios, by allowing those states to be intermeshed with broader contexts for acting and interacting.

This subsection has provided only a bare sketch of some of the key issues bound up with research on folk psychology and how it bears, in turn, on studies of the structure of fictional minds. But my larger point is that what I have termed the Exceptionality Thesis can be questioned from two directions: on the one hand, by arguing that encounters with fictional minds are mediated by the same heuristics used to interpret everyday minds (call this the Mediation argument); on the other hand, by arguing that everyday minds can be experienced in ways that the Cartesian premises of commentators like Hamburger and Cohn disallow (call this the Accessibility argument). Furthermore, the questioning of the Exceptionality Thesis is in a sense the starting point for all the approaches to fictional minds outlined by the chapters in this volume—approaches that diversify the routes along which both the Mediation and Accessibility arguments can be pursued. In the following subsection, I therefore provide a synopsis of the chapters viewed as contributions to a more general case against Exceptionality. I should stress that the authors themselves do not cast their analyses in these terms. Nonetheless, I believe that linking their chapters to the issues under discussion may help highlight interconnections among the contributors' framing assumptions, interpretive procedures, and conclusions.

A Synopsis of the Chapters

The two chapters in part 1 of the volume, "Representing Minds in Old and Middle English Narrative," provide support for both Mediation and Accessibility. Leslie Lockett's chapter explores how folk models of mind circulating in the broader culture can both inform and be buttressed (or else undercut) by fictional and other narratives. More specifically, Lockett argues that the Old English narratives that she discusses are grounded in a nondualist, corporeal conception of mind. Previous scholars have sought to use conceptual metaphor theory to characterize Old English representations of the mind as metaphoric projections of the source domain of bodily, physical processes into the target domain of mental phenomena. According to these accounts, conceptual metaphors facilitated the interpretation of the nature, causes, and signs of mental distress—for example, by affording a construal scheme based on the mechanisms of heat energy. By contrast, Lockett suggests that Old English narratives were shaped by and in turn helped shape folk understandings of the mind as literally corporeal, or localized in and inextricably interconnected with the body. Such folk models predated and conflicted with "Neoplatonic philosophy and early Christian anthropologies that emphasize the ontological and moral opposition between the fleshly body and the soul." Not only are pre-Christian representations of fictional minds mediated by the corporeal model, then; what is more, those represented minds helped consolidate the model itself and make other minds legible—accessible—via observed bodily processes and behaviors.

Monika Fludernik's chapter on Middle English narratives likewise gives support to both the Mediation and Accessibility arguments. She extends Palmer's (2004) critique of the verbal bias of the speech-category approach, arguing that the heuristics used to make sense of representations of speech in medieval narratives need to be supplemented with other strategies when it comes to interpreting Middle English methods for presenting fictional minds. But at the same time, Fludernik's approach points up how the mind-relevant heuristics straddle the divide between fictional and nonfictional contexts. For example, basic and general folk-psychological abilities are needed to parse fictional presentations of—as well as ordinary encounters with—gestures and bodily movements indicative of emotional disturbance; the same goes for the discourse cues used by medieval writers to prompt inferences about collective or group minds. The folk-psychological abilities activated by such cues are arguably trans-situational, and hence support Mediation while also accounting for the Accessibility of everyday minds.

Meanwhile, in an interesting twist on both arguments against Exceptionality, F. Elizabeth Hart, in the first of the two chapters contained in part 2, "Sixteenth- and Seventeenth-Century Minds," suggests that the spread of literacy had by the 1500s created a new, "reading-based consciousness," leading to new possibilities for immersion in storyworlds such as those evoked by the late sixteenth-century romances Hart discusses. In turn, these unprecedented narrative engagements led to new strategies for representing human interiority; characters now exhibited mental traits and aptitudes that were encountered for the first time (on a large scale) by early modern readers, thanks to the cognition-extending and-enhancing nature of written language itself.[19] On Hart's account, then, engagements with fictional minds, far from being Exceptional, afforded prototypes for emergent forms of mental activity, while the written texts in which those fictional consciousnesses were presented afforded a new form of scaffolding for memory and for thinking—and thus new routes of access to the everyday mind. Bradburn's approach, too, is at odds with the Exceptionality Thesis. Drawing on the cognitive-linguistic work on conceptual metaphors, to which Lockett also alludes, Bradburn's chapter explores how fictional texts from the seventeenth century deploy, at multiple levels, imagery deriving from humans' embodied experience—specifically, imagery allowing the mind to be construed, across any number of discourse environments, as A BODY MOVING IN SPACE. Representations of fictional minds, in other words, are mediated by the same body-anchored and -oriented imagery as representations of minds circulating in other, nonfictional contexts. What is more, by allowing for the sustained elaboration of conceptual metaphors and in-depth exploration of their semantic entailments, fictional narratives like the ones Bradburn discusses extend and strengthen the semiotic web in which our own and other minds can be situated, both within and outside of the domain of fiction.

Part 3 of the volume turns to eighteenth- and nineteenth-century methods for presenting fictional minds. Zunshine draws explicitly on the theory-based approach to folk psychology characterized earlier in this introduction to explore ubiquitous scenes of triangulated mind reading in contexts of benefaction; such scenes, in eighteenth-century narratives as well as other texts, involve constellations of more or less deeply layered attributions of mental states by givers, receivers, and observers. Zunshine's approach is anti-Exceptionalist not only because it uses a general account of folk-psychological competence to investigate fictional representations of characters engaged in efforts to read other minds, but also because it combines this approach with a historicist argument that "the fictional hierarchy of mental complexity involving the giver, the receiver, and the observer was co-implicated in eighteenth-century constructions of class boundaries and social mobility." Fictional minds must be read via the same folk-psychological abilities used to attribute mental states to nonfictional minds; in turn, those abilities both shape and are shaped by sociocultural situations in which they are more or less commonly exercised.

The two chapters devoted to nineteenth-century representations of fictional minds develop other strands of the Mediation argument. David Vallins suggests that in contrast with realist narratives, where characters' physical environments color but do not constitute their subjectivities, in Romantic storyworlds landscapes and the moods they evoke are mutually implicated in one another, such that experiences of the natural world afford an indissoluble nexus of perceptual and affective states. Hence, following up on Lockett's and Bradburn's analyses of the links between metaphor and mind, Vallins points to complex metaphorical equations between landscapes and psychological states, in which the mind is at once tenor and vehicle. Engaging with Romantic minds requires engaging with the landscapes for action and interaction—and vice versa. Nicholas Dames, meanwhile, shows how narrative representations of interiority later in the nineteenth century were influenced by emergent materialist or physiological understandings of the mind-brain. Here the Mediation argument doubles back on an extreme form of the Accessibility argument. Demonstrating how physiological psychology impinged on novelists' strategies for representing fictional minds, Dames's chapter also explores ideas that contributed to the development of behaviorist models in the early twentieth century, in which mental states are evacuated—as merely epiphenomenal, of no explanatory value, vis-à-vis observed conduct.[20]

Part 4 of the volume, finally, focuses on models of the mind in modernist and postmodernist narratives, with my own and Alan Palmer's chapters outlining anti-Exceptionalist approaches to fictional consciousnesses created from 1880 to 1945 and from 1945 to the present, respectively. My chapter disputes accounts of modernism based on the claim that early twentieth-century writers participated in and radicalized an "inward turn," a movement away from the external, material world into an internal, mental domain.[21] Rather, taking issue both with internalist or cognitivist conceptions of the mind and with efforts to align modernist narratives with such internalist models, my chapter explores parallels between early twentieth-century texts and "enactivist" theories of mind premised on tight linkages among action, perception, and cognition. In a way that offers support to both the Mediation and Accessibility arguments, I contend that, like enactivist theories, modernist narratives foreground "action loops" (Clark 1997, 35) that arise from the way intelligent agents are embedded in their surrounding environments. Per Accessibility, minds are lodged in, knowable from, what people do; per Mediation, the quality or character of fictional minds, like that of everyday minds, is a function of how they are understood to be situated in broader contexts of action and interaction. Finally, Palmer's discussion of postmodern fictional minds uses attribution theory—or the study of "how narrators, characters, and readers attribute states of mind to others and to themselves"—to explore instances of "attributional unreliability" in texts marked by ontological playfulness, or a foregrounding of issues related to the making and unmaking of worlds. Rooted in part in theory-based approaches to folk psychology, Palmer's concern with procedures for attributing mental states provides direct support for the Mediation argument. At the same time, his emphasis on the discursive contexts of attribution, or how minds are grounded in certain ways of producing and interpreting discourse, also connects up with the Accessibility argument.

From Synchronic to Diachronic Approaches

In the previous section, I emphasized how the volume features a number of different approaches to the study of fictional minds—though those approaches are arguably linked by shared presuppositions about the structure of such minds and by shared aims when it comes to explicating them. Yet the volume foregrounds another important issue facing theorists who seek to outline new directions in the study of fictional minds. Along with intratextual variation of the kind discussed in my earlier use of Cohn's ideas to analyze the passage from *Middlemarch*, in which different sorts of mind-evoking cues are employed in different parts of the same text, and along with differences in methods of presenting minds that may obtain among different narratives (e.g., different narrative subgenres) produced during the same time period, scholars of story also need to consider changes in methods of mind representation that have occurred over time, across texts written in different epochs. Here the distinction between synchronic and diachronic methods of analysis, originally proposed by Saussure in the context of linguistic study, can be brought to bear. Synchronic approaches, which have predominated in the study of consciousness representation up to now, focus on the range of narrative strategies for representing minds available to writers at a given time; such approaches thereby seek to capture the state of (this aspect of) the narrative system at a specific phase of its emergence. In turn, by characterizing the set of options for mind representation that are available at that phase, the analyst can specify which options were chosen from a broader constellation of possibilities and with what (meaning-generating) effects.[22] But approaches of this sort need to be complemented with diachronic study of the historical development of the system in question. A diachronic perspective focuses on the evolution, or changing distribution, of the strategies for mind representation that are built into narrative viewed as a system for worldmaking. At issue is whether the system has been used differently, at different times, to build storyworlds populated with minds.

Diachronic research, then, allows the methods of mind representation found in a given text to be compared with those used in earlier and later narratives; the focus is now on commonalities and contrasts among narratives from different epochs and any trajectory of change that the narratives might reveal when examined together.[23] Over the longer term, story analysts will need to employ—and ideally combine—many kinds of investigative tools to study patterns of change of this sort. Some of relevant tools are those being developed as part of quantitative, corpus-based research that uses large, often multimillion-word narrative corpora either to test or to generate hypotheses about the structure of stories—including hypotheses about changing distributions of mind-evoking cues in stories written at different times. Also relevant are tools of the kind deployed by contributors to the present volume. Rather than involving calculations of the rates of occurrence of targeted features in large collections of narrative data, these tools have been developed as part of qualitative approaches based on in-depth examinations of case studies. Such approaches and the tools developed under their auspices can help model how communities of readers (as represented by the analyst) typically engage with or experience fictional minds; identify which textual cues bear most saliently on that process of engagement; and thereby create a broader framework for inquiry in which the quantitative methods just mentioned can also be rooted—as a means for testing and refining concepts that grow out of the phenomenology of reading.[24]

Reading the chapters of this volume in sequence will afford a sense of how qualitative approaches grounded in a small cluster of sample narratives can help generate new research questions for studying the development of techniques for representing fictional minds.[25] These research questions can be probed more fully either through further elaboration of the models in which they were formulated or by expanding the corpora under consideration and using quantitative methods to test the robustness of the patterns of constancy and change identified on the basis of qualitative analysis. Hence, taken together, the volume's chapters provide the foundation for an entire program for research, or several such programs, focused on mapping trajectories of change in narrative methods for mind presentation. In order to crystallize just a few of the issues at stake, the passage from *Middlemarch*, which I reproduce here as passage B, can be compared with the following two excerpts. Passage A is from a text published about 125 years before Eliot's: namely, Henry Fielding's 1749 novel *Tom Jones*; passage C is from a narrative published 135 years later: namely, Ian McEwan's 2007 novel *On Chesil Beach*. Taken from chapter 3 of Fielding's narrative, passage A registers the reaction of Deborah Wilkins, Squire Allworthy's servant, to the initial discovery of the foundling (Tom Jones) in the squire's bedroom. Passage C is the final paragraph of McEwan's text. In this part of the novel, set some four decades after the disastrous attempt at sexual intercourse on their wedding night that effectively ended Edward and Florence Mayhew's marriage, Edward reevaluates events associated with that night and his own subsequent response to those events.

Passage A: *[1] It will not be wondered at that a creature who had so strict a regard to decency in her own person, should be shocked at the least deviation from it in another. [2] She therefore no sooner opened the door, and saw her master standing by the bedside in his shirt, with a candle in his hand, than she started back in a most terrible fright, and might perhaps have swooned away, had he not now recollected his being undrest, and put an end to her terrors by desiring her to stay without the door till he had thrown some cloathes over his back, and was become incapable of shocking the pure eyes of Mrs Deborah Wilkins, who, though in the fifty-second year of her age, vowed she had never beheld a man without his coat. [3] Sneerers and prophane wits may perhaps laugh at her first fright; yet my graver reader, when he considers the time of night, the summons from her bed, and the situation in which she found her master, will highly justify and applaud her conduct, unless the prudence which must* be supposed to attend maidens at that period of life at which Mrs Deborah had arrived, should a little lessen his admiration. (Fielding 1861 [1749], 56–57)

Passage B: *[1] Celia thought privately, "Dorothea quite despises Sir James Chettam; I believe she would not accept him." [2] Celia felt that this was a pity. [3] She had never been deceived as to the object of the baronet's [Sir James Chettam's] interest. [4] Sometimes, indeed, she had reflected that Dodo would perhaps not make a husband happy who had not her way of looking at things; and stifled in the depths of her heart was the feeling that her sister was too religious for family comfort. [5] Notions and scruples were like spilt needles, making one afraid of treading, or sitting down, or even eating.* (Eliot 1910 [1872], 25)

Passage C: *[1] When he thought of her, it rather amazed him, that he had let that girl with her violin go. [2] Now, of course, he saw that her self-effacing proposal [Florence's unorthodox but well-meant suggestion that they remain married but that Edward sleep with other women] was quite irrelevant. [3] All she had needed was the certainty of his love, and his reassurance that there was no hurry when a lifetime lay ahead of them. [4] Love and patience—if only he had had them both at once—would surely have seen them through. [5] And then what unborn children might have had their chances, what young girl with a headband might have become his loved familiar? [6] This is how the entire course of a life can be changed—by doing nothing. [7] On Chesil Beach he could have called out to Florence, he could have gone after her. [8] He did not know, or would not have cared to know, that as she ran away from him, certain in her distress that she was about to lose him, she had never loved him more, or more hopelessly, and that the sound of his voice would have been a deliverance, and she would have turned back. [9] Instead, he stood in cold and righteous silence in the summer's dusk, watching her hurry along the shore, the sound of her difficult progress lost to the breaking of small waves, until she was a blurred, receding point against the immense straight road of shingle gleaming in the pallid light.* (McEwan 2007, 202–3)

Compared with passage B's treatment of Celia Brooke, passage A features assessments of Deborah Wilkins's responses that are more detached from her vantage point on and stance toward the unfolding events. As mentioned before, sentence B5 anchors a generalized or gnomic sentiment about religious "notions and scruples" in Celia's own take on Dorothea's attitudes and behaviors. By contrast, in sentence A1 narration of Deborah's response is subordinated to the statement of a general maxim about how people tend to be shocked in direct proportion with the degree to which they hold themselves to a strict regimen of conduct—and, by implication, the degree to which they are anxious about deviating from that regimen themselves. Sentence A2, spanning ten clauses, redescends into the particulars of the situation and the characters' reactions to it. The sentence moves from an event sequence involving Deborah's action (opening the door to Squire Allworthy's bedroom), perception (seeing Allworthy in his nightshirt), and emotional response (starting back in fright), to a report of the Squire's own reaction via a counterfactual statement; this statement highlights what might have happened had Allworthy not recalled his state of undress and requested that Deborah wait outside the door till he could clothe himself more fully. But even here the final three clauses of A2 detach themselves from the characters' vantage points, ironizing Deborah's response by alluding to her "pure eyes," despite her relatively advanced age. Sentence A3 continues this movement away from reporting the specifics of the characters' perceptions, inferences, and emotional reactions. The first part of the sentence contrasts the mocking reactions of "sneerers and prophane wits," who are likely to laugh at Deborah's elaborate show of modesty, with the approving reactions of "graver readers," who are likely to view her conduct as warranted by the circumstances. But the rest of the sentence then appeals to broader social norms regarding "prudence," thereby aligning the evaluative standpoint of the narration more closely with that of the prophane wits than that of the graver readers. More generally, whereas sentence B5 restricts the scope of its assessment of religion and its effects, embedding that evaluation in Celia's attitudinal stance, sentence A3 subordinates the narrated events to broader social frameworks for evaluating them.

But does passage C continue the trajectory that can be discerned in the movement from passage A to passage B? In other words, when the excerpt from McEwan is compared with the passage from Eliot, are storyworld events—and assessments of those events—anchored even more firmly in standpoints situated within the world of the narrative? The first part of the passage does ground the worldmaking process in Edward's vantage point on events. Sentences c_1 and c_2 exemplify what speech-category theorists would call thought report, though the phrase "of course" in c_2 is ambiguous in scope: does it reflect Edward's own sense of how far he has come in his understanding and evaluation of the events involving Florence, or is this assessment relatively detached from Edward's thought-processes, growing out of the narrative report of that mental activity? Sentences c_3–c_5 continue to anchor the narration in Edward's retrospective evaluation of the events of his wedding night, with discourse cues included in c_4 functioning especially overtly as markers of Edward's subjectivity. Relevant here is the use of the counterfactual, "if only" construction, embedded in another, larger counterfactual statement. The "if only" clause underscores the ongoing regret that Edward can be assumed to feel about this unactualized combination of traits (love plus patience). Then the subsequent use of the hedge "surely" affixes a degree of doubt to the supposition that that same combination of traits, if Edward had possessed them both simultaneously when he was married to Florence, would in fact have seen the newlyweds through any difficulties.

But with sentences c_6 and c_7 the excerpt's center of gravity begins to shift. True, the generalized diagnosis, in c_6, that an entire life course can be changed by inaction, is followed in c_7 by further counterfactual statements of what Edward himself might have done on Chesil Beach that night so long ago. Yet sentence c_8 detaches itself from Edward's vantage point, using more counterfactual constructions to report what he did not know (or would not have cared to know) about Florence's own state of mind on that occasion. Here readers learn that the sound of Edward's voice would have been a deliverance to Florence, and that she would indeed have turned back had he called out to her. Finally, in sentence c9 the first part of the report provides an externalized evaluation of Edward's "cold and righteous silence"; arguably this assessment issues neither from Florence's standpoint on their wedding night nor from Edward's retrospective standpoint four decades later. As the sentence proceeds, however, the narration is again tied to Edward's mental activity, specifically to his past visual and auditory perceptions when Florence walked away, on her route back to the hotel and then out of Edward's life altogether.

Overall, then, no direct, linear trajectory of change describes the variation in methods of mind presentation used in passages A, B, and C. Excerpts A and C both deploy modes of narration in which generalized reports or assessments become detached from characters' vantage points on the storyworld, meaning that the degree to which the narratives are perspectively grounded does not, in these three excerpts, increase steadily over time. And a different pattern characterizes the changes in the *amplitude* of variation within each passage. To synopsize: passage A reveals considerable variation in the degree to which parts of the narration are grounded in characters' perceptions and evaluations; passage B, less variation on this score; and passage C, even wider variation than A when it comes to shifts in the degree to which reports are tied to characters' standpoints.

Clearly, the foregoing comments about trajectories of change are impressionistic, based on three short excerpts taken from a very limited corpus of stories from a comparatively narrow temporal span of narrative discourse in English. Hence the patterns just outlined are of dubious robustness; they may not bear up when subjected to further scrutiny through a wider sampling of mind-representing passages from these three texts or through cross-comparisons between these texts and the many other narratives that can be used as data points—both within the time span at issue and also across a wider range of periods. These brief remarks nonetheless indicate the *kinds* of questions that can be asked, and potentially translated into quantitative, corpus-based procedures of analysis, when one adopts a diachronic perspective on consciousness representation. My discussion also suggests why this book is more than just the sum of its parts. Each of the chapters that follows contributes to the larger, collaborative project of building a corpus of period-typical mind representations and using that corpus to try to understand better what (fictional) minds are and how they have evolved.

Notes

I would like to express my gratitude to Jan Alber and Henrik Skov Nielsen for their astute comments on an earlier draft of this introduction.

1. There is of course an extensive philosophical literature devoted to consciousness as an aspect or dimension of mind, sometimes characterized in terms of mental states that one is aware of or that involve raw sensory feels (see van Gulick 2009 for fuller discussion). This research supports Palmer's (2004) claim that "the mind refers to much more than what is normally thought of as consciousness or thought" (19). Nonetheless, I here use the terms "mind" and "consciousness" more or less interchangeably—for example, in locutions such as "methods for presenting minds" and "techniques of consciousness representation." I alternate between these expressions partly for the sake of variety and partly because previous narrative scholars have used the term "consciousness representation" to refer globally to all aspects of the portrayal of mental experiences in stories.

2. In Jucker's (2008) account, the aim of historical pragmatics is "to understand the patterns of intentional human interaction (as conditioned by society) of earlier periods, the historical [development] of these patterns, and the principles underlying such [development]" (895). Meanwhile, Kern (2004) exemplifies work in intellectual history that extrapolates from written narratives (among other sources) to make claims about broader cultural developments.

3. As this formulation suggests, the scope of this volume encompasses both the structure of the minds evoked in (English-language) narrative discourse from 700 to the present and the techniques or discourse strategies used to evoke those minds. Thus the term "representation," as it is used in the subtitle of the book, refers both to what is being represented (fictional minds) and to how interpreters are cued to reconstruct that "what" (via narrative strategies and techniques). Indeed, whereas a reviewer of an earlier version of this volume drew a sharp line between "mind or consciousness as literary theme" and techniques for evoking minds, and suggested that properly narratological treatments should limit their focus to tech-

niques for consciousness representation, my own working assumption is that the study of mind as theme or narrative topic and the study of strategies used to portray minds are interdependent areas of inquiry. Techniques for consciousness representation are rooted in and shaped by conceptions of what the mind is and how it works, while, conversely, understandings of the mind cannot be studied in isolation from the methods by which they are figured in fictional and other narratives. See Alan Palmer's chapter for a parallel argument: namely, that considering how fictional minds are presented in narratives (at the discourse level) entails considering their structure and contents (at the story level). See also note 8 below.

4. For an especially rich treatment of issues of speech and thought representation from a cross-linguistic and cross-disciplinary perspective, see Tammi and Tommola (2006).

5. For her part, Maria Mäkelä (2006) questions what she views as a "referential bias" both in earlier research on consciousness representation and in later reassessments of the research that adapt ideas from the cognitive sciences. As Mäkelä puts it, "recent cognitive approaches tend to regard fictional and actual minds as being based on precisely the same cognitive schemata" (231). In developing her critique (see also Alber et al. 2010, 119–24), Mäkelä articulates a version of what I term the "Exceptionality Thesis," or the claim that readers' engagements with fictional minds are different in kind than their engagements with minds outside the domain of narrative fiction. In what follows I sketch counterarguments to this thesis.

6. As discussed in F. Elizabeth Hart's contribution to this volume, "storyworlds" can be defined as the worlds evoked by narratives, while, reciprocally, narratives can be defined as blueprints for a specific mode of worldmaking. For an account of narrative as a system for creating, transforming, and aggregating storyworlds, see Herman (2009a, 105–36).

7. Here I follow other commentators (e.g., Fludernik 1993, 227–79; McHale 1978; Toolan 2001 [1988], 130–40) in acknowledging the role of context in decisions about what counts as an instance of free indirect discourse. Furthermore, I should note that in suggesting that free indirect speech, though couched as a narrative report, also contains expressivity markers that point to the speech patterns of a particular character, my comments resonate with the "dual-voice hypothesis" disputed by Banfield (1982, 2005). Arguing that "certain sentences of fiction do not occur in the spoken language and cannot be said to be enunciated by a narrator" (2005, 396; cf. 1982, 183–89), Banfield takes issue with the assumption that narrative fiction is a form of communication. Instead, she subdivides fictional narratives into two kinds of sentences, "both distinct from sentences of discourse [which are in fact

governed by a logic of communication]: sentences of narration *per se* and sentences which represent consciousness" (1982, 143). Drawing on the ideas of Hamburger and the linguist Emile Benveniste, Banfield contends that sentences of third-person narration present events without the mediation of a narrator, their "tenses . . . anchored to no NOW" (164). Sentences of free indirect thought are similarly speakerless, or not governed by the rules of communicative discourse, because for Banfield it is impossible for a speaker's discourse and another's subjectivity or "SELF" to co-occur (1982, 94). Though I will not take up Banfield's arguments in detail in what follows, I do see them as harmonizing with the Exceptionality Thesis regarding fictional minds—a thesis against which this volume I think militates.

8. For further discussion of the geography of mind at work in this tradition of research—that is, the assumption that modes of thought representation can be arranged along a scale corresponding to degrees of distance from the interior domain of the mind—see my chapter in this volume. Note, too, that this scalar model exemplifies the entanglement of the "what" and "how" aspects of mind representation, as described earlier. The scale at issue, like the claim that particular narrative techniques occupy increments upon it, is interlinked with a conception of the mind as situated on the proximal end of an axis that stretches between the realm of individual consciousness or subjectivity "in here" and the realm of the larger social and material world "out there."

9. Daniel Dennett characterizes such folk-psychological rules of thumb in the following way: "very roughly, folk psychology has it that *beliefs* are information-bearing states of people that arise from perceptions and that, together with appropriately related *desires*, lead to intelligent *action*" (1987, 46). In my discussion the term "folk psychology" is meant to refer in a generic way to the heuristics used to make sense of the conduct of self and other. By contrast, the term "theory of mind" effectively predecides the nature of the heuristics at issue by suggesting that they have the same structure as (scientific) theories. But as Jens Brockmeier pointed out in a personal communication, the term "folk psychology" carries potentially problematic connotations of its own. Specifically, it may be used to draw an invidious distinction between a properly scientific psychology, on the one hand, and everyday understandings of how actions relate to reasons for acting, on the other hand (see, e.g., Stich 1983). In contrast with pejorative usages of this sort, I construe the concepts, classifications, and reasoning procedures bound up with folk psychology as comparable to those at work in a broad range of folk-taxonomic systems, ethnobotanical, ethnolinguistic, and other (cf. Herman 2007). Like these other systems, ethnopsychology,

as it might be called, comprises methods for interpreting minds that need to be studied in parallel with—rather than viewed as a deficient precursor to—the methods of interpretation that have been developed in scientific or academic psychology (see also Sorrell 1991, 147–48).

10. Nor am I suggesting that interpreters of fictional narratives adopt the same stance toward the situations portrayed in those texts that they adopt toward situations in narratives that make a claim to fact. Rather, as analysts such as Doležel (1998), Cohn (1999), Pavel (1986), and Ryan (1991) have argued, interpreters orient differently to stories that evoke what is taken to be a (falsifiable) version of our more or less shared, public world than they do to fictional narratives, which evoke what Doležel (1998) terms "sovereign" worlds. In connection with the autonomous, stand-alone worlds of fiction, it simply does not make sense to try to confirm or falsify reports about what goes on, in the way that a prosecuting attorney seeks to corroborate via the testimony of multiple witnesses a version of what happened during the commission of a crime. Hence it would be a category mistake to attempt to characterize as true or false the events surrounding Dorothea Brooke's marriage with Edward Casaubon in *Middlemarch*; any additional retellings of these events would, rather than provide corroborating or disconfirmatory evidence vis-à-vis what happens in Eliot's narrative, instead create new fictional worlds. However, acknowledging the ontological autonomy or nonfalsifiability of storyworlds like Eliot's does not provide warrant for the further claim that only fictional narratives afford access to the I-originarity of another. Granted, fictional narratives have the power to stipulate as true reports about characters' mind-contents. But the onus is on Exceptionalists to demonstrate that readers have to use different interpretive protocols to make sense of such stipulated mental states and dispositions, in comparison with the protocols they use for construing actual minds. Again, then, I stress the need to disentangle questions about the authentication of reports about minds from questions about how to interpret those reports in order to gain access to the minds at issue.

11. Thus, Richardson (2006) argues that "the trajectory of recent literary practice" reveals "extreme narrators and acts of narration [that] have continued to move ever further beyond the established boundaries of realism, humanism, and conventional representation, and these new works pose severe problems for narratological models that are solely based on mimetic works" (138). Earlier, Richardson describes as follows the conventions for representing minds in texts he characterizes as mimetic: "A first person narrator cannot know what is in the minds of others, and a third person narrator may perform this, and a few other such acts, but may not

stray beyond the established conventions of depicting such perceptions: the thought of one character may not be lodged within the mind of another without any intervening plausible explanation" (6–7). I would argue by contrast that, in light of the research on folk psychology that I discuss in this section, the modes of narration that Richardson characterizes as unnatural or "anti-mimetic" converge with present-day understandings of how minds actually work. Especially pertinent in this connection are accounts of the accessibility of others' minds via the embodied, socially situated practices in which they are lodged.

12. Hence the volume seeks to avoid the unidirectional borrowing—that is, the importation of ideas from the cognitive sciences into traditions of narrative study but not vice versa—that Sternberg (2003) rightly characterizes as problematic.

13. As Sodian (2005) puts it, Premack and Woodruff "argued that the ability to attribute mental states to oneself and others requires theoretical knowledge because mental states are unobservable and are inferred, like theoretical terms in the sciences. Because the attribution of mental states improves our predictions and explanations of human behavior, the conceptual system underlying these attributions has the explanatory power of a theory" (95).

14. I am grateful to Dan Hutto for discussions about some of the ideas developed in this paragraph. For more details about the two accounts of folk psychology, see Gallagher (2005), Hutto (2008), Hutto and Ratcliffe (2007), Nichols and Stich (2003), Slors and Macdonald (2008), and Zahavi (2007).

15. For more on the concept of attribution and the way attributions play out in narrative contexts, see Alan Palmer's chapter in this volume.

16. Currie (2004) argues that, although engagement with narrative fiction requires simulation of some kind, and often involves imaginative projections into the situation of characters (species of simulation for which Currie reserves the term "empathy" [179–88]), simulative responses can also sometimes be of a more impersonal sort. In such impersonal simulation, I will, while interpreting a narrative like Eliot's, engage in "belief-like imaginings" or "desire-like imaginings" but without simulating a specific character's mental state. For example, having encountered Casaubon prior to the passage I have excerpted, readers (especially rereaders of the novel) may experience desire-like imaginings that Dorothea not fall under Casaubon's spell—imaginings that extend beyond Celia's desires, for example.

17. Stawarska (2007) characterizes this bias as follows: "received thinking about folk psychology . . . privileges *a third-person approach* towards one's fel-

low beings, *about* whom one needs to theorize or whom one needs to model by means of simulational routines, [to] the exclusion of the *second-person* approach, where the interaction is a direct source of mutual understanding" (79). That same bias is evident in Wimmer and Perner's (1983) classic study of false beliefs. In one version of the study children observe, from a distanced position, others engaging in activities that require a modification of the observer's beliefs about what the observed parties believe.

18. Compare here Bruner's remark: "Only by replacing [a] transactional model of mind with an isolating individualistic one have Anglo-American philosophers been able to make Other Minds seem so opaque and impenetrable" (1990, 33).

19. Hart bases her analysis, in part, on Donald's (1991) account of the development of written language as an especially powerful support system for, and transformer of, cognitive processes and abilities. Along the same lines, Clark (1997) has argued that the use of linguistic and other props as tools for thinking provides grounds for a view of the mind as extended or crisscrossing between intelligent agents and their surrounding environments: "Just as a neural-network controller for moving an arm to a target in space will define its commands to factor in the spring of muscles and the effects of gravity, so the processes of onboard reason may learn to factor in the potential contributions of textual offloading and reorganization, and vocal rehearsal and exchange" (214).

20. See Herman (2010) for further discussion of the place of this extreme form of the Accessibility argument in the broader context of recent research on the mind.

21. Indeed, this understanding of modernism and the Exceptionality Thesis are mutually reinforcing, with the thesis positioning narratives of the period as paradigmatically concerned with otherwise inaccessible psychological depths and the narratives of the period ostensibly foregrounding the experiences of interiority that are taken, by Exceptionalists, to be the hallmark of readerly engagements with fictional minds. See Cohn (1978, 8–9) and, for counterarguments, my chapter in this volume.

22. For an analysis of focalization strategies along these lines, see Herman (2003b, 310–17).

23. As Palmer (2004) puts it, "the diachronic study of fictional minds might . . . suggest some answers to the following two questions: What are the features of the fictional-mind constructions of a particular historical period that are characteristic of that period and different from other periods? What are the similarities in fictional-mind constructions that obtain across

some, most, or all periods?" (240–41). See also Fludernik's (2003) suggestive account of the benefits of the "diachronization of narratology."

24. See Herman (2005) and Salway and Herman (2011) for further discussion of the possibilities and limitations of quantitative methods of this sort,
including both top-down or hypothesis-driven methods, and bottom-up or
data-driven methods. For a corpus-based approach to thought (and speech)
representation specifically, see Semino and Short (2004). For more general
discussion of the qualitative/quantitative distinction itself, see Johnstone
(2000). To paraphrase Johnstone's account, whereas qualitative methods
address questions about how and why data have the particular character
that they do, quantitative methods address questions about how much (the
degree to which) and how often (the frequency with which) those data display a given property or set of properties.

25. The contributors' chapters can be read in tandem with wider-scope accounts of the development of consciousness representation, such as Lodge's
(2002) and Wood's (2008, 139–68). These commentators' bird's-eye perspectives complement the finer-grained, more historically localized analyses presented here.

References

Abbott, H. Porter, ed. 2001. "On the Origins of Fiction: Interdisciplinary
   Perspectives." Special issue, *SubStance* 94/95.
Alber, Jan, Stefan Iversen, Henrik Skov Nielsen, and Brian Richardson. 2010.
   "Unnatural Narratives, Unnatural Narratology: Beyond Mimetic Mod-
   els." *Narrative* 18 (2): 113–36.
Banfield, Ann. 1982. *Unspeakable Sentences: Narration and Representation in the
   Language of Fiction*. Boston: Routledge & Kegan Paul.
———. 2005. "No-narrator Theory." In *Routledge Encyclopedia of Narrative
   Theory*, ed. David Herman, Manfred Jahn, and Marie-Laure Ryan, 396–
   97. London: Routledge.
Boyd, Brian. 2009. *On the Origin of Stories: Evolution, Cognition, and Fiction*.
   Cambridge MA: Harvard University Press.
Bruner, Jerome. 1990. *Acts of Meaning*. Cambridge MA: Harvard University
   Press.
Butte, George. 2004. *I Know that You Know that I Know: Narrating Subjects from
   Moll Flanders to Marnie*. Columbus: Ohio State University Press.
Clark, Andy. 1997. *Being There: Putting Brain, Body, and World Together*. Cam-
   bridge MA: MIT Press.
Cohn, Dorrit. 1978. *Transparent Minds: Narrative Modes for Presenting Conscious-
   ness in Fiction*. Princeton: Princeton University Press.

————. 1999. *The Distinction of Fiction*. Baltimore: Johns Hopkins University Press.

Currie, Gregory. 2004. *Arts and Minds*. Oxford: Oxford University Press.

Dennett, Daniel C. 1987. *The Intentional Stance*. Cambridge MA: MIT Press.

Doležel, Lubomír. 1998. *Heterocosmica: Fiction and Possible Worlds*. Baltimore: Johns Hopkins University Press.

Donald, Merlin. 1991. *Origins of the Modern Mind*. Cambridge MA: Harvard University Press.

Eliot, George. 1910 [1872]. *Middlemarch*. New York: Century.

Fielding, Henry. 1861 [1749]. *Tom Jones*. New York: H. W. Derby.

Fludernik, Monika. 1993. *The Fictions of Language and the Languages of Fiction: The Linguistic Representation of Speech and Consciousness*. London: Routledge.

————. 1996. *Towards a "Natural" Narratology*. London: Routledge.

————. 2003. "The Diachronization of Narratology." *Narrative* 11 (3): 331–48.

Gallagher, Shaun. 2005. *How the Body Shapes the Mind*. Oxford: Oxford University Press.

Gorman, David. 2005. "Fiction, Theories of." In *Routledge Encyclopedia of Narrative Theory*, ed. David Herman, Manfred Jahn, and Marie-Laure Ryan, 163–67. London: Routledge.

Hamburger, Käte. 1993 [1957]. *The Logic of Literature*. 2nd ed. Trans. Marilynn J. Rose. Bloomington: Indiana University Press.

Harris, Paul L. 1991. "The Work of the Imagination." In *Natural Theories of Mind: Evolution, Development, and Simulation of Everyday Mindreading*, ed. Andrew Whiten, 238–304. Oxford: Blackwell.

Herman, David, ed. 2003a. *Narrative Theory and the Cognitive Sciences*. Stanford CA: Center for the Study of Language and Information.

————. 2003b. "Regrounding Narratology: The Study of Narratively Organized Systems for Thinking." In *What Is Narratology? Questions and Answers Regarding the Status of a Theory*, ed. Tom Kindt and Hans-Harald Müller, 303–32. Berlin: de Gruyter.

————. 2005. "Quantitative Methods in Narratology: A Corpus-Based Study of Motion Events in Stories." In *Narratology beyond Literary Criticism*, ed. Jan-Christoph Meister, with Tom Kindt, Wilhelm Schernus, and Malte Stein, 125–49. Berlin: de Gruyter.

————. 2007. "Ethnolinguistic Identity and Social Cognition." *Sign Systems Studies* 35 (1–2): 217–29.

————. 2008. "Narrative Theory and the Intentional Stance." *Partial Answers* 6 (2): 233–60.

————. 2009a. *Basic Elements of Narrative*. Oxford: Wiley-Blackwell.

———. 2009b. "Storied Minds: Narrative Scaffolding for Folk Psychology." In "Narrative and Folk Psychology," special issue, *Journal of Consciousness Studies* 16 (6–8): 40–68.

———. 2010. "Narrative Theory and the Second Cognitive Revolution." In *Introduction to Cognitive Cultural Studies*, ed. Lisa Zunshine, 155–75. Baltimore: Johns Hopkins University Press.

Hobson, Peter. 2002. *The Cradle of Thought*. London: Macmillan.

———. 2007. "We Share, Therefore We Think." In *Folk Psychology Reassessed*, ed. Daniel D. Hutto and Matthew Ratcliffe, 41–61. Dordrecht, The Netherlands: Springer.

Hogan, Patrick Colm. 2003. *The Mind and Its Stories: Narrative Universals and Human Emotion*. Cambridge: Cambridge University Press.

———. 2005. "Narrative Universals." In *Routledge Encyclopedia of Narrative Theory*, ed. David Herman, Manfred Jahn, and Marie-Laure Ryan, 384–85. London: Routledge.

Hutto, Daniel D. 2008. *Folk Psychological Narratives: The Sociocultural Basis of Understanding Reasons*. Cambridge MA: MIT Press.

Hutto, Daniel D., and Matthew Ratcliffe, eds. 2007. *Folk Psychology Reassessed*. Dordrecht, The Netherlands: Springer.

Johnstone, Barbara. 2000. *Qualitative Methods in Sociolinguistics*. Oxford: Oxford University Press.

Jucker, Andreas H. 2008. "Historical Pragmatics." *Language and Linguistics Compass* 2 (5): 894–906.

Kern, Stephen. 2004. *A Cultural History of Causality: Science, Murder Novels, and Systems of Thought*. Princeton: Princeton University Press.

Leech, Geoffrey, and Michael Short. 2007 [1981]. *Style in Fiction: A Linguistic Introduction to English Fictional Prose*. 2nd ed. Harlow: Pearson/Longman.

Leslie, Alan. 1987. "Pretense and Representation: The Origins of the Theory of Mind." *Psychological Review* 94:412–26.

Lodge, David. 2002. "Consciousness and the Novel." In *Consciousness and the Novel: Connected Essays*, 1–91. Cambridge MA: Harvard University Press.

Mäkelä, Maria. 2006. "Possible Minds: Constructing—and Reading—Another Consciousness as Fiction." In *Free Indirect Discourse: Literature, Translation, Narratology*, ed. Pekka Tammi and Hannu Tommola, 231–60. Tampere, Finland: Tampere University Press.

McEwan, Ian. 2007. *On Chesil Beach*. New York: Anchor.

McHale, Brian. 1978. "Free Indirect Discourse: A Survey of Recent Accounts." *Poetics and Theory of Literature* 3 (2): 249–87.

Nicols, Shaun, and Stephen P. Stich. 2003. *Mindreading: An Integrated Account of Pretence, Self-Awareness and Understanding of Other Minds*. Oxford: Oxford University Press.

Palmer, Alan. 2004. *Fictional Minds*. Lincoln: University of Nebraska Press.

Pavel, Thomas. 1986. *Fictional Worlds*. Cambridge MA: Harvard University Press.

Premack, David, and Guy Woodruff. 1978. "Does the Chimpanzee Have a Theory of Mind?" *Behavioral and Brain Sciences* 1:515–26.

Richardson, Brian. 2006. *Unnatural Voices: Extreme Narration in Modern and Contemporary Fiction*. Columbus: Ohio State University Press.

Ryan, Marie-Laure. 1991. *Possible Worlds, Artificial Intelligence, and Narrative Theory*. Bloomington: Indiana University.

Salway, Andrew, and David Herman. 2011. "Digitized Corpora as Theory-Building Resource: New Methods for Narrative Inquiry." In *New Narratives: Stories and Storytelling in the Digital Age*, ed. Ruth Page and Bronwen Thomas. Forthcoming.

Semino, Elena, and Michael Short. 2004. *Corpus Stylistics: Speech, Writing and Thought Presentation in a Corpus of English Narratives*. London: Routledge.

Slors, Marc, and Cynthia Macdonald. 2008. "Rethinking Folk-Psychology: Alternatives to Theories of Mind." *Philosophical Explorations* 11 (3): 153–61.

Sodian, Beate. 2005. "Theory of Mind: The Case for Conceptual Development." In *Young Children's Cognitive Development*, ed. Wolfgang Schneider, Ruth Schumann-Hengsteler, and Beate Sodian, 95–129. Mahwah NJ: Erlbaum.

Sorrell, Tom. 1991. *Scientism: Philosophy and the Infatuation with Science*. London: Routledge.

Stanzel, F. K. 1984 [1979]. *A Theory of Narrative*. Trans. Charlotte Goedsche. Cambridge: Cambridge University Press.

Stawarska, Beata. 2007. "Persons, Pronouns, and Perspectives." In *Folk Psychology Re-assessed*, ed. Daniel D. Hutto and Matthew Ratcliffe, 79–99. Dordrecht, The Netherlands: Springer.

Sternberg, Meir. 2003. "Universals of Narrative and Their Cognitivist Fortunes (I)." *Poetics Today* 24:297–395.

Stich, Stephen. 1983. *From Folk Psychology to Cognitive Science*. Cambridge MA: MIT Press.

Strawson, P. F. 1959. *Individuals: An Essay in Descriptive Metaphysics*. London: Methuen.

Tammi, Pekka, and Hannu Tommola, eds. 2006. *Free Indirect Discourse: Literature, Translation, Narratology*. Tampere, Finland: Tampere University Press.

Tooby, John, and Leda Cosmides. 2001. "Does Beauty Build Adapted Minds? Toward an Evolutionary Theory of Aesthetics, Fiction and the Arts." In "On the Origins of Fiction: Interdisciplinary Perspectives," special issue, *SubStance* 94/95:6–27.

Toolan, Michael. 2001 [1988]. *Narrative: A Critical Linguistic Introduction*. 2nd ed. London: Routledge.

van Gulick, Robert. 2009. "Consciousness." In *Stanford Encyclopedia of Philosophy*, ed. Edward N. Zalta. Spring ed. http://plato.stanford.edu/archives/spr2009/entries/consciousness/.

Vygotsky, Lev S. 1978. *Mind in Society: The Development of Higher Psychological Processes*. Ed. Michael Cole, Vera John-Steiner, Sylvia Scribner, and Ellen Souberman. Cambridge MA: Harvard University Press.

Werth, Paul. 1999. *Text Worlds: Representing Conceptual Space in Discourse*. Ed. Michael Short. London: Longman.

Wimmer, Heinz, and Joseph Perner. 1983. "Beliefs about Beliefs: Representation and Constraining Function of Wrong Beliefs in Young Children's Understanding of Deception." *Cognition* 13:41–68.

Wood, James. 2008. *How Fiction Works*. New York: Farrar, Straus, and Giroux.

Zahavi, Dan. 2007. "Expression and Empathy." In *Folk Psychology Reassessed*, ed. Daniel D. Hutto and Matthew Ratcliffe, 25–40. Dordrecht, The Netherlands: Springer.

Zunshine, Lisa. 2006. *Why We Read Fiction: Theory of Mind and the Novel*. Columbus: Ohio State University Press.

Part I

Representing Minds in
Old and Middle English Narrative

1. 700–1050
Embodiment, Metaphor, and
the Mind in Old English Narrative

LESLIE LOCKETT

Old English narratives habitually represent the mind as a material entity, residing in the chest cavity and subject to thermal and spatial changes that correspond to changing mental states. For example, in the poetic dialogue *Solomon and Saturn*, one of the interlocutors describes what happens to his mind (*hige*) when he is overwhelmed by his studies:

> *Nænig manna wat,*
> *hæleða under hefenum,   hu min hige dreoseð,*
> *bysig æfter bocum;   hwilum me bryne stigeð,*
> *hige heortan neah   hædre wealleð.*

No man, no hero under heaven, knows how my mind fails, occupied with books; sometimes a flame rises up in me, my mind seethes oppressively near my heart. (ASPR 6:33, ll. 59b–62)[1]

Since the late 1990s, most studies of Old English (OE) representations of the mind interpret such passages as manifestations of conceptual metaphors, such as MENTAL DISTRESS IS HEAT ENERGY (see, for example, Low 1998 and Mize 2008). Although the application of conceptual metaphor theory has shed valuable light on OE narratives of mental activity, it is worth pausing to consider whether it is entirely appropriate to use the term "metaphor" in this context. To do so presupposes that the Anglo-Saxons regarded mind and body as discrete domains and that the supposedly abstract mind takes on concrete characteristics solely by virtue of metaphorical mappings from the domain of the human body or of other objects observed in nature. Current

43

metaphor theory, insofar as it interprets all forms of conceptualization as blends of source and target domains, seems to render moot the question of whether a given conceptual system is viewed as literal or metaphorical by those who deploy it in discourse. In this chapter, however, I maintain that it is profitable to distinguish between conceptual systems that have literal versus metaphorical status for members of particular textual communities. OE narrative abounds in depictions of an embodied mind, and I maintain that for the Anglo-Saxon audience, this mind was not only "embodied" in the sense used by metaphor theorists but also literally corporeal; they thought of the mind as the part of the body responsible for thought. Modern audiences misconstrue this model of the mind as a conceptual metaphor because our own habitual mind-body dualism predisposes us to expect that our linguistic forerunners likewise believed the mind was incorporeal and intangible.[2]

In the first part of this chapter I survey typical characterizations of the mind in OE narratives of mental distress. Next, in support of my argument that these texts depict a literally embodied mind, I draw on ideas proposed by Lakoff and Johnson under the rubric of embodied realism, which they define briefly as "the view that the locus of experience, meaning, and thought is the ongoing series of embodied organism-environment interactions that constitute our understanding of the world" (Johnson and Lakoff 2002, 249). Embodied realism, although typically invoked in nonhistorical discussions of the cognitive processes behind metaphor generation, also suggests a mechanism by which a particular model of mind might begin as a literal expression of folk psychology but gradually become metaphorical. Finally, I turn to the discipline of transcultural psychiatry, which aims to remedy the tendency of Western psychiatric practitioners to impose upon non-Western patients illness categories based on their own mind-body dualism. I argue that readers of OE narratives should similarly set aside their preconceptions about the mind-body relationship, including the assumption that Anglo-Saxon narratives of the embodied mind were necessarily metaphorical.

Learned and Folk Definitions of the Mind

Because users of OE had no exact equivalent for our Modern English word "mind," it is useful to begin with a few remarks about what the mind was in the surviving texts of the Anglo-Saxon period. OE texts of all genres use the word *mod* to refer to that part of the human being responsible for all kinds of mental activity—rational, emotional, contemplative, mnemonic, and so forth—and poets also had recourse to the near-synonyms *hyge*, *sefa*, and *ferhð*. However, as Malcolm Godden first demonstrated, the corpus of OE literature preserves two mutually irreconcilable opinions on the relationship of the mind to the other elements of the human being. A few texts by highly learned Anglo-Saxon authors subscribe to the "classical tradition," informed by Neoplatonic philosophy and early Christian anthropologies that emphasize the ontological and moral opposition between the fleshly body and the soul. In this tradition, the *mod* is merely one component of the soul (OE *sawol* or *gast*); this soul serves the multiple functions of enlivening the flesh, carrying out all mental activities including the governance of the body, and participating in the afterlife when the body has died (Godden 1985, 271–85). Straightforward textual evidence for the classical tradition is easily identified, because this tradition characteristically inhabits nonnarrative, explicitly didactic texts whose express purpose is to render a model of the human being that can be considered theologically or scientifically authoritative (Low 1998, 43–44).

In the "vernacular tradition" (Godden 1985), by contrast, the *sawol* has an exceedingly limited role as long as it resides in the living body; its chief function is to represent the individual in the afterlife. In this tradition, all types of thought are carried out by the mind (*mod*, *hyge*, *sefa*, *ferhð*, and related compounds), which is substantially and functionally separate from the soul (Godden 1985, 285–95). If this understanding of the human being can be considered dualistic, it is a dualism that pits the soul against a close-knit partnership of mind and body. "[T]he soul . . . is the helpless victim (or beneficiary) of a separate mental faculty which is associated with the body," says Godden in his analysis of the OE *Soul and Body* poems (1985, 289); his observation holds true for nearly all OE narratives that deal with mind, soul, and body. Because the vernacular tradition tends to inhabit narrative and lyric texts that deal with diverse subjects, this model of the mind-body relationship is not presented as a scientifically or theologically authoritative and systematic concept; rather, individual passages describing the mind-body complex are only as integral and specific as is necessary to explain human behaviors pertinent to the main narrative (Low 1998, 36–37).

Old English Narratives of Intense Mental Activity

While OE texts preserve two distinct perspectives on what the mind *is*, there is one dominant OE characterization of how the mind behaves during episodes of intense mental activity. It resides in the chest cavity or in the organ of the heart, and it endures increased temperature, size, and pressure in conjunction with episodes of intense distress and desire. Both acute and chronic mental states heat the mind, leading in turn to mental boiling and swelling, which presses inward on the heart and outward on the walls of the chest cavity. When distress dissipates, so do the heat and constriction within the chest cavity, such that emotions cool and the heart becomes roomy. This pattern of behaviors attributed to the mind-in-the-breast is often called the hydraulic model of the mind, because the stages of the pattern resemble the behavior of a sealed container of fluid under the influence of heat.[3] From among the hundreds of OE invocations of the hydraulic model, I have selected a few passages to illustrate each stage and the variety of ways in which spatial and thermal changes are mapped onto the mind, the organ of the heart, and the mental states themselves.[4]

Cardiocentrism

Mental activity of all kinds occurs within the container of the breast (*breost* or *hreðer*) or within the organ of the heart (*heorte*). One may perform a mental function in the breast, as when Satan urges Eve, "gehyge on þinum breostum þæt þu inc bam twam meaht / wite bewarigan" (consider in your breast that you both can guard yourselves from punishment) (*Genesis B*, ASPR 1:20, ll. 562–63a). Alternatively, a mental state may impinge directly upon the chest cavity, as when the *Andreas*-narrator says, "Sar eft gewod / ymb þæs beornes breost" (Grief again traveled throughout the man's breast) (*ASPR* 2:36, ll. 1246b–47a), or when the narrator of *The Rhyming Poem* complains, "Nu min hreþer is hreoh, heofsiþum sceoh, / nydbysgum neah" (Now my breast is troubled, fearful in its mournful journeys, close to troubles) (*ASPR* 3:167–68, ll. 43–44a). Mental activity may also belong to the heart and breast by virtue of genitive constructions (*heortan geþoht*) and compound nouns (*breostceare*):

> *A scyle geong mon   wesan geomormod,*
> *heard heortan geþoht,   swylce habban sceal*
> *bliþe gebæro,   eac þon breostceare,*
> *sinsorgna gedreag.*

A young man must always be sorrowful in mind, the thought of his heart must be cruel. Likewise must he have a cheerful countenance as well as anxiety in his breast, a multitude of endless miseries. (*Wife's Lament*, *ASPR* 3:211, ll. 42–45a)

Although the Anglo-Saxons portrayed no consistent relationship among the participants (mind, heart, mental state, self) in such narratives, the localization of all mental activity in the vicinity of the heart is constant. Moreover, this localization was doubtless interpreted literally by the Anglo-Saxon audience, for whom the psychological function of the brain was not common knowledge prior to the eleventh century; we cannot impute to them the modern conventional allocation of rational thought to the head and emotions to the heart.[5]

Cardiocentric Heat

Heating of the mind and heart occurs in conjunction with many intense mental states: anger, aggression, love, licit and illicit desires, anxiety, grief (but compare Gevaert 2005, 10), intellectual frustration, and cognitive impairment. The heart may be heated while the mind experiences distress, as when the eponymous heroine of the poem *Judith* says, "þearle ys me nu ða / heorte on-hæted ond hige geomor" (Now my heart is severely heated and my mind miserable) (*ASPR* 4:101, ll. 86b–87). This utterance conforms to the division of labor that the modern reader expects: the fleshly organ of the heart suffers from the tangible affliction of heat, while the supposedly more abstract mind endures the abstract emotion of being *geomor* (sorrowful). Yet in OE narrative the mind itself can also be hot; the narrator of *Christ II* remarks, "Him wæs geomor sefa / hat æt heortan" (Their mind was miserable, hot near the heart) (*ASPR* 3:17, ll. 499b–500a). Even emotions such as *nið* (hatred) and *gnornsorge* (sorrow) can heat up; thus the narrator of *Guthlac B* reports that once his master dies, Guthlac's disciple "gnornsorge wæg / hate æt heortan" (bore sorrow, hot at his heart) (*ASPR* 3:87, ll. 1335b–36a), and in *Andreas*, it is said of the savage Mermedonians that "man wridode / geond beorna breost, brandhata nið / weoll on gewitte" (malice blossomed throughout the breast of the men; a fiery hot hostility boiled up in their mind) (*ASPR* 2:24, ll. 767b–69a).

Mental Boiling and Swelling

Just as heat causes liquids to boil or seethe and solids to swell, so does mental heat cause the mind and its contents to swell: for instance, in the foregoing lines from *Andreas*, the Mermedonians' hot hatred "boiled up" (*weoll*) in the mind. The intransitive verb *weallan* "to surge, swell, or boil," and the related noun *wylm*, "an upsurge, swelling, or boiling," belong to a family of words that can refer to swelling and boiling observed externally in nature (e.g., of sea water, boiling water, fire) as well as the invisible seething of the mind. The passage from *Andreas* demonstrates that this seething may be predicated of a mental state (such as *nið*); elsewhere in the same poem, seething is predicated of the mind instead: "þær manegum wæs / hat æt heortan hyge weallende" (There many a man's mind was seething, hot at his heart) (*ASPR* 2:50, ll. 1708b–9). In the passage from *Solomon and Saturn* that I quoted at the opening of this chapter, the mind seethes under the influence of an internal flame: "hwilum me bryne stigeð, / hige heortan neah hædre wealleð." Emotional "surges," represented by the noun *wylm* or a related compound, may afflict the heart, as when the *Exodus*-narrator reports that "wæron heaðowylmas heortan getenge, / mihtmod wera" (surges of aggression, the rage of men, were touching their heart) (ASPR 1:95, ll. 148–49a); or the whole chest cavity may seethe under the influence of mental distress, as when Beowulf's "breost innan weoll / þeostrum geþoncum, swa him geþywe ne wæs" (breast seethed inwardly with dark thoughts, which was unusual for him) (Fulk, Bjork, and Niles 2008, 80, ll. 2331b–32). OE authors also commonly signified mental swelling with words related to the intransitive verb *belgan* "to swell (with rage)."[6] Ælfric retells the Old Testament episode in which Naboth refuses to sell his vineyard to King Ahab, which sends the king to bed in a rage: "þa gebealh hine se cynincg and to his bedde eode, wende hine to wage, wodlice gebolgen" (Then the king swelled up [with rage] and went to bed, turned to face the wall, insanely swollen [with rage]) (Skeat 1966 [1881–1900], 1:394). Conversely, according to Vercelli Homily 4, the virtuous man is "ne eaðbilge ne hatheort" (neither easily swollen nor hot-hearted) (Scragg 1992, 96). Less frequently, the verb *seoðan*, whose primary meaning is "to cook in boiling liquid" (usually in culinary and medical contexts), appears in narratives of mental activity, where it suggests a prolonged state of "stewing" in one's own misery. When Hygelac admits to having harbored doubts and anxieties about the undertakings of his nephew Beowulf, for instance, he says, "Ic ðæs modceare / sorhwylmum seað, siðe ne truwode / leofes mannes" (I simmered my worry about him in surges of sorrow; I did not have faith in the journey of the dear man) (Fulk, Bjork, and Niles 2008, 67, ll. 1992b–94a).

Seething and Swelling Lead to Constriction

When the mind and its contents seethe in the breast, they increase the internal pressure of the chest cavity, creating a constricted environment. In the poem known as *Christ II (Ascension)*, the disciples suffer mental constriction after seeing Christ ascend into heaven: "torne bitolden wæs seo treowlufu / hat æt heortan, hreðer innan weoll, / beorn breostsefa" (that faithful love, bitterly oppressed, was hot at the heart; the breast welled inwardly, the mind-in-the-breast burned) (*ASPR* 3:18, ll. 538–40a).[7] Although these lines are devoid of conjunctions and adverbs that would subordinate one of these cardiocentric changes to another, either temporally or causally, it is difficult to avoid interpreting these changes as a natural mechanism like that which one would observe in a kettle set on the stovetop. When the disciples' "faithful love" (here a source of distress as well as desire) brings on mental heat, the mind-in-the-breast is kindled to burning and the container of the breast swells or boils, causing their mental contents to be "constricted."

Most of my illustrations of the hydraulic model thus far have come from verse texts, which may give the misleading impression that the hydraulic model is no more than a poetic trope. This is not the case; hydraulic-model imagery is simply more vivid and concise, and less constrained by the diction of Latin source texts, in OE poems than in prose. One prose text in which the hydraulic model is rendered quite vividly is the anonymous early tenth-century translation of the Latin *Ecclesiastical History of the English People* by Bede (d. 735), who was himself an Anglo-Saxon. This passage narrates the changing mental states of Eadwine, the future king of Northumbria, when he has just been warned that his protector intends to betray him:

[S]æt swiðe unrot on stane beforan þære healle, & ongon mid monegum hætum his geþohta swenced beon: & ne wiste, hwider he eode oðþe hwæt him selest to donne wære. þa he þa longe mid swigendum nearonissum his modes & mid þy blindan fyre soden wæs, þa geseah he semninga on midre niht sumne mon.[8]

Very unhappy, Eadwine sat on a stone in front of the hall, and he began to be oppressed by the manifold heat of his thoughts, and he did not know where he should go or what would be best for him to do. Then when he had for a long time been stewed in the silent constrictions of his mind and by the inward fire, then suddenly in the middle of the night he spied a certain man. (Miller 1959–63 [1890–98], 1:128)

Elements of the hydraulic model are already present in Bede's Latin but are amplified by the OE translator. Bede reports that Eadwine "is troubled by the manifold heat of the thoughts" (*multis . . . cogitationum aestibus affici*), but where Bede says Eadwine is "troubled," the OE translator says he is "burdened" or "oppressed" (*geswenced*). Bede's Latin also mentions Eadwine's "constrictions of mind" and "inward fire" (*mentis angoribus et caeco . . . igni*), but where Bede says that Eadwine "was devoured" (*carperetur*) by these forces, the OE translator writes that Eadwine was *soden*, that is, "cooked" or "stewed" (*soden* is the past participle of the verb *seoðans*, discussed earlier). (For the text of Bede's Latin, see Colgrave and Mynors 1969, 178.)

If the translator of the OE *Bede* has merely fleshed out hydraulic-model imagery found in his Latin source, the translator of the Latin *De consolatione Philosophiae* by Boethius (d. 524) has gone further, inserting a complex hydraulic-model narrative where Boethius has none. In the Latin, Lady Philosophy explains that those who are superficially the most powerful and wealthy suffer from other insidious psychological afflictions:

> *hinc enim libido uersat auidis corda uenenis,*
> *hinc flagellat ira mentem fluctus turbida tollens,*
> *maeror aut captus fatigat aut spes lubrica torquet.*

For here desire overthrows the heart with avaricious poisons; here roiling anger brings on surges that batter the mind, which is worn down by repressed sorrow or tormented by slippery hope. (Bieler 1957, 70, IV m. 2, ll. 6–8)

Despite the mixing of metaphors, this cluster of images lends urgency to what might otherwise be a fairly dry, moralizing observation that immoderate desire leads to further psychological disorder. The OE prose rendering of this passage departs significantly from the original, not only in diction but also in meaning:

Forþam of þam unmette and þam ungemetlican gegerelan, of þam swetmettum and of misclicum dryncum þæs liþes onwæcnað sio wode þrag

*þære wrænnesse and gedrefð hiora mod swiðe swiðlice. þonne weaxað eac
þa ofermetta and ungeþwærnes, and þonne hi weorðað gebolgen þonne
wyrð þæt mod beswungen mid þam welme þære hatheortnesse oððæt hi
weorþað geræpte mid þære unrotnesse and swa gehæfte.*

*Therefore because of extravagance and immoderate dress, because of sweet-
meats and wines of all kinds, there arises an insane moment of wanton-
ness that agitates their mind very powerfully. Then excess and impatience
increase too, and when they [i.e., excess and impatience] grow swollen,
then the mind is battered by the boiling up of hotheartedness, until these
men become constrained by their distress and are thus imprisoned.* (Godden and Irvine 2009, 1:346, ll. 15–21)

The OE translator has omitted the images of poison and slip-
periness and consolidated the remaining images into a coherent mechanism, in which the mind, directly affected by what is
put on and into the body, warms and expands under the influence of psychological distress, culminating in the "constricted"
(*geræpte*) condition of the distressed individuals.

Cardiocentric Cooling and Roominess

When distress and desire dissipate, the cardiocentric environs
of the mind become cool or roomy, reversing the thermal and
spatial changes associated with intense mental activity. For instance, Beowulf offers to cool Hrothgar's anxieties: he promises
to show him how to get rid of the monster,

> gyf him edwenden   æfre scolde
> bealuwa bisigu   bot eft cuman—,
> ond þa cearwylmas   colran wurðaþ.

*if ever a change should come to him later on, a remedy for the trouble of
his injuries, and if his seething cares should become cooler.* (Fulk, Bjork,
and Niles 2008, 12, ll. 280–83)

Beowulf even uses the word *cearwylmas* ("anxiety-surges" or
"seething cares") to underscore that Hrothgar suffers from car-

diocentric heat that Beowulf hopes to assuage by cooling. Likewise, in *Genesis B*, when Satan is bitterly envious of the first human beings, the narrator reports that "weoll him on innan / hyge ymb his heortan" (his [i.e., Satan's] mind swelled inwardly around his heart) (*ASPR* 1:14, ll. 353b–54a). Later, pleased to have caused Adam and Eve's downfall, Satan's messenger says, "Forþon is min mod gehæled, / hyge ymb heortan gerume" (Therefore my mind is healed; my mind is roomy around my heart) (*ASPR* 1:26, ll. 758b–59a). The association of cardiocentric roominess with calmness has not survived in Modern English, but when we set these two passages together as before-and-after snapshots of the devils' mental condition, the meaning of *gerume* becomes clear: the seething and spatial constriction concomitant with their earlier distress have ceased to squeeze the heart. Similarly, when the Old Testament heroine Judith must slay Holofernes, she prays to God for an end to the psychological heat that afflicts her breast, and God grants her relief in the form of mental spaciousness: "þa wearð hyre rume on mode, / haligre hyht geniwod" (Then it became roomier in her mind; hope was renewed in the holy woman) (*ASPR* 4:102, ll. 97b–98a).

The Hydraulic Model and Metaphor Theory

It is easy to see why conceptual metaphor theory has provided the most popular analytical framework for OE narratives of mental activity over the past two decades. For the modern reader who might not otherwise be able to understand what it means for Hrothgar to have "simmered [his] worry in surges of sorrow" or for a devil's mind to be "roomy around [his] heart," it is useful to posit that these are figures of speech that transfer to the concept of mind certain concrete characteristics that facilitate the narration of its behaviors, which would otherwise remain difficult to narrate, being obscured by invisibility and abstraction. Moreover, the simplest explanation for the existence of dozens of cross-cultural and diachronic analogues of the hydraulic model is embodied realism: the theory that interactions between the body and the environment influence the generation of conceptual metaphors.[9] As Lakoff and Johnson explain, this influence operates "on the basis of 'conflations' in our experience—cases where source and target domains are coactive in our experience. For example, verticality and quantity are coactive whenever we pour juice into a glass or pile up objects. This is the experiential grounding for [the conceptual metaphor] MORE IS UP" (2002, 245–46). Likewise, the coactivity of intense mental activity with chest-centered sensations of heat and pressure provides the "experiential grounding" for the hydraulic model. Zoltán Kövecses has focused particularly on the embodied roots of the conceptual metaphors ANGER IS HEAT and THE MIND IS A PRESSURIZED CONTAINER; while accommodating criticisms from those who claim that embodied realism underestimates the role of cultural variability in the generation of metaphors, he still maintains that certain physiological responses to intense mental experiences must be non-culture-bound in order to account for the presence of these metaphors in many unrelated cultures.

The universality of actual physiology might be seen as leading to the similarities (though not equivalence) in conceptualized physiology (i.e., the conceptual metonymies), which might then lead to the similarity (though again not equivalence) in the metaphorical conceptualization of anger and its counterparts. . . . [I]t is not suggested, however, that embodiment actually produces the [ANGER IS HOT FLUID IN A] PRESSURIZED CONTAINER metaphor but that it makes a large number of other possible metaphorical conceptualizations either incompatible or unnatural. (Kövecses 2000, 159–60)

Although there is still debate over the amount of influence exerted by embodied experience and cultural variation on the process of metaphor generation, a moderate version of embodied realism is now accepted as a premise in much current work on metaphorical models of mind.[10]

Embodied Realism and Emergent Metaphoricity

Perhaps because it arose as a corollary to Lakoff and Johnson's theory of conceptual metaphor, embodied realism is usually invoked only in conjunction with theories of metaphor and conceptual blending. A serious consideration of the relationship between embodied realism and *literal* conceptual formation has been discouraged by the cognitive-linguistic turn in metaphor studies, which emphasizes the processes of mapping and blending that dominate the human brain's methods of conceptualization. This ahistorical, process-oriented approach sets aside content- and context-based distinctions among literal, metonymic, and metaphorical language—that is, distinctions that depend upon whether a given community of language users might perceive the semantic content of an utterance to be literally true within the framework of contemporary folk or learned bodies of knowledge (see Fludernik, Freeman, and Freeman 1999, 384–85; Hogan 2003, 91).

Yet literary and intellectual historians cannot ignore these content- and context-based categories, because many of the textual communities that we study *did* maintain a sharp distinction between figurative and truth-bearing utterances. The responsible literary or intellectual historian neither throws out the distinction that his historical subjects might have made between figurative and truth-bearing utterances, nor imposes upon historical subjects his own framework for assessing metaphoricity, but rather aims to interpret his historical subjects' literal and figurative utterances according to a historically appropriate framework. In what follows, I suggest that Lakoff and Johnson's account of embodied realism (whatever its stated purpose or goals) can be recruited for this endeavor.

To begin, consider a spectrum of possible relationships between source and target domains, *as perceived by the historical user* of a given concept. At one end of the spectrum, where source and target domains are perceived to be wholly discrete, we have metaphors (be they conceptual or ornamental), or statements of the type "X is not -X." At the other end of the spectrum, we have statements that are perceived to be literally true, in which source and target domains are not wholly discrete (e.g., "X_1 is an X"). In this case, the mapping of one conceptual domain onto another, as happens in deductive arguments, does not involve metaphoric extension of the domains in question. Metonymies *may* occupy intermediate positions on this spectrum, when source and target domains are not wholly discrete—say, in a statement of the type "X is a salient part of X"—but the character of the relationship between domains is as important in metonymy as is the perceived degree of discreteness between them, so a spectrum model can only partially accommodate metonymy.[11]

For Lakoff and Johnson, embodied experience shapes and constrains the blending of source and target domains, regardless of their semantic content—or whether the processes of conceptualization count as literal or metaphorical for a given culture or population. But how does embodied realism affect the intellectual status, historical longevity, and textual record of a particular concept? First, where the generation of a concept has been strongly constrained by embodied perception, and there exists (in the pertinent textual community) no viable challenge to the perception that this embodied reality is literally true, then there is no reason to call that concept a metaphor, *whether a modern observer would regard it as literally true or not.* Second, this concept could move toward the metaphorical end of the spectrum if some cultural influence were to trigger a new recognition that the target domain is not accurately described by those experientially constrained features of the source domain. Eventually the two domains might come to be acknowledged as wholly discrete, but if the mapping of features from source to target continued at the level of language alone, ornamental metaphors would emerge, and if mapping continued at the conceptual level, conceptual metaphors would emerge.

I propose that, in the case of concepts shaped or strongly constrained by embodied experience, it is difficult to bring about any shift along the spectrum toward metaphoricity. Suppose that a concept rooted in embodiment generates everyday idioms: the use of those idioms will reinforce the culture's predisposition to accept the embodied perception as literally true, while everyday experience of the embodied perception will reinforce the "naturalness" of the idioms. Consequently, if a concept is regularly reinforced by both embodied experience and everyday idioms, it will be very difficult for a rival concept to supplant the embodied concept or to usurp its status as a literal truth. Thus in order for that embodied concept to be transformed from a literal to a metaphorical usage, it must be challenged by an extremely persuasive and authoritative rival conceptualization. If a rival concept that does not conform to embodied experience merely coexists with the embodied concept, without being either inherently more persuasive or backed by a greater figure of authority, it will be unable to supersede the embodied concept, which is continually reinforced by subjective experience (now strongly culturally conditioned) and everyday language.[12]

If I am correct in these propositions, ideas of embodied realism can benefit historical study of processes by which literal concepts acquire the status of metaphors. The metaphorization of an embodied concept can scarcely begin to occur without a sustained challenge from a scientifically or theologically authoritative rival, which (in the case of any culture whose scientific and theological learning are transmitted in writing) we would expect to leave discernible traces in the textual record. It may be easier to identify the point when a rival concept first arises in discourse than when it actually eclipses the literal use of the embodied concept in narrative, because the textual communities that produce learned discourses may embrace a counterintuitive rival concept more readily than the less learned general public, depending on the degree to which the rival theory is promoted as authoritative. During the period when counterintuitive concepts coexist with embodied concepts, the historian might expect to find evidence of conceptual stratification, with the embodied concept remaining in literal use in narrative and other discourse types even while the counterintuitive rival has supplanted the embodied concept in specialized modes of discourse.

My hypothesis is that the hydraulic model of the mind (including the corollary notion of a corporealized mind located in the chest cavity) has undergone a transformation of this sort in the history of the English language: this model of mind originated as a series of literal articulations of how the mind-body complex was perceived to behave, and over several centuries new medical and theological doctrines divided the single domain of the mind-body complex into separate domains of mind and body. A defense of the historical part of this hypothesis falls outside the scope of this chapter but is, in theory, a straightforward problem of intellectual history: one need only identify when and how firmly the Anglo-Saxons (or specific Anglo-Saxon textual communities) assimilated doctrines that would have challenged the status of the hydraulic model and the mind-body complex as literal truths. Foremost among such doctrines would have been incorporealist theories of mind (e.g., the classical tradition of Anglo-Saxon psychology) and cephalocentric theories of mind (as promulgated in Galenic medical doctrine). In Lockett (2011), I conclude that such a transformation affected the folk psychology of ordinary Anglo-Saxons no earlier than the early to mid-eleventh century, after nearly all surviving OE poetry was already recorded.

This historical argument, however, rests upon a premise that is more difficult for the modern audience to accept, namely that the hydraulic model and the concept of the mind-body complex originally had the status of literal truth among the Anglo-Saxons. Because many parts of the hydraulic model persist in Modern English usage as conceptual metaphors (e.g., EMOTIONS RESIDE IN THE HEART; ANGER IS HEAT; THE MIND IS A CONTAINER), we tend to assume they have always been metaphors: this is the position taken, rather uncritically, by Kay (2000), among others. Moreover, the typical modern reader has inherited a deeply ingrained mind-body dualism: we are so accustomed to thinking of the mind-body relationship as one of opposition that it is difficult to conceive of the Anglo-Saxons attributing bodily characteristics to the mind for any reason other than metaphorical mapping. For an unbiased view of the status of the hydraulic model and the mind-body complex in OE narrative, we need to set aside our dualist presuppositions.

It is not easy to reorient our habits of perception and analysis, but recent work in the field of transcultural psychiatry demonstrates how profitable such a reorientation can be for observers of other cultures' notions of mind. The subdiscipline of transcultural psychiatry was developed in the first half of the twentieth century, initially to increase the efficacy of Western medical and mental-health practitioners who served non-Western populations, either in non-Western countries or in immigrant communities, by heightening these practitioners' awareness that Western views of the mind-body relationship are neither "natural" nor "objectively true" but culturally constructed and idiosyncratic. The rationale that supports their approach to synchronic, cross-cultural studies of models of mind and mental illness can be equally useful in our diachronic, cross-cultural study, for although the Anglo-Saxons are our linguistic ancestors, they can hardly be said to inhabit the same *culture* as modern-day speakers of English (who are, in any case, inhabitants of many disparate cultures).

Transcultural Psychiatry and the Dualist Minority

Early work in transcultural psychiatry approached non-Western psychological disorders as cultural variants of disorders acknowledged in Western psychiatry, such as depression and schizophrenia. Yet the results garnered by such studies were often vitiated by what Kleinman calls a *category fallacy*: "Having dispensed with indigenous illness categories because they are culture-specific, studies of this kind go on to superimpose their own cultural categories on some sample of deviant behavior in other cultures, as if their own illness categories were culture-free" (1977, 4). The reification of Western illness categories is but one of many category fallacies that the field of transcultural psychiatry calls attention to, and aims to correct, in both clinical and academic contexts. Among these, the most germane to my analysis is the tendency to impose uncritically upon non-Western cultures the rigid Western separation, even opposition, between mind and body. Among medical and mental-health practitioners, this tendency manifests itself in an overly rigid distinction between psychological and somatic disorders, obscuring how non-Western patients frequently present with bodily complaints when their disorder is one that Western psychiatrists would view as essentially mental. Additionally, the use of Western frameworks in the evaluation of non-Western modes of experiencing and communicating illness has led to some particularly short-sighted arguments, including the frequently repeated generalization that non-Westerners are especially prone to somatization, that is, the articulation of mental distress in terms of bodily symptoms with no known organic etiology. Laurence J. Kirmayer and Arthur M. Kleinman are among the most vocal critics of this generalization, which furthermore has proven untenable in clinical settings (see Kirmayer, Dao, and Smith 1998; Kleinman and Kleinman 1985; and Alexander et al. 1994, among others). The Western insistence on separating psychological and somatic disorders "largely reflects the persistent mind-body dualism of Western medicine: psychiatric disorders are perceived as mental disorders, notwithstanding their prominent somatic symptoms," according to Kirmayer, Dao, and Smith (1998). "The label of somatization then serves to fit the recalcitrant patient and problem into the overall system of medicine (even if it offers little in the way of clarity)" (258, 236). The implications for treatment are significant because, "notwithstanding the current biological turn in psychiatry," Westerners have a hard time shedding the suspicion that those who somatize their mental distress are either deluded or deceitful, either hysterical or malingering (258). In order to provide successful treatment to patients with a holistic understanding of mental and physical disorders, Western practitioners are encouraged to set aside their own engrained mind-body dualism and to understand the nature and causes of other cultures' mind-body holism.

Just as the discipline of transcultural psychiatry endeavors to improve psychiatric care by reorienting practitioners' perspectives on other cultures' concepts of mind, so can its fundamental principles improve the modern reader's grasp of historically disparate cultures' concepts of mind. Studies generated in the field of transcultural psychiatry demonstrate that mind-body dualists are actually a minority within the contemporary global community: "In other parts of the world, and in the experience of patients from many ethnocultural groups, the sharp distinction between psychological and somatic symptoms is far from obvious" (Kirmayer, Dao, and Smith 1998, 236). Fabrega (1991) extends the same argument to encompass the diachronic global community of cultures whose psychologies we can study in written records: specifically, in the Indian medical tradition known as Ayurveda and in Chinese traditional medicine (which are both still highly influential today). In Ayurveda, "every facet of illness and disease can involve phenomena that cross the mind-body duality of the West": for instance, the migration of excess humors to the heart, where the mind resides, may result in both epilepsy (*apasmara*), typically treated as a physical disorder in the West, and mental insanity (*unmada*) (Fabrega 1991, 186). It is crucial to clarify that the Ayurvedic etiology of epilepsy and insanity is not the product of a naive or "primitive" understanding of the coactivity of chest-centered sensations with pathological mental distress; rather, a sophisticated series of cultural mediations has shaped the interpretation of chest-centered sensations within an elaborate theoretical framework. Yet the mediating cultural influences, despite many centuries' contacts with Western concepts of mind-body opposition, have not themselves brought about the widespread assimilation of body-mind dualism or the splitting of the mind-body complex into discrete domains, a transformation that would presumably have relegated Ayurvedic holism to the status of conceptual metaphor. Instead, the "ontological distinction between mental and physical disease," which is a prerequisite to the category of somatization, "did not gain dominance in India. The theory of Ayurvedic medicine is powerfully unitary and functional in nature and does not distinguish ontologically among types or nature of medical disease" (Fabrega 1991, 185).

Fabrega extends a similar historical observation to traditional Chinese medicine, in which the organ of the heart is "responsible for the expressions of a person's individuality, including consciousness, concentration, reasoning, and organized social action" (1991, 188). Cardiocentric psychology "underscores the holism implicit in Chinese medicine," and this holism explains why "in classical Chinese medicine the idea of somatization as exaggerated, excessive, displaced, or peculiarly manufactured bodily symptoms simply does not exist" (188–89). Kirmayer, Dao, and Smith (1998) likewise assert that the lack of distinction between mental and physical illness "does not mean that Chinese medicine . . . dissolved the mind-body dualism of Western medicine: they never treated it in the first place. The holism of Chinese medicine does not develop psychology as a separate realm of discourse" (258–59).

In sum, the mind-body holism of the Ayurvedic and Chinese medical traditions is not the result of some cultural influence on an originally dualist psychology; on the contrary, dualism never formed a part of these medicines, because neither philosophy, nor theology, nor natural science, nor any other potentially authoritative rival system of thought has sufficiently challenged these cultures' phenomenologically based concept of the mental and the physical as a single domain. If modern Westerners think that patients steeped in the Ayurvedic or Chinese medical traditions are prone to somatizing their mental distress, this perspective is the product of our own assumption that mental and physical distress are ontologically discrete. Kirmayer (2001) usefully turns the Western perspective on its head when he writes that "if there is any validity to this generalization [i.e., that non-Westerners are more prone to somatization], it can only be because Westerners (who themselves comprise extremely diverse and divergent cultural groups) share some distinctive values or practices that contribute to the obverse of somatization, which has been termed *psychologization*" (23). I find Kirmayer's articulation of the problem helpful because it urges the Western observer of other cultures' mind-body concepts to recognize that psychologization is stranger and more counterintuitive than somatization, and that dualism is not a "default" view of mind and body but a product of "distinctive values or practices." Kleinman and Kleinman (1985) likewise maintain that "from the crosscultural perspective, it is not somatization in China and the West but psychologization in the West that appears unusual and requires explanation" (435).

A Reorientation of Our Approach
to Old English Psychological Narratives

Were the Anglo-Saxons not culturally "Western"? With respect to their outlook on the mind-body relationship, the short answer is no. Prior to the eleventh century, the vast majority of ordinary Anglo-Saxons, including the ruling class and those of modest education and middling literacy, had no sustained exposure to the key texts of the "classical tradition" of Neoplatonist-Christian psychology, nor was there widespread practical or theoretical use of Galenic medicine (Lockett 2011). Other "distinctive values and practices" that helped to relegate the corporeal mind and the hydraulic model to the status of metaphor in Modern English postdate the Anglo-Saxon period altogether (e.g., Cartesian dualism, knowledge of the circulatory system, and the many modern Western social teachings that are founded firmly upon the premise that one's will and intellect thrive or fail independent of the conditions of one's bodily and material existence; see Johnson 2007, 1–4). Transcultural psychology and embodied realism can be used to bring these historical observations to bear on the issue of the metaphorization of the hydraulic model. Transcultural psychology uproots the dualist prejudices that we typically bring to our reading of other cultures' psychologies, while embodied realism allows us to predict that a folk belief rooted in embodied experience will be long lived in the face of counterintuitive rival theories, and that in literate cultures the battle between rival theories will be detectible in the textual record.

To clarify, I am not suggesting that *all* OE hydraulic-model narratives were intended or interpreted by their target audiences as literal articulations of the mind-body relationship. Instead, my recommendation is that readers of OE approach the hydraulic model with the expectation that it is probably a literal usage unless it can be demonstrated otherwise—essentially, we should shift the burden of proof to those who would maintain that the hydraulic model is a metaphor, rather than taking its metaphoricity for granted.

Consider, for instance, the poem *Beowulf* and the prose OE *Boethius*, both quoted above. Neither the text of *Beowulf* nor the other works copied alongside it in the same manuscript suggest that the author(s), copyists, or audience of this poem had been exposed to learned philosophical discourse on the soul or medical discourse on the mind. I will remain convinced that the vivid hydraulic-model imagery of *Beowulf* represents literal articulations of an Anglo-Saxon folk model of the mind unless further investigation demonstrates that the poem was either created or copied or read in an environment where rival models of mind had been assimilated. This criterion is far more specific than the mere demonstration that the *Beowulf* poet(s) possessed classical or Christian learning of any variety: signs of an author's exposure to Vergil's *Aeneid* or Isidore's *Etymologies* in no way guarantee that he had absorbed the doctrine of the incorporeal, unitary soul. By contrast, the OE *Boethius* is translated from a sophisticated work of Neoplatonic philosophy and, moreover, it emanated from King Alfred's circle (if not necessarily from his own pen), a milieu that demonstrably read and digested patristic teachings that the mind formed part of the incorporeal soul. Consequently, hydraulic-model imagery in this prose work is, though purposeful, probably not a literal representation of the translator's understanding of mental activity.

More generally, reorienting our initial approach to OE hydraulic-model narratives does not relieve us of the burden of further investigating whether a specific Anglo-Saxon textual community might have used or interpreted the hydraulic model metaphorically, but it does reframe the problem and establishes how the textual record can help us solve it.

Notes

I am very grateful to Ethan Knapp, Lisa Kiser, Drew Jones, and especially David Herman for their insightful comments on drafts of this chapter; any errors that remain are entirely my own.

1. Quotations from Old English (OE) poems, except *Beowulf*, are drawn from the six volumes of *The Anglo-Saxon Poetic Records* (Krapp and Dobbie 1931–42), hereafter called *ASPR* and referenced by volume and page numbers. All translations of OE and Latin texts are my own.

2. For more information about conceptual metaphor theory, see my discussion below as well as Elizabeth Bradburn's contribution to this volume. Stanley (1956), predating the cognitive turn in metaphor theory, questions whether the modern observer is able to distinguish poetic embellishments (i.e., metaphors in the old "literary" sense) from statements that would have held up to the Anglo-Saxons' standards of scientific or theological veracity. Low (1998), focusing on OE poetic representations of the mind, invokes Lakoff and Johnson's work on conceptual metaphor but, like Stanley, con-

cludes that we cannot know whether certain expressions were metaphorical from the point of view of the Anglo-Saxons.

3. The term "hydraulic model" is employed in numerous disciplines' studies of the mind, including cognitive linguistics (see Kövecses 2000, 142–63), transcultural psychiatry, and the philosophy of emotions.

4. Nearly all extant OE poetry resists attempts to assign dates of composition; however, manuscript copies of OE poetry are roughly datable and provide a *terminus ante quem* for the poems' composition. I have quoted passages from the following poems and manuscripts: *Andreas* from the Vercelli Book (Vercelli, Biblioteca Capitolare, Cod. CXVII), copied circa 975 AD; *Christ II (Ascension)*, *The Rhyming Poem*, *Guthlac B*, and *The Wife's Lament* from the Exeter Book (Exeter, Cathedral Library, 3501), circa 975; *Genesis B* and *Exodus* from Oxford, Bodleian Library, Junius 11, the first part of which was compiled circa 960–990; *Beowulf* and *Judith* from the Nowell Codex (London, British Library, Cotton Vitellius A.xv, fols. 94–209), circa 1000; and *Solomon and Saturn* from Cambridge, Corpus Christi College, manuscripts 422 (late tenth century) and 41 (early eleventh century). I also quote from several prose texts: Homily 4 in the Vercelli Book (see above); Ælfric's *Lives of Saints* (composed within a brief span just before and after the year 1000); and the OE *Boethius* and the OE *Bede*, associated with the circle of King Alfred (d. 899) and composed during the late ninth or early tenth century (see Godden 2007).

5. Recent studies of the mind in OE generally agree with Godden's (1985) claim that the Anglo-Saxons regarded the heart as the literal seat of all mental activity; compare with McIlwain (2006), whose claim that the Anglo-Saxons had both direct and indirect knowledge of cephalocentric theories of mind is most persuasive for the period from around 990 onward.

6. Extant occurrences of the verb *(ge)belgan* refer strictly to the psychological condition of being "swollen with rage" (Cameron, Amos, and Healey 2003; s.v. *belgan, gebelgan, bylgan²*, *gebylgan, gebylged*). This raises the possibility that the Anglo-Saxons would not have recognized the connection between *(ge)belgan* and its spatial swelling.

7. I have removed the editors' semicolon after *bitolden*.

8. At the words "þa he þa lange mid," I follow the reading of Cambridge, Corpus Christi College 41 (Miller 1959–63 [1890–98], 3:121) because the reading preserved in Miller's base text (Oxford, Bodleian Library, Tanner 10) is syntactically awkward.

9. A full chapter of Lockett (2011) is devoted to discussion of the ancient, medieval, and modern analogues of the hydraulic model.

10. One notable exception is the work of Caroline Gevaert, who argues that OE representations of the mind refute Kövecses's claims of diachronic

stability in the conceptual metaphors ANGER IS HEAT and THE MIND IS A PRESSURIZED CONTAINER and therefore undermine the validity of embodied realism itself. Gevaert's argument is, unfortunately, flawed in several respects: she oversimplifies the claims of cognitive linguists (2005, 2–3), is unaware of the significant body of scholarship on the mind in OE literature (4, 11n1), and bases her analysis on a search for words signifying anger in the Corpus of OE database (5), a method that in no way accounts for the rich OE lexicon of emotional distress. As an alternative to Kövecses's explanation, which is in turn based on embodied realism, Gevaert proposes that the concept ANGER IS FIRE maps onto a volatile emotion the characteristic temperature and volatile nature of ordinary fire observed in nature or in domestic settings. Of course, this explanation in no way accounts for the cross-cultural and diachronic consistency of anger's *bodily* localization in the chest or abdomen.

11. The chief reason why I do not consider the possible role of metonymy in the OE hydraulic model is that syntactic variation in the linguistic expression of each stage of the hydraulic model makes it difficult if not impossible to identify stable boundaries between domains or dominant patterns of interdomain relationships. Certainly the OE evidence as a whole does not conform to a single metonymic structure such as THE PHYSIOLOGICAL EFFECTS OF AN EMOTION STAND FOR THE EMOTION (on which, see Lakoff and Kövecses 1987, 196–97).

12. As an illustration of this process, consider that the modern concepts of sunrise and sunset rely on the conceptual metaphor THE SUN IS A SATELLITE OF THE EARTH, which is not literally true but which arises from the embodied perception that the earth stands still while the sun goes up in the morning and down in the evening. Although the heliocentric model of the solar system is now taught to schoolchildren, the metaphorization of sunrise and sunset is not yet complete; indeed, one in five Americans still believes that the sun orbits the earth (Dean 2005), doubtless due in part to the mutual reinforcement of our perception that the sun moves around the earth and our everyday use of the terms "sunrise" and "sunset."

References

Alexander, J. P., S. G. S. Prabhu, E. S. Krishnamoorthy, and P. C. Halkatti. 1994. "Mental Disorders in Patients with Non-Cardiac Chest Pain." *Acta Psychiatrica Scandinavica* 89:291–93.

Bieler, Ludwig, ed. 1957. *Anicii Manlii Severini Boethii Philosophiae consolatio.* Corpus Christianorum Series Latina 94. Turnhout: Brepols.

Cameron, Angus, Ashley Crandell Amos, and Antonette diPaolo Healey, eds. 2003. *The Dictionary of Old English: Fascicles A–F.* CD-ROM, version 1.0. Toronto: Pontifical Institute of Mediaeval Studies.

Colgrave, Bertram, and R. A. B. Mynors, eds. 1969. *Bede's Ecclesiastical History of the English People.* Oxford: Clarendon Press.

Dean, Cornelia. 2005. "Scientific Savvy? In the U.S., Not Much." *New York Times,* August 30, 2005. http://www.nytimes.com/2005/08/30/science/30 profile.html.

Fabrega, Horacio, Jr. 1991. "Somatization in Cultural and Historical Perspective." In *Current Concepts of Somatization: Research and Clinical Perspectives,* ed. Laurence J. Kirmayer and James M. Robbins, 181–99. Washington DC: American Psychiatric Press.

Fludernik, Monika, Donald C. Freeman, and Margaret H. Freeman. 1999. "Metaphor and Beyond: An Introduction." *Poetics Today* 20:383–96.

Fulk, R. D., Robert E. Bjork, and John D. Niles, eds. 2008. *Klaeber's Beowulf and the Fight at Finnsburg.* 4th ed. Toronto: University of Toronto Press.

Gevaert, Caroline. 2005. "The ANGER IS HEAT Question: Detecting Cultural Influence on the Conceptualization of Anger through Diachronic Corpus Analysis." In *Perspectives on Variation: Sociolinguistic, Historical, Comparative,* ed. Nicole Delbecque, Johan van der Auwera, and Dirk Geeraerts, 195–208. Berlin: Mouton de Gruyter.

Godden, Malcolm R. 1985. "Anglo-Saxons on the Mind." In *Learning and Literature in Anglo-Saxon England,* ed. Michael Lapidge and Peter Clemoes, 271–98. Cambridge: Cambridge University Press.

———. 2007. "Did King Alfred Write Anything?" *Medium Ævum* 76:1–23.

Godden, Malcolm, and Susan Irvine, eds. 2009. *The Old English Boethius: An Edition of the Old English Versions of Boethius's* De Consolatione Philosophiae. 2 vols. Oxford: Oxford University Press.

Hogan, Patrick Colm. 2003. *Cognitive Science, Literature, and the Arts: A Guide for Humanists.* New York: Routledge.

Johnson, Mark. 2007. *The Meaning of the Body: Aesthetics of Human Understanding.* Chicago: University of Chicago Press.

Johnson, Mark, and George Lakoff. 2002. "Why Cognitive Linguistics Requires Embodied Realism." *Cognitive Linguistics* 13:245–63.

Kay, Christian J. 2000. "Metaphors We Lived By." In *Essays on Anglo-Saxon and Related Themes,* ed. Jane Roberts and Janet Nelson, 273–85. London: King's College London Centre for Late Antique and Medieval Studies.

Kirmayer, Laurence J. 2001. "Cultural Variations in the Clinical Presentation of Depression and Anxiety: Implications for Diagnosis and Treatment." *Journal of Clinical Psychiatry* 62 (suppl. 13): 22–28.

Kirmayer, Laurence J., Thi Hong Trang Dao, and André Smith. 1998. "Somatization and Psychologization: Understanding Cultural Idioms of Distress." In *Clinical Methods in Transcultural Psychiatry*, ed. Samuel O. Okpaku, 233–65. Washington DC: American Psychiatric Press.

Kleinman, Arthur M. 1977. "Depression, Somatization, and the 'New Cross-Cultural Psychiatry.'" *Social Science and Medicine* 11:3–10.

Kleinman, Arthur, and Joan Kleinman. 1985. "Somatization: The Interconnections in Chinese Society among Culture, Depressive Experiences, and the Meanings of Pain." In *Culture and Depression: Studies in the Anthropology and Cross-Cultural Psychiatry of Affect and Disorder*, ed. Arthur Kleinman and Byron Good, 429–90. Berkeley: University of California Press.

Kövecses, Zoltán. 2000. *Metaphor and Emotion: Language, Culture, and Body in Human Feeling*. Cambridge: Cambridge University Press.

Krapp, George Philip, and Elliott Van Kirk Dobbie, eds. 1931–42. *The Anglo-Saxon Poetic Records*. 6 vols. New York: Columbia University Press.

Lakoff, George, and Mark Johnson. 1980. "Conceptual Metaphor in Everyday Language." *Journal of Philosophy* 77:453–86.

Lakoff, George, and Zoltán Kövecses. 1987. "The Cognitive Model of Anger Inherent in American English." In *Cultural Models in Language and Thought*, ed. Dorothy Holland and Naomi Quinn, 195–221. Cambridge: Cambridge University Press.

Lockett, Leslie. 2011. *Anglo-Saxon Psychologies in the Vernacular and Latin Traditions*. Toronto Anglo-Saxon Series. Toronto: University of Toronto Press.

Low, Soon Ai. 1998. "The Anglo-Saxon Mind: Metaphor and Common Sense Psychology in Old English Literature." PhD diss., University of Toronto.

McIlwain, James T. 2006. "Brain and Mind in Anglo-Saxon Medicine." *Viator* 37:103–12.

Miller, Thomas, ed. and trans. 1959–63 [1890–98]. *The Old English Version of Bede's Ecclesiastical History of the English People*. Early English Text Society original series 95, 96, 110, 111. London: Oxford University Press.

Mize, Britt. 2008. "Manipulations of the Mind-as-Container Motif in *Beowulf, Homiletic Fragment II*, and Alfred's *Metrical Epilogue to the Pastoral Care*." *Journal of English and Germanic Philology* 107:25–56.

Scragg, D. G., ed. 1992. *The Vercelli Homilies and Related Texts*. Early English Text Society original series 300. Oxford: Oxford University Press.

Skeat, Walter W., ed. 1966 [1881–1900]. *Ælfric's Lives of Saints*. Early English Text Society original series 76, 82, 94, 114. Reprinted as 2 volumes. London: Oxford University Press.

Stanley, Eric G. 1956. "Old English Poetic Diction and the Interpretation of *The Wanderer, The Seafarer*, and *The Penitent's Prayer*." *Anglia* 73:413–66.

2. 1050–1500
Through a Glass Darkly;
or, the Emergence of Mind in Medieval Narrative

MONIKA FLUDERNIK

The representation of consciousness in medieval literature is an underexplored area of narratological research. Partly, this is the result of a general failure of classical narratology to engage with narratives before the early eighteenth century (the beginning of the novel). Partly, too, the neglect of this issue stems from a general belief that the representation of consciousness does not properly start before the late eighteenth century at the earliest, and only comes into its own with the novel of consciousness in the late nineteenth century (starting with Thomas Hardy).

As Alan Palmer has demonstrated so convincingly in *Fictional Minds* (2004), the study of speech and thought representation has been biased in favor of speech defined in terms of four categories: direct speech (*"How are you?"*), interior monologue (*Nice bit of pudding, that*), free indirect discourse (FID) (*How was she?*), and indirect speech (*Jim said the boat was gone*); psychonarration—that is, the narrator's presentation of a character's mind (*He mulled it over*)—has barely received any attention. Arguing against what he termed the "speech-category approach," Palmer was able to document the importance of thought report (or what Cohn [1978] calls psychonarration) in the nineteenth-century realist novel, and this proportional and functional preference can also be found in the eighteenth-century Gothic novel and in Virginia Woolf's narratives, for example. Thus, in the following passage from Radcliffe (1998 [1794]), I have highlighted the instances of psychonarration: "these united circumstances **disposed her mind to tenderness**, and **her thoughts were with Valancout**" (123).

Building on Palmer's account as well as my own previous work (Fludernik 1993, 1996), the present chapter will rethink

69

prior scholarship on the representation of consciousness in medieval English narrative, and it will also question the categories we have been using for analyzing the emergence of mind. More specifically, my chapter will begin by discussing how categories of thought representation have relied on a preconception that all thought is verbal. I will then outline six categories of thought representation used in Middle English texts from the thirteenth century onward, exploring the broader implications of those categories for the study of consciousness representation in narrative.

The Verbal Bias in Studies
of Speech and Thought Representation

As the history of the study of speech and thought representation shows, there has always been a bias toward verbalized thought. Prototypically, one conceives of consciousness as consisting of words and sentences rather than, say, images or inchoate feelings. This appears most forcefully in the very term "speech and thought representation," the standard narratological label for the analysis of embedded discourse, or discourse quoted or otherwise alluded to in the framing narrative. This bias reveals itself in two respects. On the one hand, consciousness is treated as internal utterance, as speech that is not articulated aloud but produced silently in the manner of a soliloquy. On the other hand, the bias causes narratologists to treat characters' mental and verbal acts as material situated on a level below the primary diegetic level. When two characters speak with one another, they may also tell one another stories. Such stories are therefore embedded insets, stories within a story, located on a framed or hypodiegetic level. When characters have a vision or dream, these are likewise treated as hypodiegetic. In the first case, the embedded narrative is narrated; in the second case it is imagined or visualized in the mind of the protagonist. Whereas, therefore, in the story-within-the-story mode, the character *tells* the story, in the case of visions or dreams, this is not the case. The protagonist either has to *tell* what he or she perceived in the dream, thus verbalizing the dream narrative and converting it into the embedded story category; or the dreamer's mental experience is narrated by the primary narrator as an extended passage of narrated perception and psychonarration. In the second case, the character's conscious experiences do not form a story within the story but are rather (mental) events reported by the primary narrator. Hence, techniques for representing characters' mental experiences are not completely coextensive with techniques for representing their spoken utterances.

Criticism of the speech and thought parallelism was first articulated by linguists, in particular by Leech and Short in *Style in Fiction* (2007 [1981]). In this book the authors demonstrate (255–81) that in the English language direct speech is by far the most common form of speech representation ("'He must be off,' he said, getting up"), whereas in the rendering of consciousness it is the narrative report of thought acts (NRTA) ("He wondered about her love for him"). Even more strikingly, thought representation lacks one of the most common forms of speech representation, indirect discourse. After all, phrases like *He pondered whether he could tell her the truth* are not necessarily equivalent to, "He said to himself: Can I tell her the truth?"; rather, because of the *verbum cogitandi,* or verb of thinking, the phrasing supports a nonliteral reading of the sentence—that is, a process of weighing whether and how one might admit to having wrecked the car, had an affair, and so forth.[1] The parallel between speech and thought was additionally questioned, though only implicitly, by Ann Banfield in her *Unspeakable Sentences* (1982), a study that demonstrated conclusively that sentences of indirect speech and FID are not the result of a transformation of direct into (free) indirect speech but a separate syntactical construct (26–37). In other words, Banfield contested the traditional view that (free) indirect speech emerges from a transposition of verbatim utterances that are merely shifted into (usually) third-person reference, past tense, and deictic alignment with the surrounding narrative (thus direct speech *I love you* turns into indirect speech *He told her that he loved her; I am going to Paris tomorrow* into *She exclaimed that she was going to Paris the next day*). Moreover, indirect speech, as demonstrated by logical semanticists, preserves the propositional but not the lexical meanings of direct speech. (Banfield's research is based on work on logical semantics by Kripke and Putnam, among others.) Thus, *He told her that he loved her* may be a rendering of a wide variety of utterances such as *Honey, I am your teddy bear* or *Well, you know I've been trying to say this for quite a while, mh, I . . . I really like you, you're the nicest person I've ever met.*

If indirect speech is already a more or less free rewriting of an original utterance, this caveat against what might be called the transcription theory applies even more stringently to thoughts which—unlike speech—cannot be tested against tape recordings of the original. And, for obvious reasons, fictional speech representation is even more "invented" since the "original" utterances do not have any prior existence.

My own analysis of the inventedness of direct speech (Fludernik 1993, 398–433) likewise questions the notion of verbatim rendering. Building on work by previous discourse analysts (especially Chafe 1980; Tannen 1984, 1989), I demonstrated that much direct speech in conversational narrative is clearly invented and does not render original utterances in verbatim fashion, most pointedly so because there never was an original utterance in the first place. As Short, Wynne, and Semino (2004) have argued, this fact of course does not at all undermine standard norms and expectations: speech reports in newspapers like the *Times* and the *Guardian* are certainly held to the requirement of verbatim quotation, and the same is true in the witness box and similar contexts (see also Short 2003; Short, Semino, and Culpeper 1996). However, this does not mean that all direct speech is actually a verbatim reproduction; in less legally binding circumstances, in general conversation or the tabloid press, the general tenor of an utterance may be sufficient, or the reproduction may focus on certain phrases and disregard other parts of the original. For our present purposes, the main point is that even in the case of direct speech one cannot expect complete faithfulness; to do so in the case of thought processes, which are not directly transparent to others and not necessarily immediately recoverable even by the mind that generated them, is patently absurd.

Since indirect or free indirect discourse cannot be traced back to a unique source utterance, it makes even less sense to treat thought representation as a transformation of a verbalized thought. The narratological equation between speech and thought representation on both a formal and a substantive level is therefore a fallacy. Medieval literature provides even further corroboration of the necessity of treating thought differently from speech. In what follows, I will first frame some general remarks about aspects of the Middle English rendering of consciousness and then proceed to provide example passages for a variety of different categories of thought representation. Overall, my analysis suggests that current narratological models might require some modification when they are brought into dialogue with medieval texts.

Forms of Consciousness

Since consciousness comprises areas of mental activity that are not verbal, it may be helpful to start out with a list of verbal and nonverbalized states and processes of consciousness. In my usage, thoughts are understood to be units of verbalized mind sufficiently concrete to be articulated in propositional form, as for instance in arguments and actual internal speech (in literature soliloquies could be argued to provide a generic mold for internal speech and self-debate). Beyond this realm, there are unarticulated, vague half-thoughts that flit across the mind without being captured and pressed into specific syntactic shape. Thoughts of this sort are less pertinent to medieval literature than they are to Modernist texts, where they sometimes appear in the one-word sentences of interior monologues—as is the case with many of Leopold Bloom's thoughts in Joyce's *Ulysses* (1922). Secondly, *emotions* clearly fall outside the verbalized realm (although they are verbaliz*able*), and these may include anything from moods and predispositions to more specific feelings such as fear, joy, anger, frustration, or jealousy. I here take the lexemes emotions, feelings, and sentiments to be largely synonymous, but cognitive scientists sometimes distinguish between them.[2] Emotion is often treated as the hyperconcept, with moods and feelings the subordinate categories. Attitudes, beliefs, and views belong to another category of mind content. They are often verbalized (especially if they relate to frequently articulated maxims such as *All politicians are corrupt*), but may also include vague antipathies typical of racist attitudes, optimistic or pessimistic views of life (or would that be a mood or disposition?), or idealized expectations, suspicions, and so on. Sensations constitute yet another category (hunger, pain, dizziness), and the experience of color and light or darkness may also fall under this heading. Finally, there are ideas and memories, both aspects of consciousness that are difficult to place. Ideas can be spontaneous and not yet verbalizable, although they are usually propositional, verbalized elements of consciousness and treated as part of the rational mind. Memories *include* the other categories—for example, thoughts, feelings, sensations, ideas, and beliefs—so they reproduce mental categories under a separate index or in a different mode.

Literary scholars in general, and narratologists in particular, have only begun to come to terms with the traditions of research surrounding these aspects of conscious experience.[3] In what follows, I seek to extend this project of synthesis and integration by focusing on the verbal as well as nonverbal reflexes of consciousness found in medieval texts. Study of these reflexes can help bring to light part of the genealogy of techniques used to evoke minds—or mental activity—in narrative discourse. Building on the arguments of Palmer (2004), who notes the importance of thought report for presenting nonverbal elements of consciousness, I suggest that psychonarration is also a crucial category in Middle English texts and that Middle English is also able to express nonverbalized consciousness.

The Representation of
Consciousness in Middle English Narrative

This section explores how various types of mental activity manifest themselves in Middle English narrative. In particular, I focus on two thirteenth-century, two fourteenth-century, and several fifteenth-century texts in order to suggest how medieval writers evoked consciousness and also to sketch the trajectory of change in these techniques over the centuries from which my case studies are taken. The texts are the two early romances *King Horn* and *Sir Orfeo*; *The South English Legendary*; Chaucer's "Knight's Tale"; Capgrave's *The Life of St. Katharine*; and two prose romances (extracts from Malory's *Morte D'Arthur* and *The Three Kings' Sons*). The types of mental activity that I explore in these narratives include descriptions of gestures and movements indicative of emotional disturbance; the presentation of consciousness via direct discourse; psychonarration; narratorial empathy; free indirect discourse; collective group consciousness; and virtual direct speech.

1. Descriptions of Gestures and Other Behaviors Indicative of Emotional States

My first category is one that is clearly new to our traditional type of analysis: descriptions of gesture and physical movement indicative of emotional disturbance, what I would like to call narrative indexes of interiority. This correlates with what psychologists call affect display. It is an extremely natural category, as a comparison with drama demonstrates. We all observe other people express their emotions in body language. Stage directions are full of sentences like "She faints" and "He raises his hand in despair." Traditionally, in narrative these signals of consciousness have been treated as part of the plot (fainting) or as descriptive elements in the narrator's discourse that frame characters' speech (dialogue) or more extensive renderings of thought processes and feelings. Again, the plot-centered bias of narratology can be said to have been responsible for marginalizing an awareness that such passages might have anything at all to do with consciousness.

Let us now look at some typical examples from Middle English narrative.

> (1.1) *The children hi broghte to stronde,*
> *Wringinde here honde . . .*
> (*MEVR* 1993, *King Horn*, ll. 115–18)

1.1. They took the children, who were wringing their hands, *to the beach.*[4]

(1.2) Tho gan Rymenhild mislike
And sore gan to sike.
Armes heo gan buwe;
Adun heo feol y-swowe.
Horn in herte was full wo
(ll. 429–33)

1.2. Then Rymenhild began to worry and to sigh. She started to move
her arms [to and fro] and fell down fainting. *Horn was very sorry
in his heart [grieved to see it].*

In both passages from the thirteenth-century romance *King Horn*
we have a reference to gestures—the wringing of hands, the moving of the arms in a gesture of despair. In the second example,
Rymenhild also sighs, and this is followed by the heroine's fit of
fainting. The second passage, moreover, contains two clear cases
of psychonarration (*gan . . . mislike*, "She started to be afraid,"
and *was full wo*, "Horn grieved to see it").

(1.3) *The King into his chaumber is go*
And oft swooned *opon the ston*
And made swiche diol and swiche mon
That neighe his lif was y-spent.
(*MEVR* 1993, *Sir Orfeo*, ll. 172–75)

1.3. The King went to his chamber and repeatedly collapsed fainting
on the floor and made such grieving moans *that [it seemed as if] his life
were almost spent.*

In this example from *Sir Orfeo*, the king, who has just lost his
queen, faints and then loudly laments his situation; it remains
unclear, however, whether the *diol* and *mon* ("doleful cry" and
"moan") are to be taken as the verbal or nonverbal expression
of woe. Even more difficult is the decision of how to categorize
the final line ("so that he nearly died [with grief]"). This is an
expressive narrative comment on the depth of Orfeo's emotional
prostration, which can (but need not) be read as an instance of
psychonarration.

2. The Presentation of
Consciousness via Direct Discourse

The second most common form of rendering consciousness in my sample corpus is by means of direct discourse.[5] The verbalization of thought is here underlined by the repeated use of the inquit *said*. These soliloquy-like internal speeches also often go unframed by a *verbum dicendi* of this sort, though, as well as varying significantly in length and complexity. Let us look at an example from Malory:

(2.1) And so the nyght fell on hym, and than was he ware in a slade of a pavylyon of rede sendele. "Be my feyth," seyde sir Launcelot, "in that pavylyon woll I lodge all this nyght." (Malory 1971, VI 153, ll. 19–21)

2.1. And then it turned night and he saw a pavilion of red sandalwood in a glade. "By my faith," said Sir Launcelot, "in this pavilion will I rest this night."

Here we have an interposed inquit tag (*seyde sir Launcelot*) and a direct discourse rendering of Lancelot's decision to spend the night in the pavilion. Note the interjection "By my feyth," which lends a colloquial quality to the internal speech.

The marked rhetorical quality of these soliloquies also shows up in the following example from "St. Katherine" in *The South English Legendary*. Maxence, the evil despot, here laments the treachery of his followers and his wife, who have all converted to Christianity:

(2.2) þemperour þo gan drawe his her . & sore sike & grone Mahoun he seide hou schal ich do . schal ich beleue alone Whi neltou raþere fecche me . & bringe me of þis lyue þan suffri to leose alle mi men . after mi leoue wyue (SEL 1967–69, "St. Katherine" 541, ll. 267–70)

2.2. Then the emperor began to pull his hair and to sigh and moan. "Mahomet," he said, "what shall I do? Must I be left by myself? Why won't you rather fetch me and take my life away than allow [me] to lose all my men after [I have already lost] my dear wife?"

Quite a few of the internal speeches in this corpus are apostrophes to absent addressees. Thus, in (2.2) Maxence calls on Mahomet ("Mahoun"), and in (2.3) Arcite in the "Knight's Tale" directly addresses the absent Emily when he laments how much he suffers from his love:

> (2.3) *Love hath his firy dart so brennyngly*
> *Ystiked thurgh my trewe, careful herte,*
> *That shapen was my deeth erst than my sherte.*
> *Ye sleen me with youre eyen, Emelye!*
> (Chaucer 1988, A, ll. 1564–67)

2.3. *Love has sent his fiery arrow so smartingly through my faithful and anxious heart that I was killed even before the arrow reached my shirt. You slay me with your eyes, Emily!*

Rymenhild in *King Horn*, too, apostrophizes her heart—"Herte, nu thu berste" (l. 1202)—and her brother Athulf, who has waited in vain for Horn to return and prevent Rymenhild's forced marriage, directs his soliloquy to Horn:

> (2.4) *"Horn, nu thu ert well longe.*
> *Rymenhild thu me toke*
> *That I sholde loke.*
> *Ich habbe y-kept hure evre;*
> *Com nu other nevre—*
> *I nemay no leng hure kepe.*
> For sorewe nu I wepe."
> (MEVR 1993, *King Horn*, ll. 1106–13)

2.4. "Horn, you have now been gone a great while. You gave me Rymenhild to take care of her. I have kept her [safe] all this time. Come now or never—I can no longer safeguard her. For sorrow I now weep."

This passage is particularly interesting since it self-referentially has Athulf analyze his emotions: "For sorewe nu I wepe" (l. 1113). Rather than merely repressing his woe and anxiety, like the steward in (2.2), Athulf draws attention to the external signs of his emotional turmoil ("I cry") and specifies the emotion signified by his tears as "sorrow." This analysis of one's own emotions is an interesting aspect of the rendering of consciousness that deserves narratological attention. In particular, I would like to point out the affinity of such self-reflexive analysis with what psychologists have termed "meta-emotions" (Jäger and Bartsch 2006), although this concept was developed for different contexts and does not include the case given in (2.4).[6]

It is worth pointing out that the one passage bearing a similarity to modern interior monologue is the extract from Malory, and that all the other examples are cases of direct internal speech, clearly articulated as if they were to be uttered on stage. The early modern soliloquies in the romances of Robert Greene (1558–92) or Thomas Lodge (1558–1625) are therefore not inventions of the sixteenth century but remnants and elaborations of a thriving Middle English tradition of soliloquizing protagonists.

3. Psychonarration in Middle English Narrative

Psychonarration is an extremely common form of mind depiction in medieval narrative. However, in contrast to direct thought, Middle English writers tend to use only brief passages of psychonarration. Two typical examples are (3.1) and (3.2):

> *(3.1) The children* dradde *therof.*
> *Hi* wenden *to wisse*
> *Of here lif to misse*
> (*MEVR* 1993, *King Horn*, l. 124)

3.1. The children were afraid of this *["grew afraid"]. They* thought they knew *that they would be killed [literally: "to miss their lives"].*

> *(3.2) And in a tour,* in angwissh and in wo,
> *This Palamon and his felawe Arcite . . .*
> (Chaucer 1988, A, ll. 1030–31)

3.2. And in a tower, in anguish and in woe this Palamon and his friend Arcite . . .

In (3.1) the children "were afraid" and "thought they would be killed." Here the *verba sentiendi et cogitandi* are used to describe mental turmoil—fear and anxious expectation. By contrast, Chaucer condenses the mental reference by using noun phrases ("in anguish and in wo") rather than fuller verbal descriptions. Now consider example (3.3) from *King Horn*:

> *(3.3) Heo* luvede *so Horn child*
> *That negh heo gan* wexe wild
> (ll. 255–56)
> *Of folk heo* hadde drede . . .
> *Hire sorewe ne hire pine*
> *Ne mighte nevre fine.*
> (ll. 262, 265–66)

3.3. She loved *Horn so much that she nearly* went mad. *She* was afraid *of people. . . . Her* sorrow *and her* woe *seemed neverending.*

In this passage Rymenhild's love of Horn is represented dramatically: at the beginning of the passage she is said to "love Horn so much, she nearly went mad." Lines 265–66 are, however, difficult to interpret. Rather than reading this as the narrator's or bard's depiction of Rymenhild's emotional embattlement, which, as he proleptically notes, will endure ("ne mighte nevre fine"), one could also interpret the lines as indicating Rymenhild's own awareness of the apparent interminability of her anguish, thereby construing it as a stretch of free indirect discourse (a transposition, so to speak, of "Never will my sorrow and grief end"). This interpretation is supported by the use of *mighte* (might), which only makes sense in a subjective reading of the sentence.

Slightly more extensive representations of consciousness can be found in (3.4)–(3.6). In (3.4) Horn keenly smarts when he has to watch Rymenhild faint:

> *(3.4) He makede Rymenhilde lay—*
> *And he makede walaway.*
> *Rymenhild feol y-swowe . . .*

Hit smot to Hornes herte
So bitere that hit smerte.
(ll. 1489–94)

3.4. He sang Rymenhild's song and he expressed his grief ("sang wala-way") Rymenhild fainted. . . . It smote Horn's heart so keenly that it hurt.

Horn has here returned from abroad in disguise to wed Rymenhild and rescue her from a marriage to the evil Fikenhild. In the cited passage the emotional intensity is signaled not indexically by an external gesture but by reference to Horn's mental pain, which the narrative aligns with Horn's shock at Rymenhild's fainting fit. The two final lines of this extract present Horn's feelings from an external perspective in omniscient fashion, only describing the keenness of his anguish rather than allowing him to express it in direct internal speech. Chaucer, at least 150 years later, is much more imaginative in showing Palamon's love and jealousy in the image of a sword piercing his heart (cf. passage [2.3] and [4.5]), and this extravagant image is aligned with Palamon's own sensations when he discovers the beautiful Emily:

> *(3.5) This Palamoun, that* thoughte *that thurgh his herte*
> *He* felte *a coold swerd sodeynliche glyde,*
> *For ire* he quook *. . .*
> (Chaucer 1988, A, ll. 1574–76)

3.5. Palamon, who imagined that he felt a cold sword suddenly pierce his heart, shook with anger . . .

The one really extensive passage of psychonarration that I came across in my preliminary corpus is also from Chaucer's "Knight's Tale." Theseus here has to come to a decision about the two knights encountered dueling one another because of their love of Emily. He is beset by the women in his entourage who plead for the two knights, but his anger soon gives way to compassion when he understands that it was love that motivated the one knight to escape from prison and the other to risk death by returning from exile. The two competitors had met one another, incidentally, in a wood where Palamon overheard Arcite's soliloquy articulating his love for Emily ("'Allas,' quod he, 'that day I was bore!'" [see A, ll. 1542–71]). Theseus's ruminations are reproduced as (3.8):

> (*3.8*) *Til at the laste aslaked was his [Theseus's] mood,*
> *For pitee renneth soone in gentil herte.*
> And though he first for ire quook and sterte,
> He hath considered shortly, in a clause,
> The trespas of hem bothe, and eek the cause,
> *And although that his ire* hir gilt accused,
> *Yet in his resoun he* hem bothe excused,
> *As thus:* he thoghte wel *that every man*
> *Wol helpe hymself in love, if that he kan,*
> *And eek delivere hymself out of prisoun.*
> And eek his herte hadde compassioun
> *Of wommen, for they wepen evere in oon;*
> *And in his gentil herte he* thoughte *anon,*
> *And* <u>*softe unto hymself he seyde,*</u> *"Fy*
> *Upon a lord that wol have no mercy,*
> *But been a leon, bothe in word and dede,*
> *To hem that been in repentaunce and drede,*
> *As wel as to a proud despitous man*
> *That wol mayntene that he first began.*
> *That lord hath litel of discrecioun,*
> *That in swich cas kan no divisioun,*
> *But weyeth pride and humblesse after oon."*
> (Chaucer 1988, A, ll. 1760–81)

3.8. Finally his anger was assuaged, for pity soon flows through a gentle heart. Though he first quaked and shook for anger, to state the case in brief, he soon considered *[historical present]* their crime and its cause. *Although his anger accused them, his reason excused them, in the following manner:* he reflected *that every man in love will help himself, if possible, and will deliver himself from prison.* His heart, too, had compassion for women, *because of their common tendency to weep. And in his kind heart he then* considered, *and said to himself softly: "Fie upon a lord that will have no mercy, but acts like a lion, both in word and deed, to those that have repented [their ways] and are in fear. [Fie] also [to] the man who is proud and pitiless and who insists on his course of action without compromise! That lord must surely lack proper judgment who can make no distinction between pride and humility in such cases."*

The passage starts with psychonarration and a narrative summary of Theseus's mental state: his wrath has disappeared. This is followed by a gnomic statement by the narrator about gentle hearts (l. 1761), to be applied to noble Theseus, who exemplifies the general truth about kind hearts being full of mercy. The passage then develops into an extremely detailed psychological analysis, rendering the several stages of Theseus's emotions, his rationale for excusing knights, and his eventual decision motivated by an ideal of behavior that he wishes to follow. From psychonarration (*hath considered*), the account turns to near-allegorical explication: both his wrath (*ire*) and reason are cast as agents of his change in mood. He then goes on to outline further thoughts. The passage continues with more analysis of Theseus's feelings (*compassion*), and after the reiteration of the "gentle heart" (l. 1772) we move into a soliloquy in which he weighs the advantages of pity and mercy for the ideal ruler. All in all, Chaucer presents Theseus's mental activities as fundamentally verbal processes.

Such long and complex passages of psychonarration are rare except in Chaucer and in the prose romances in the late fifteenth century, as in the following passage from *The Three Kings' Sons*, where Prince Philip joins Fferant incognito:

(3.9) thus departed fferant the Senesshall . . . til that he approched the Reaume of Sizile, auisyng *alwey his newe seruaunt /* consideryng *withyn hym self / his persone, his beaute / his maner, his humbles / wherof he was* moche ameruailed */ for he* wende *not that yn the body of any one man might haue ben so many vertues to-gedir / So* thought *he wele / that if he had as moche worthynesse and prowes as he had persone & maner, he*

shold be the moost perfit thinge that euer god made sith tyme of his pas-
sion. (*Three Kings' Sons* 1895, 13.39–14.9)

3.9. And so Fferant the Seneschal departed . . . until he came to the realm
of Sicily. He considered again and again his new servant [Prince Philip],
weighing in his mind his handsomeness, his comportment [and] his hu-
mility. He wondered at these, since he could not believe that in any man's
body so many virtues could be lodged together. So he thought that if he
should have as much nobility and valor as handsome features and proper
conduct he would be the most perfect man that God [Christ] had made
since his passion.

4. Narratorial Empathy

A fourth method for representing consciousness in Middle English narrative, one that does not have a place in traditional narratological accounts, is the empathetic assumption of a protagonist's
feelings by the narrator or bard. Narratorial addresses to the
narratee vicariously sympathizing with the protagonist also occur in texts with an "engaging narrator" (Warhol 1986), but the
narrative status of such empathetic exclamations has received
no detailed analysis as far as I am aware. Moreover, the possible connection of such passages with the representation of consciousness is a narratological lacuna. A character's supposed
verbal mind-content has always been taken to be prior to its
narrative representation. Yet in the empathetic exclamations to
be discussed in this section, it is impossible to tell whether the
narrator is reporting the feelings of a character, expressing his
own analogous emotions, or fantasizing about what the character might have felt in the circumstances.

For example, (4.1) can be read as an omniscient statement
by the narrator, yet the exclamation mark and emotional expressivity of the two lines indicate the narrator's empathy for
Horn's situation.

(4.1) *Ofte hadde Horn beo wo*
Ac nevre wurs than him was tho!
(*MEVR* 1993, *King Horn*, ll. 119–20)

To paraphrase: the narrator omnisciently remarks that Horn has had a lot of grief in his life, but never as much as at this moment. The passage could—from a present-day perspective—be categorized as free indirect discourse, but that is perhaps an unlikely reading given the scarcity of FID in Middle English literature. (See excerpts [5.1]–[5.3] for examples.) In particular, the use of the name Horn (rather than a pronominal reference) makes a FID reading of the two lines less likely. The temporal adverb *tho* ("then"), as a distal deictic, likewise militates against a FID analysis of the passage (proximal *nu* being very common in this romance and therefore likely to have been used to signal internal focalization from Horn's perspective).

In (4.2) and (4.3), on the other hand, the empathetic involvement of the narrator is quite unambiguous:

> *(4.2) Lord! Who may telle the sore*
> *This King sufferd ten yere and more!*
> (*MEVR* 1993, *Sir Orfeo*, ll. 239–40)

4.2. Lord! Who can tell the pain that this King suffered for ten years or more!

> *(4.3) Nou God helpe sein Thomas . for he was al one*
> (*SEL* 1967–69, 2:627, l. 521)

4.3. Now God help Saint Thomas, for he was [left] all to himself.

In the first case, the narrator's exclamations underline Sir Orfeo's sufferings; in the second, the narrator sympathizes with Saint Thomas's situation and wishes that God might assist him. A more extended passage occurs in *The Knight's Tale*. The narrator moves from a condensed summary of seven years' imprisonment to rendering Palamon's mental condition in psychonarration ("forpyned," "wo," "distresse") and then launches into a rhetorical question whose sole purpose, it seems, is to underline his compassionate empathy with the protagonist:

(4.4) In derknesse and horrible and strong prisoun
Thise seven yeer hath seten Palamoun
Forpyned, *what for* **wo** *and for* **distresse.**
Who feeleth double soor and hevynesse
But Palamon, that love destreyneth so
That wood out of his wit he goth for wo?
(Chaucer 1988, A, ll. 1451–56)

4.4. *In darkness, in the horrible strong prison Palamon has sat for seven years,* **wasted** *by* **woe** *and by* **distress.** Who but Palamon, so afflicted by love that he is almost out of his mind with grief, feels double pain and depression?

The empathy of the narrator is here further underlined by the use of the present tense, which emphasizes the state of Palamon's unhappiness by turning it into an enduring picture of woe.[7]

Finally, I would also like to note the narrator's frequent use of simile—for example, in (4.5), where the narrative provides access to the emotional quality of the character's interiority via a comparative scenario, here the wounding of Palamon's heart by Amor's arrow as a correlative of his exclamation of pain and his blanching to the bones:

(4.5) That thurgh a wyndow, thikke of many a barre
Of iren greet and square as any sparre,
He cast his eye upon Emelya
And therwithal he bleynte *and cride, "A!"*
As though he stongen *were unto the herte.*
(Chaucer 1988, A, ll. 1075–79)

In (4.5), rather than preexisting the act of narration, the quality of Palamon's suffering emerges only through the narrator's figurative language; the cause of the physical signs of suffering is not named explicitly but implied through a metaphorical scenario of physical pain that occurs in a telling position, the heart. Chaucer elsewhere uses even more inventive similes, and I will deal with a much longer and complex passage later in a different context (7.1).

5. Free Indirect Discourse

In the case studies on which my analysis is based, there were only two unambiguous instances of FID and one passage that might or might not involve this technique for representing consciousness. The doubtful example comes from *King Horn* (compare my discussion of [4.1]). Here Horn's father, about to be murdered by an overwhelming majority of Saracens, enters the battle against them with the two knights that happen to accompany him.

> (*5.1*) *The king alighte off his stede,* . . .
> *And his gode knightes two,*
> All too fewe he hadde tho!
> (*MEVR* 1993, *King Horn*, ll. 51–54)

5.1. The king descended from his horse, . . . *and [so did] his two knights. All too few they were [literally: had he then].*

The exclamation "All too fewe he hadde tho!" represents a lamentation about the clearly fatal situation of the king. One can read this exclamation as the king's realization of his hazardous position in being so strongly outnumbered by his enemies (hence FID); but it is more plausible to take the line as the omniscient narrator's empathetic remark that gives utterance to his anguish about the impending disaster. We would then have another instance of narratorial empathy. This second reading is supported by the distal *tho* ("then"), though this deictic certainly does not entirely rule out a FID reading; after all, in early instances of FID one cannot expect to see all the "rules" later associated with this technique being observed in full.

By contrast, (5.2) and (5.3), interestingly both from the more colloquial saints' legends, are more obvious examples of FID.

> (*5.2*) "*Now hath Porfir me forsake,*
> *That was wardain of al mi liif!*"
> *Oft he seyd* allas allas
> That euer was he born of wiif!
> ("Seynt Katerine," Ms.Auchil.fol.21;
> Horstmann 1881, 256, ll. 597–600)

5.2. "Now has Porfir forsaken me, who was the guardian of all my life." He often said: Alas, alas, that he had ever been born by a woman.

Here the relevant sentence reads: "Allas, allas, that he had ever been born [by a woman]." This is clearly *not* direct discourse, since the ruler's presumptive *I* has been shifted into alignment with the surrounding third-person past-tense narrative. The absence of a past perfect, a relatively rare form in Middle English, is no counterargument to the reading. The passage cannot be interpreted as indirect speech (if one takes *seyd* to be "he said [to himself]"): indirect speech usually does not include interjections. More important, if one removes the interjection, the resulting meaning contradicts the original passage: *he seyd that ever he was born of wiif* would in fact mean "He said that he had ever been born of a woman." Since all humans are born of women, that utterance makes no sense, and the *ever* loses its function in the clause. In fact, the *that* clause depends on the interjection *allas* (*Alas that he was ever born*), and as such is syntactically a complete exclamatory sentence ("O that I should ever have been born"). As a consequence, the introductory *seyd* does not serve as an introductory verb whose object is the *that* clause, but as a *verbum dicendi* introducing direct speech. In modern English one would place a colon after *seyd*; what follows is a separate clause with shifted reference, hence: FID. There is even the remote possibility of interpreting *seyd* not as "said" but as "sighed," but this is too contentious a reading of the past tense of *siʒen* "sigh."

The most obvious example of FID in my case studies is (5.3). The passage deals with Thomas à Becket in his struggle against King Henry II:

> (5.3) *Sein Thomas isei wel þo . þat þer nas wei bote on*
> *þat he moste stif wiþstonde . oþer is riʒtes forgon*
> *He þoʒte þat Holy Churche . he nolde neuere bitraye*
> *And þat he nolde neuere in such seruage . hure*
> *bringe bi is daye*
> Raþer he wolde [as] oþer were . to martirdom be ido
> þane Holy Churche were so bineþe . iredi he was þerto

Neuere ne miȝte þe kyng and he . acordi noþing þer
Ac departede al in wraþþe . as hi ofte dude er
(SEL 1967–69, 2, ll. 723–30)

The passage starts with two sentences of psychonarration: "St. Thomas *saw that* there was but one way, that he had to resist stoutly, or forgo his rights. He *thought that* [decided] he would never betray the Holy Church and that he would never [consent to] bring her into such slavery [to the state] during his life time." This is followed by two lines of FID, italicized above, in which Thomas's commitment to martyrdom is reflected in an internal argument following on from the two previous ones: "He would rather be martyred, as others were before him, than allow the Holy Church to be humiliated in such a way [i.e., by bringing it into slavery]; he was ready for it [martyrdom]." The passage is entirely convincing as an instance of FID because it occurs in continuation of a relative *that* clause.

More generally, as this passage suggests, although free indirect discourse is not a common form of the representation of consciousness in Middle English, it exists (and there are more numerous examples of FID used for the purposes of *speech* representation).[8] Yet the overall importance of FID in Middle English narrative is difficult to gauge. Passages in FID are very brief and modulate in and out of reports of characters' actions or in and out of direct speech or thought. Unlike the extensive stretches of FID for the representation of consciousness with which one is familiar from the Gothic novel and especially after Thomas Hardy, FID here does not effect a focalization on the characters' psyche and a concomitant backgrounding of the narrator's voice. What one can observe here are simply first traces of a technique used extensively in conversational narrative, preponderantly for the representation of utterances (compare Fludernik 1993). It is hard to see such examples as a deliberate device chosen for a particular effect. As in conversational narrative, FID passages first arise from more convenient ways of continuing the previous clauses—from a perhaps inadvertent mixing of narratorial discourse and the performatively enhanced projection of the protagonists' utterances or thoughts.

6. Collective or Group Consciousness

I would like to conclude my survey with two special cases that I found very interesting and that may be well worth keeping in mind as a template when looking at more Middle English texts and how they represent different modes of consciousness. These two cases are, first, instances of collective consciousness and, second, virtual direct speech.

Palmer has devoted some attention to the collective mind in his book *Fictional Minds* (2004) and in recent essays (2005, 2010). The representation of collective consciousness (a village's attitudes, a family's opinions, etc.) is, however, not a phenomenon invented by George Eliot, or even by Jane Austen; one can, surprisingly, find it in Middle English narrative, though I hasten to add that so far I only know of one example text, Capgrave's novelistic saint epic *The Life of Saint Katharine* (c. 1445). Capgrave's text emphasizes collective uniformity of opinion and contrasts it with the troublesome singularity of Katharine. The two briefer examples cited below are both ambiguous in the sense that they might be read either as utterances or as thought processes, but since both passages depict people's attitudes, they *could* conceivably represent consciousness rather than speech.[9] In any case, my discussion of the two passages is only a preliminary attempt at clarifying the key issues. Additional research will be required to ascertain the scope and functions of such representations of group consciousness in medieval narrative more generally.

The first of my two example passages, from Capgrave's text, conveys a sense of the gossip at court when Katharine's mother becomes pregnant. Since this happens when she is already quite old, Katharine's birth is a miracle.

> *(6.1) Many a man & woman at þis thyng low,*
> *Sume of hem sayd, "it is but a lye,*
> *þe kyng is ful febyll, þe qwen ful eld now:*
> *Schall sche now grone, schal sche now crye?*
> *schal sche in þis age in chyldebede lye?*

þis thyng is not lykly," þus seyd þei alle,
ladyes in þe chaumbyr' & lordys in þe halle.
(Capgrave 1973 [1893], I, ll. 204–10)

6.1. Many a man and woman laughed at this; some of them said, "It is only a lie! The king is quite feeble, the queen is rather old: [how] could she now groan [in childbirth], [how] could she now scream? Is it possible that she at her age could lie in childbed? This is not likely at all!" So they all said, the ladies in the chamber and the lords in the hall.

A number of reasons for doubting the pregnancy of the queen are listed in very expressive direct discourse. The men and the women in court agree in their disbelief of the signs of the queen's pregnancy. Literally, they all utter (*sayd, seyd*) their doubts to one another; hence, the passage most likely is real gossip (speech representation). However, since the attitudes of a great number of people are being described, one need not assume that any actual utterance, produced by any particular member of the court, is being quoted verbatim. It is quite impossible for all people to have uttered exactly the same speech. Rather, the passage summarizes the general opinion of the courtiers and ladies at court, and many of these opinions may not have been put into words.

The second example passage of group consciousness gives us the reaction of the scholars who have been called to repudiate St. Katharine's theological views by means of their arguments and have instead succumbed to her logic.

> (6.2) *"O good godd," seyd þeis clerkes thane,*
> *"þis mayd hath lerned mor' thyng in her' lyue*
> *Than we supposyd, for mor' than we sche canne.*
> *We woundyr who sche may our' argumentis dryue*
> *ffor hyr conclusyon now in ʒerys fyue*
> *Cune we not lerne þat sche doth in one" —*
> *Thus seyd þeis wysmen be row euerychon.*
> (Capgrave 1973 [1893], I, ll. 414–20)

6.2. *"O good God,"* the scholars then said, *"This maiden has understood more things in her life than we had thought, for she is more knowledgeable than we are. We are quite surprised at how she is able to handle our arguments, and in five years' time we could not learn to reach the conclusion that she does [did] in one." So spoke ["said"] these scholars one after another.*

Again, it is likely that the scholars tell one another of their conviction that St. Katharine is superior to them in intelligence and knowledge; but it also makes sense for each of them to come to this realization one by one singly, and then this would be a representation of consciousness versus speech.

7. Virtual Direct Speech

The final mode of mind representation that I will examine here occurs in a quite complex passage from Chaucer, involving an extended simile that results in an invented virtual soliloquy on the part of the character in the world that constitutes the source domain for the analogy. The situation is again Palamon's and Arcite's duel. At the point when these two knights are about to pounce on one another, the narrator says that their color rose in their faces, and then he launches into an extended simile, comparing the two knights with hunters about to face a dangerous animal that threatens to kill them. This tension experienced by a hunter observing a bear or lion rush at him causes the same kind of change in color observable in the two knights. The simile suggests that the change of color arises from an awareness of danger and the fear of imminent death at the hands of an enemy, the possibility that one of them may die in this decisive battle:

(7.1) *And in a grove, at tyme and place yset,*
This Arcite and this Palamoun ben met.
<u>*Tho chaungen gan the colour in hir face,*</u>
Right as the hunters in the regne of Trace,
That stondeth at the gappe with a spere,
Whan hunted is the leon or the bere,
And hereth hym come russhyng in the greves,

> *And breketh bothe bowes and the leves,*
> And thynketh, *"Heere cometh my mortal enemy!*
> *Withoute faille, he moot be deed, or I:*
> *For outher I moot sleen hym at the gappe,*
> *Or he moot sleen me, if that me myshappe."*
> So ferden they in chaungyng of hir hewe,
> *As fer as everich of hem oother knewe.*
> (Chaucer 1988, A, ll. 1635–48)

7.1. And in a grove, at the time and place that they had set, Arcite and Palamon met. The color in their faces then began to change, just like the hunters *in the realm of Thrace who* stand with a spear at the clearing *when lions or bears are being hunted. They hear the animal rush forward in the thicket, breaking [through] the boughs and leaves, and* think: *"Here comes my mortal enemy! Now, without fail, either he or I must be dead: for either I must kill him in the clearing or he may kill me, if I am unlucky"*—just so behaved these two men as their color rose *as they looked one on the other.*

Clearly, what we have here is a soliloquy—formally speaking; so from that perspective the passage merits little comment. What makes it noteworthy is the fact that Chaucer—and in this he significantly anticipates features of the novel—concentrates extensively on his protagonists' emotions and goes out of his way to portray them in an extensive, elaborated fashion. The second remarkable aspect of this passage is its literariness. This kind of simile is unlikely to occur in the more popular genres of Middle English literature, and (as far as I am aware) does not emerge again in prose until Gascoigne, Sidney, and the other Elizabethan writers of romance. From a European perspective, the use of such elaborate rhetorical figures at this time is not such a surprise—Dante's *Divina commedia* of course contains hoards of such similes. Nevertheless, in terms of the Middle English texts at our disposal, such inventive and complex similes, which even integrate fictive soliloquies, stand out and point toward later developments in narrative, particularly toward Elizabethan depictions of characters' emotions in the romance genre.

Concluding Remarks

My survey of Middle English literature, based on the small corpus of texts discussed in this chapter, has already yielded some important insights. To start with, the radical distinction between speech and thought that has dominated narratological discussions of consciousness representation in the novel does not necessarily apply *mutatis mutandis* to medieval texts. The internal speech of characters when cited in direct discourse is always highly articulate and resembles dramatic soliloquies. In fact, late sixteenth-century dramatic soliloquies in Marlowe, Kyd, or Shakespeare presumably imitated the earlier narrative soliloquy. Not only can characters overhear another person's soliloquy without this being felt to infringe on the readers' notions of realism; the soliloquies themselves are introduced consistently by inquit tags of *seyd* and *quath*, with the result that one should perhaps translate them as "said to him/herself" or "articulated" (rather than "thought"). One way of solving this problem might be to separate verbalized from nonverbalized states of mind, and to locate verbalized internal speech on the side of speech representation, leaving the representation of consciousness to deal with inchoate feelings, emotions, and sensations.

Secondly, the parallelism between the forms of speech and thought representation, as found in present-day English, cannot be assumed to hold for Middle English. The most important type of representation of consciousness for twenty-first-century expectations is the description of gestures and body language indicating emotional states of mind, especially disturbance or turmoil. Given the sheer number of passages involved, this must be treated as a separate category of the representation of consciousness in Middle English. Moreover, it would be an interesting subject of research to compare the distribution and functions of gestural and bodily representations of this kind in texts from the Renaissance to the present day. (Hearken, PhD students working on narratological topics!) Further, as we have seen, psychonarration, a form of thought representation that is highly prominent in the novel, also occurs frequently in Middle English; but until the fifteenth century it tends to consist of discrete brief clauses, a verb or noun in isolation, rather than lengthy passages, as becomes the rule later. In Semino and Short's (2004) terminology, most psychonarration in Middle English narrative is therefore NRT (narrative report of thoughts or consciousness) rather than NRTA (narrative representation of thought acts). The latter category does not emerge fully until the late fourteenth century.

As I have noted, there also exist a number of passages in which the narrator empathetically reproduces the protagonist's emotions *in propria persona* for the benefit of the audience, which is asked to chime in with these sentiments. Here, too, an analysis of the frequency with which this technique is used after 1500 might yield interesting insights into a buried history of narratorial involvement.

Finally, there are a few cases of free indirect thought in Middle English, though they are nowhere near as pervasive as in Old French.[10] In addition, representations of collective speech (and possibly thought) also can be found at this early stage of development. Again, this is an interesting result largely because of the later prominence of these techniques in the nineteenth-century novel, and I am noting them here merely by way of a complete presentation of the formal varieties found in my corpus.

Two broad points can be underscored at this juncture. First, Middle English displays much more extensive narrative depictions of subjectivity and interiority than it is usually credited with (particularly by specialists on the Renaissance, who claim a rise in subjectivity in the later sixteenth century).[11] Despite the clichéd character of most of the reactions portrayed in Middle English narratives, protagonists are shown to suffer, experience joy, and endure doubt or anxiety, and the aesthetic effect of their feelings and thoughts is clearly meant to involve the audience emotionally as well.

Secondly, more theoretical questions about the applicability of current models of speech and thought representation to earlier texts have been raised in this article. My hunch is that by taking account of the development of consciousness-signaling gestures and narratorial comments in postmedieval texts, one could perhaps arrive at a model that integrates medieval and modern forms of the representation of speech and consciousness across the board, emphasizing dominant devices for different periods in turn. More research on this topic is clearly needed before the outlines of such a model become visible.

Notes

1. On the problematic status of indirect thought, see Fludernik (1993, 311–12).

2. For instance, emotions are sometimes treated as "measurable physical responses to salient stimuli," whereas feelings are considered to be "the subjective experiences that sometimes accompany these processes" (*Wikipedia*, entry on "Emotion"). Some scientists include hunger among feelings and therefore do not see the categories of emotions and feelings as coinciding entirely, and dispositions and moods are also set apart from the former two categories (cf. the discussion in Robinson 2007, 5–6). Other distinctions are those between affect, affect display, disposition, feeling, and mood. The terminology also crucially depends on which emotion theory one takes as one's basis; judgment theories tend to foreground the cognitive aspect of emotions, whereas appraisal theories encompass other dimensions of emotions.

3. See, for instance, Hogan (2003) and Keen (2007).

4. All translations are mine. Also, italics, bold italics, and underlining are all emphases added by me to distinguish between different forms of thought representation or to highlight individual words or phrases.

5. Obviously, this count takes each case of direct speech as *one* instance; when counting lines of text (since these internal speeches often extend over several lines), direct speech becomes the most prominent category. Only a rough estimate is here provided for the texts analyzed. For a more robust statistical analysis, more texts would need to be analyzed and utterance/word counts compared across the corpus.

6. Jäger and Bartsch (2006) employ the concept of meta-emotion to characterize conflicting feelings such as guilt and malicious joy, which require a superordinate emotional level from which the subject can resolve the conflict between them.

7. Another example from Chaucer, this time from *The Man of Law's Tale* is: "O blood royal, thet stondeth in this drede, / Fer been thy freendes at thy grete neede!" (O royal blood [i.e., Custance], you who are in dread [of your life], far away are your friends when you need them most urgently) (1988, B, ll. 657–58). The narrator here empathizes with Custance, who has been accused of murder.

8. Compare Fludernik (1993, 93–95, 194–95).

9. In *Fictions of Language* (1993), I cited another example from Chaucer's *Man of Law's Tale* (1988, B, ll. 621–25), which is also ambiguous between speech and thought.

10. See Fleischman (1990) and Marnette (2005). The existence of FID in Old French is a matter of dispute since scholars have different definitions of what counts as a proper example of FID.

11. See, for instance, Hanson (1998), Lobsien (1999), Grady (2000), Pye (2000), Dyck and Martin (2002), Lobsien and Lobsien (2003), as well as Amodio (1995) and Eagleton (1997). Counterarguments against the notion of a specifically modern subjectivity can be found in Aers (1992), Baisch et al. (2005), Knapp (2002), and Spearing (2005).

References

Source Texts

Capgrave, John. 1973 [1893]. *The Life of St. Katharine of Alexandria*. Ed. Carl Horstmann. EETS OS 100. Millwood NY: Kraus Reprint Co.

Chaucer, Geoffrey. 1988. *The Riverside Chaucer*. 3rd ed. Oxford: Oxford University Press.

Horstmann, Carl. 1881. *Altenglische legenden. Neve Folge*. Heilbronn: Henninger.

Malory, Sir Thomas. 1971. *Works*. Ed. Eugène Vinaver. 2nd ed. Oxford: Oxford University Press.

Middle English Verse Romances. 1993. Ed. Donald B. Sands. Exeter Medieval English Texts and Studies. Exeter: University of Exeter Press.

Radcliffe, Ann Ward. 1998 [1794]. *The Mysteries of Udolpho*. Ed. Bonamy Dobreé. Oxford: Oxford University Press.

The South English Legendary. 1967–69. Corpus Christi College Cambridge MS 145. Ed. Charlotte D'Evelyn and Anna J. Mill. 3 vols. EETS 234, 235, 244. Oxford: Oxford University Press.

The Three Kings' Sons. 1895. Ed. Frederick James Furnivall. EETS ES 67. London: Kegan Paul.

Scholarly Works

Aers, David. 1992. "A Whisper in the Ear of Early Modernists; or, Reflections on Literary Critics Writing the 'History of the Subject.'" In *Culture and History 1350–1600: Essays on English Communities, Identities and Writing*, ed. David Aers, 177–201. New York: Harvester Wheatsheaf.

Amodio, Mark C. 1995. "Tradition, Modernity, and the Emergence of the Self in *Sir Gawain and the Green Knight*." *Assays: Critical Approaches to Medieval and Renaissance Texts* 8:47–68.

Baisch, Martin, Jutta Eming, Hendrikje Haufe, and Andrea Sieber, eds. 2005. *Inszenierungen von Subjektivität in der Literatur des Mittelalters*. Königstein: Helmer.

Banfield, Ann. 1982. *Unspeakable Sentences: Narration and Representation in the Language of Fiction*. Boston MA: Routledge.

Chafe, Wallace. 1980. "The Deployment of Consciousness in the Production of a Narrative." In *The Pear Stories: Cognitive, Cultural, and Linguistic Aspects of Narrative Production*, ed. Wallace Chafe, 9–50. Norwood NJ: Ablex.

Cohn, Dorrit. 1978. *Transparent Minds: Narrative Modes for Presenting Consciousness in Fiction*. Princeton NJ: Princeton University Press.

Dyck, Paul, and Matthew Martin, eds. 2002. "Constructions of the Early Modern Subject." Special issue, *Early Modern Literary Studies: A Journal of Sixteenth- and Seventeenth-Century English Literature* 9.

Eagleton, Terry. 1997. "Self-Undoing Subjects." In *Rewriting the Self: Histories from the Renaissance to the Present*, ed. Roy Porter, 262–69. London: Routledge.

Fleischman, Suzanne. 1990. *Tense and Narrativity: From Medieval Performance to Modern Fiction*. Austin: University of Texas Press.

Fludernik, Monika. 1991. "The Historical Present Tense Yet Again: Tense Switching and Narrative Dynamics in Oral and Quasi-oral Storytelling." *Text* 11 (3): 365–98.

———. 1993. *The Fictions of Language and the Languages of Fiction: The Linguistic Representation of Speech and Consciousness*. London: Routledge.

———. 1995. "Middle English *tho* and Other Narrative Discourse Markers." In *Historical Pragmatics*, ed. Andreas Jucker, 341–74. Amsterdam: John Benjamins.

———. 1996. *Towards a "Natural" Narratology*. London: Routledge.

———. 2000. "Discourse Markers in Malory's *Morte D'Arthur*." *Journal of Historical Pragmatics* 1 (2): 231–62.

———. 2003. "The Diachronization of Narratology." *Narrative* 11 (3): 331–48.

———. 2005. "Narrative Structure in the Middle English Prose Romance." In *Anglistentag Aachen 2004: Proceedings*, ed. Lilo Moessner and Christa M. Schmidt, 43–51. Trier, Germany: WVT.

Grady, Hugh. 2000. "Our Need for a Differentiated Theory of (Early) Modern Subjects." In *Philosophical Shakespeares*, ed. John J. Joughin, 34–50. London: Routledge.

Hanson, Elizabeth. 1998. *Discovering the Subject in Renaissance England*. Cambridge: Cambridge University Press.

Hogan, Patrick. 2003. *The Mind and Its Stories: Narrative Universals and Human Emotion*. Cambridge: Cambridge University Press.

Jäger, Christoph, and Anne Bartsch. 2006. "Meta-Emotions." *Grazer Philosophische Studien* 73:179–204.

Keen, Suzanne. 2007. *Empathy and the Novel*. Oxford: Oxford University Press.

Knapp, Fritz Peter. 2002. "Subjektivität des Erzählers und Fiktionalität der Erzählung bei Wolfram von Eschenbach und anderen Autoren des 12. und 13. Jahrhunderts." In *Wolfram-Studien, XVII: Wolfram von Eschenbach—Bilanzen und Perspektiven*, ed. Wolfgang Haubrichs, Eckart Conrad Lutz, and Klaus Ridder, 10–29. Berlin: Schmidt.

Leech, Geoffrey N., and Mick Short. 2007 [1981]. *Style in Fiction*. 2nd ed. London: Longman.

Lobsien, Verena Olejniczak. 1999. *Skeptische Phantasie: Eine andere Geschichte der frühneuzeitlichen Literatur*. München: Fink.

Lobsien, Verena Olejniczak, and Eckhard Lobsien. 2003. *Die unsichtbare Imagination: Literarisches Denken im 16. Jahrhundert*. München: Fink.

Marnette, Sophie. 2005. *Speech and Thought Presentation in French*. Amsterdam: John Benjamins.

Müller, Wolfgang G. 1982. "Das Ich im Dialog mit sich selbst: Bemerkungen zur Struktur des dramatischen Monologs von Shakespeare bis zu Samuel Beckett." *Deutsche Vierteljahrsschrift* 56 (2): 314–33.

Neuse, Werner. 1990. *Geschichte der erlebten Rede und des inneren Monologs in der deutschen Prosa*. New York: Peter Lang.

Orth, Eva-Maria. 2000. *Das Selbstgespräch: Untersuchungen zum dialogisierten Monolog am Beispiel englischsprachiger Romane*. Trier, Germany: WVT.

Palmer, Alan. 2004. *Fictional Minds*. Lincoln: University of Nebraska Press.

———. 2005. "Intermental Thought in the Novel: The Middlemarch Mind." *Style* 39 (4): 427–39.

———. 2010. "Large Intermental Units in *Middlemarch*." In *Postclassical Narratology: Approaches and Analyses*, ed. Jan Alber and Monika Fludernik, 83–104. Columbus: Ohio State University Press.

Pascal, Roy. 1977. *The Dual Voice: Free Indirect Speech and Its Functioning in the Nineteenth-Century European Novel*. Manchester: Manchester University Press.

Pye, Christopher. 2000. *The Vanishing: Shakespeare, the Subject, and Early Modern Culture*. Durham NC: Duke University Press.

Robinson, Jenefer. 2007. *Deeper Than Reason: Emotion and Its Role in Literature, Music and Art*. Oxford: Clarendon Press.

Semino, Elena, and Michael H. Short. 2004. *Corpus Stylistics: Speech, Writ-*

ing and Thought Presentation in a Corpus of English Writing. London: Routledge.

Short, Michael H. 2003. "A Corpus-Based Approach to Speech, Thought and Writing Presentation." In *Corpus Linguistics by the Lune: A Festschrift for Geoffrey Leech,* ed. A. Wilson, P. Rayson, and T. McEnery, 241–71. Frankfurt am Main: Peter Lang.

Short, Michael H., Elena Semino, and Jonathan Culpepper. 1996. "Using a Corpus for Stylistics Research: Speech and Thought Presentation." In *Using Corpora in Language Research,* ed. Jenny Thomas and Michael Short, 110–31. London: Longman.

Short, Michael H., Martin Wynne, and Elena Semino. 2004. "Revisiting the Notion of Faithfulness in Discourse Presentation Using a Corpus Approach." *Language and Literature* 11 (4): 325–55.

Spearing, Anthony C. 2005. *Textual Subjectivity: The Encoding of Subjectivity in Medieval Narratives and Lyrics.* Oxford: Oxford University Press.

Steinberg, Erwin R. 1973. *The Stream of Consciousness and Beyond in Ulysses.* Pittsburgh: University of Pittsburgh Press.

Steinberg, Günter. 1971. *Erlebte Rede: Ihre Eigenart und ihre Formen in neuerer deutscher, französischer und englischer Erzählliteratur.* Göppingen: Alfred Kümmerle.

Tannen, Deborah. 1984. *Conversational Style: Analyzing Talk among Friends.* Norwood NJ: Ablex.

———. 1989. *Talking Voices: Repetition, Dialogue, and Imagery in Conversational Discourse.* Cambridge: Cambridge University Press.

Warhol, Robyn R. 1986. "Toward a Theory of the Engaging Narrator: Earnest Interventions in Gaskell, Stowe, and Eliot." *PMLA* 101 (5): 811–18.

Part II

Sixteenth- and
Seventeenth-Century Minds

3. 1500–1620
Reading, Consciousness, and Romance in the Sixteenth Century

F. ELIZABETH HART

Between the late fifteenth and early seventeenth centuries in England, the concept of human consciousness became increasingly linked to the question of what goes on inside the human head. The early modern *minde*—seat of reason, soul, will, and even passion—had long been known to be connected corporeally to the *braine*, although the exact nature of their relationship was (and remains) a mystery.[1] Human figures in the literature of the period gradually assumed more of the outlines of Renaissance individuality, especially by comparison with their medieval counterparts, and one of the ways this individuality was expressed, I contend, was through a narrowing of focus toward the mind as an object and as an adjunct to the head—the latter now a wellspring of imagined realities.

To be sure, the English had important precedents for representing interiority and for understanding the "self" in terms of the mind's inner workings. Writings by Augustine, Boethius, and other Christian Platonists had long treated "soul" and "mind" as more or less synonymous concepts.[2] But by the sixteenth century, and owing (as Scott Manning Stevens has shown) to shifts in medical science, the discourse of interiority had begun expanding toward the more inclusive semantics of the physical—toward a sense of self that could be represented as supplemental to the metaphysical.[3] At the same time, however, and in a development that more keenly interests me in this chapter, representations of the mind also became more precise in their imagery, enacting a shift both in the etiology and the symbolic resonances of "mind" away from the heart and toward another organ altogether—the brain—and thus toward the metonym of the head-as-mind.[4]

Narratives across the period's important genres, from the Bible to romance, epic poetry, and staged drama, presented figures of humans who now possessed a head-centered (and mind-centered) interiority, a quality of inwardness that even aspires, at times, to simulate the act of thinking. In the sixteenth century, we still find representations of humans whose thoughts and emotions are expressed by the external means familiar from medieval literature—for example, spoken dialogue, gestures, or other somatic signs.[5] Only now, we also glimpse brief representations of conscious self-awareness and introspection: people pausing in the midst of action to wrestle with their inner conflicts, to speculate about others' intentions, or to lose themselves in imaginary worlds. While such representations occur only rarely throughout the sixteenth century, by the century's final decades they had become a recognizable feature of romance fiction and a distinguishing trait of the theater, particularly of Shakespeare's plays.[6] Within another half century, the impulse to inhabit purely imaginary worlds occasionally dominated such diverse literary works as Andrew Marvell's "The Garden" (ca. 1650–52) and Margaret Cavendish's The Blazing World (1666, 1668).

But might this tendency toward richer portraits of interiority in the early modern period indicate a phenomenological as well as a literary sea change? In this chapter, I argue that it does. Specifically, I claim that the heightened impulse to represent consciousness bespeaks a shift in people's actual experiences of themselves, insofar as the act of engaging one's consciousness as such became an aspect of human life newly worth telling, writing, and reading about. The fairly obvious agency behind such a change would be the introduction of print technology to England in 1476; but the more direct cause—itself arguably an effect of print—was a massive shift in people's cognitive abilities toward reading in particular. Print technology, in conjunction with humanism and the Protestant Reformation, both of which placed enormous emphasis on text reading, supported an unprecedented increase in English literacy rates across geographical, class, and gender boundaries. Many more people learned to read—and some to write—than had previously been able to;

and still more who were not literate themselves became exposed to those who were, in towns, cities, and throughout rural areas. Today, researchers complain of the difficulty of measuring the exact rates of early modern literacy, but all basically agree that literacy increased markedly in the hundred or so years following printing.[7]

This chapter hypothesizes the development of what I will call a reading-based consciousness in England—first, by briefly surveying what historians now believe about reading literacy in the period and reflecting on how today's cognitive approaches to literacy might give that history a fresh perspective; and second, by turning to narrative text worlds or storyworlds and considering the likelihood that increased numbers of readers also meant that narrative immersion simply became a more widespread, commonly shared, and familiar experience whose effect, overall, was to focus cultural attention on the mind and on the specialized worlds that minds create. What, I ask, are the implications of this new concern with the mind? I explore here evidence that such awareness began to emerge through new kinds of representations of human interiority, manifesting in what today we term "character psychology." These representations simulate the mental processes of early modern readers made newly self-conscious *by* their reading. Such recursive experiences of consciousness would have rewarded Renaissance authors by giving them a quality of reception they could not have expected before the advent of printing—and thus my hypothesis tangentially addresses the period's noticeable proliferations in literary production and experimentation.

My examples of text-generated representations of consciousness-processing come from three important romances written near the end of the sixteenth century: Sir Philip Sidney's *New Arcadia* (composed 1578–84; published 1590/1593),[8] Robert Greene's *Pandosto* (1588), and Edmund Spenser's *Faerie Queene* (1590). Romance may seem an odd genre with which to examine this period's art of characterization, considering the richness of the drama in this regard; however, my interest is in specifically textual forms of narrative, of which romance was an especially popular example, second only to the Bible as a source of stories. Appealing to an unusually broad readership, romance crossed gender, class, and educational lines more readily than narratives composed for courtly or popular tastes (e.g., epic poetry or broadside ballads).[9] Furthermore, romance preceded the stage in terms of its innovations in characterization, starting earlier than the drama to experiment with representations of interiority. Beginning with Sidney's *Arcadia* and peaking (though hardly ending) with Shakespeare's late plays, romance offered the Renaissance its first and most influential model for narratives of fictional minds.

Sixteenth-Century Literacy

Near the end of Canto 9 in Book 2 of *The Faerie Queene*, Sir Guyon and Prince Arthur, while on a tour through Alma's Castle, stumble upon the blind sage Eumnestes surrounded in his garret chamber by books and parchment scrolls—"old records from auncient times" (57.7). The hermit antiquarian has been collecting history texts to form a small library within the castle, and the knights, pausing in the doorway, are drawn in with a sudden passion to explore. They comb the shelves; then each pulls down a title appropriate to his own personal narrative: Arthur finds *Briton moniments*, which tells how multiple "Regiments" in England became the provenance of a single gifted leader; Guyon selects *"Antiquitie of Faerie* lond," a genealogy of his Elfin peoples (59.8, 60). Sitting down immediately, Arthur and Guyon become so deeply immersed in their silent reading that all past and future quests—indeed all "action" we might consider prototypical of both epic and romance genres—are suspended for the full length of Canto 10. In the meantime, Alma, the knights' gracious tour guide, is summarily dismissed: "Wherat they burning both with feruent fire, / Their countries auncestry to vnderstond, / Crau'd leaue of *Alma*, and that aged sire, / To read those bookes; who gladly graunted their desire" (Canto 9, 60.6–9).

It is hard to imagine an English literary artist constructing this scene prior to the introduction of mass-produced printed texts. Even granting that Spenser's intended reader was probably a courtly one, someone likely to have remained as comfortable with manuscripts as with printed texts,[10] this moment in *The Faerie Queene* captures an experience now widespread enough— owing to printing—for the poet to take it for a legitimate subject for fiction: reading books. The resulting representation performs an act of framing that is unusual for the romance and unique in *The Faerie Queene*: In order to process this episode and the whole of Canto 10 that follows, Spenser's reader must construct an imaginative scenario in which Arthur and Guyon are doing exactly the same thing—that is, *constructing imaginative scenarios*. Creative framing as a narrative technique has been a distinguishing trait of the romance genre dating back to its earliest examples in the Greek prose fictions that are among Spenser's (and Sidney's and Greene's) sources.[11] But whereas these earlier romances use frames to nest stories within stories and thereby thicken their narratives, or whereas they shift laterally along time lines to add dimensions of past events to current ones before moving on to future ones (the common classical technique of beginning *in medias res*), Spenser's frame *contracts inward* through a series of scenarios set explicitly inside his two characters' heads. Guyon and Arthur wave off the world surrounding their bodies and transport themselves—just as we must do when we imagine them—to worlds much more narrowly located inside the "spaces" of their minds. Their *mind*scapes thus come into functional alignment with the many other *land*scapes and physical structures (e.g., "the plaine"; the Bower of Bliss; the Garden of Adonis; the Castle of Temperance, where this episode is set) that stage allegories of spirituality throughout the poem. Sixteenth-century semantics had maintained the medieval equation of mind with soul, allowing the mind to serve as a platform for religious allegory. Here, Spenser both adopts and expands on that tradition, presenting the mind as the locus of moral being but *also* as a processing instrument—with which we and his characters read and imagine—and as a virtual space containing worlds embedded inside worlds.

I will return to this episode at the end of the chapter. Before proceeding, however, I want to review some of the evidence regarding reading literacy in early modern England and then discuss in more detail how an early modern reading-based consciousness may be contextualized by today's science of reading—and specifically by findings that reading skill changes humans' neurological makeup and may even alter consciousness.

The difficulty of quantifying early modern literacy rates derives partly from an unsurprising scarcity of records, but also from the fact that literacy historians' understanding of what actually constitutes "literacy" has changed in recent years.[12] What historians now realize is that there was a crucial time gap during the sixteenth century between the teaching of reading and the teaching of writing (Charlton and Spufford 2002; Fox 2000; Spufford 1981; Watt 1991).[13] The two skills were apparently taught separately, with reading being offered approximately two years before writing and the latter often not at all. Additionally, it is now believed that some rudimentary, vernacular reading instruction would have been given in the home to both boys and girls (around age five or six) and to enough children whose families spanned the social spectrum to spread at least a smattering of reading ability throughout England. Kenneth Charlton and Margaret Spufford assert that even the country's poorest children—and more women across the social spectrum—may have been exposed to reading than was previously believed (Charlton and Spufford 2002, 27, 42). Given this revised scenario, historians are recognizing the profound implications of far *greater numbers* of people interacting with texts than could have been imagined until recently. Of the many aspects of our view it changes, this scenario forces us to change our model of early modern culture itself, since "it is the first skill, reading, which brings about cultural change and openness to the spread of ideas" (Charlton and Spufford 2002, 27).[14] It now seems probable that far more people could at least read, if not write, and that the many now-likely readers—more women, more tradesmen, craftsmen, laborers, yeomen, and peasants—may amount to a reading-based culture on a scale that historians are only beginning to understand.[15]

Charlton and Spufford's key statement to this effect is the following: "Between 1500 and 1700 . . . [England] was transformed into a society in which writing, and particularly reading, were widely used in many areas of human activity, including pleasure and self-education, by *many more members of the community*, including some of the labouring poor" (43, emphasis added). Here they point to a dimension of the history that might be easily undertheorized in our attempts to understand a "fundamentally literate" early modern society: the creation of "community" within a critical mass of people who hold certain cognitive skills in common. Historians and sociologists tend to examine societies as products of institutions; or as groupings of people whose shared experiences are expressed in practices deriving from ideas and ideology; or as groups whose shared identities are based on social or political categories of race, gender, class, sexual orientation, ethnicity, and nationality. It is trickier to expand such analyses to account for ways in which people also identify with one another through *shared cognitive skills*. Yet we form such alliances all the time, and as a species we probably have been doing so since our primate ancestors first turned their material world into crude forms of technology. It seems that shared habits of cognitive processing based on acquired, technology-specific skills create social groupings just as readily as other identity-forming forces. For evidence we need only point to such groupings made manifest by today's digital technologies—for example, social networks accessed by computers, phones, and other hardware intermediaries (some yet to be invented).

But learning to use a skill-specific technology is more than just a matter of conditioning oneself to press certain buttons. Rather, it requires a complex series of brain adaptations, through which the act of focusing on a task actually channels new neural pathways. Repetition enriches and eventually entrenches the pathways, to the point where the acquired skills become relatively automatic (Edelman 1987; Freeman 2000; Hebb 1949). Technology, in this sense, actually changes the morphology of individual brains and in so doing forges new bases for social interaction since any group of technology users, having made similar brain adaptations, will eventually recognize the commonality of their new experience.

The Literate Brain

Acquiring a "literacy brain" works on these same principles—only more so. The cognitive psychologist Merlin Donald cites a growing consensus among neuroscientists that literacy in general—especially reading—represents such a profound brain "innovation" that it may be comparable in impact to first-language learning (Donald 2001, 302). Like any technology, literacy alters the brain and causes changes in the general cognitive capacities of individuals that affect those individuals' social interactions:

Literacy skills change the functional organization of the brain and deeply influence how individuals and communities of literate individuals perform their cognitive work. Mass literacy has triggered two kinds of major cognitive reorganizations, one in individuals and the other in groups.

To become fully literate, [an] individual must acquire a host of neural demons that are completely absent from anyone who lacks literacy training. . . . There is no equivalent in a preliterate mind to the circuits that hold the complex neural components of a reading vocabulary or the elaborate procedural habits of formal thinking. (Donald 2001, 302)

Donald's "neural demons" underlie those aspects of consciousness that scientists call "executive functioning," referring to the frontal-lobe coordinator of attention, memory, linguistic, visual, and auditory processes, all necessary capacities for acquiring new skills. Much of human consciousness operates automatically, without the overseeing of the executive function. But *learning* new skills, especially those based in complex symbol-processing, requires conscious attention and enormous stores of short, intermediate, and long-term memory.[16] Eventually such skills do become automatic, but only after the act of processing them has permanently altered neural structures.[17]

These insights are relevant to a historical analysis because individual brains/minds develop in tandem with cultures, and—in complex feedback loops of cause and effect—cultures are shaped by the structure of individual brains/minds. A study, therefore, involving the mass acquisition of cognitive skills is also very much a culture study. Both Donald and the literacy historian David Olson have recognized this connection: "Literate culture," writes Donald, "has capitalized on untapped cerebral potential and reprogrammed the human brain in its own image" (Donald 2001, 302). Such plasticity means that "the core configuration of skills that defines a mind actually varies significantly as a function of different kinds of culture. *This is especially true of the most conscious domains of mind, such as those involved in formal thinking and representation*" (302, emphasis added). Olson's discussion supports the historical argument that a profound shift in human consciousness must have occurred specifically during the early modern period once reading had reached a point of critical mass:

> *We may think of literacy as both a cognitive and a social condition, the ability to participate actively in a community of readers who have agreed on some principles of reading . . . a set of texts to be treated as significant, and a working agreement on the appropriate or valid interpretation(s) of those texts. That definition allows us to understand how the kind of literacy developed and shared by a community of readers towards the end of the medieval period and the beginning of [the] early modern period could provide both a new way of reading texts and a new way of looking at and thinking about the world.* (Olson 1994, 274–75)

The rising number of early modern readers helped produce a trend away from "thinking about things to thinking about representations of things, that is, *thinking about thought*" (282, emphasis added), an observation in sync with the connection that Donald makes between "core skills" and a given culture's patterns of "formal thinking and representation," in the passage by him that I quoted earlier.

To complicate this scenario a bit more, let us also consider the historian Roger Chartier's (1995) observations regarding the special importance of *silent* reading as an aspect of early modern literacy change. Owing to the decline of the classical practice of *scriptio continua*—the running together of a text's letters with no space breaks to demarcate individual words—texts became friendlier to silent reading, which in turn promoted habits of reading in private.[18] While this shift in manuscript and eventually printing practice did not eliminate either reading aloud or public reading,[19] it did add to readers' repertoire of habits and in so doing invited them to participate in a different quality of reading experience. As noted by Cavallo and Chartier (1999, 7), silent reading promotes reading at one's own pace, rereading as needed for comprehension, reading selectively or in fragments, reading cross-textually, and reading hypertextually—that is, keeping track of glosses, references, commentaries, and so forth; meanwhile, privacy frees the reading mind from the demands of external sociability in order for it to focus attention internally—on itself.

Reading Storyworlds

With such focus on, and tolerance for, complexity comes the greater likelihood that readers can engage meaningfully with challenging texts involving high levels of abstraction or content-area training such as formal argumentation or debates within specific disciplines of learning. Silent, private reading thus undoubtedly supported both the rise of humanism and the spread of the Reformation, movements requiring complex interaction between readers and texts and among readers themselves. But silent, private reading must also have provided the optimal conditions for a non-content-specific form of reading that we may mistake as less challenging and therefore less instructive: the reading and processing of literary narratives.

The relative effortlessness with which humans process narrative texts as compared to texts organized by other rhetorical principles (e.g., description, declamation) belies the complexity inherent in even simple stories (whether in fiction or nonfiction, literary or popular traditions). The complexity of narrative has to do with the requirement that readers or listeners create and then immerse themselves in an *alternative reality* that springs to vivid existence out of the exchange between a narrative's formal elements—its language—and the receivers' minds. When a narrative's linguistic elements are relatively stabilized by being cast in the form of a written text, the imagined scenarios may achieve greater complexity as a function of greater flexibility.

(For instance, as Herman [2004, 62–66] has suggested, written narratives allow for more flexible processing of the temporal and spatial codes inherent to all stories, resulting in what are perhaps qualitatively different experiences of the storyworlds evoked by written texts.[20]) I argue that silent, private reading—an increasingly common activity in the sixteenth century—provided ideal conditions for constructing and then inhabiting imaginative text worlds.

The concept of the text world can be linked to Marie-Laure Ryan's (1991) work on possible-worlds approaches to narrative (cf. Semino 1997) as well as the account of "mental spaces" developed by Gilles Fauconnier (1994). The theory of text worlds proper was first outlined by Paul Werth (1999); Joanna Gavins's (2007) textbook presents an overview and systematization of the theory, which also has affinities with Catherine Emmott's (1997) "contextual frame" theory and the idea of "storyworlds" as developed by David Herman (2002). A text world is a dynamic mental construct, cued by the linguistic codes of a text, that builds upon a reader's real-world knowledge and experiences but that may also exceed the real world in its possibilities, depending on the "frames" or semantic mechanisms by which category boundaries—usually fuzzy and shifting—define both the physical and situational parameters of the imagined reality. The metaphor of the "world" is common to the various disciplines invested in the theory and has received support for its appropriateness from the empirical work of the cognitive psychologist Richard Gerrig (1993). Gerrig's experiments, designed to determine how people generally understand their experience of narratives (whether by reading, hearing, or viewing them), have consistently shown that subjects feel literally *transported* from a place of origin to a different "place," in which they as well as agents—characters—perform actions consistent with the inferred realities of the new "place." Subjects describe being transported in this way regardless of whether the narrative they are experiencing is fiction or nonfiction, its outcome unknown or known ahead of time (Gerrig 1993, 10–13).

The metaphor that such an experience constitutes a world draws on two important scientific models for how humans think: gestalt theory in cognitive psychology and mental space theory in linguistics.[21] Gestalt theory explores the ways in which the brain discerns pattern, defining a gestalt as a mental construct collected from a variety of information systems (physical, psychological, biological, and symbolic) out of which the brain distills a unified whole—although, importantly, a whole that exceeds the sum of its constituent parts. Gestalts are like mental holograms that generate the illusion of interior three-dimensionality and that predispose the brain toward constructing patterns. Mental-space theory embraces the notion that our thoughts operate through gestalt-based, virtual three-dimensionality and from this three-dimensionality deduces functions via analogy with actual space, including the very fundamental one (based on universal experience) that agents move through and express themselves in space. Thus, to combine the theories: Brains discern patterns in gestalt form and from these patterns construct illusions of spatial conditions similar to what real bodies and minds are accustomed to living in and with, including animation—that is, dynamic movement patterns unfolding in time.

Herman's concept of storyworlds seeks a rapprochement between narratological, linguistic, and cognitive approaches to narrative understanding. Whereas the structuralist narratologists, for example, characterized story as a kind of substrate of the text, Herman's storyworld actively links narrative's formal linguistic elements to the extralinguistic modeling capabilities of interpreters' minds. In Herman's analysis, the two are indistinguishable—at least practically speaking—in the moment of a mind's processing of a narrative: "It would be difficult to account for the immersive potential of stories by appeal to structuralist notions of *story*, that is, strictly in terms of events and existents arranged into a plot by the narrative presentation" (Herman 2002, 16). Instead, he argues, immersion occurs because processing minds construct holistic interior environments—that is, gestalts—into which the mind pours complex blends taken from multiple stores of knowledge and information (including, though not restrictively, the formal elements of a narrative's presentation):

Interpreters of narrative do not merely reconstruct a sequence of events and a set of existents but imaginatively (emotionally, viscerally) inhabit a world in which, besides happening and existing, things matter, agitate, exalt, repulse, provide grounds for laughter and grief, and so on. . . . [S]toryworlds are mentally and emotionally projected environments in which interpreters are called upon to live out complex blends of cognitive and imaginative response, encompassing sympathy, the drawing of causal references, identification, evaluation, suspense, and so on. (Herman 2002, 16–17)

In other words, storyworlds exploit the mind's capacity to simulate its own workings, especially the processes of "formal thinking and representation" (to quote Donald again) that encapsulate both the cognitive and the cultural dimensions of literacy.

All storyworlds simulate consciousness in these ways, but text-based storyworlds, and especially those read silently and privately, provide richer experiences of mental simulation because of the heightened complexities of readers' immersions. From a historical perspective, the fact that many *more* people than ever before could have gained access to such simulations in the early modern period suggests a subtle shift in the phenomenon of consciousness itself, in keeping with Olson's scenario. I contend that we find evidence for this shift in one of the period's main sources of narrative fiction, the romance, which appears at times to be self-consciously experimenting with representations of consciousness-in-process.

The Cognitive Frames of Ancient Romance

In the famous opening to Heliodorus's *Ethiopian Story*, the classical Greek romance that Sidney cited as a source for his *Arcadia*, a small band of brigand pirates lands on a bank of the River Nile and views a scene of slaughter from a conflict that has apparently just ended. They see strewn along the river's edge the hacked-up bodies of numerous dead men and also the overturned remnants of a banquet interrupted by the violence. Then, off in the distance, they spot a beautiful woman sitting atop a rock, staring down at a wounded man lying on the ground below her. The scene's narrator dwells on the appearance of the woman: "Her head was crowned with laurel; a quiver was slung over her shoulder; and her left arm was propped upon her bow, beyond which the hand hung negligently down. The elbow of her other arm she supported on her right thigh, while on its palm she rested her cheek; and with downcast eyes she held her head still, gazing intently on [the] prostrate youth" (Heliodorus 1997, 4). This first, emblematic image of Chariclea, the story's heroine, begs the mystery of what catastrophe has just befallen these people. It also captures the amazement of the pirates, who find in Chariclea's frozen perspective a different sort of mystery: Who is she? Who is the bleeding youth she watches?

In this summary, I have tried to convey the restrictively *visual* nature of the information that Heliodorus's narrator gives us: the sights of havoc that the pirates gaze on, the minute details of Chariclea's weaponry and physical demeanor. As the scene continues, the information switches to what is *heard* as the narrator quotes Chariclea and the wounded man speaking to each other (the man first):

"My sweet one, are you truly with me, still alive? Or have you too fallen by chance a victim to the fighting . . . ?" "On you," she answered, "it rests whether I live or die. Now, do you see this?" she added, showing a sword that lay upon her knees. "Hitherto it has been idle, withheld by your breathing." As she spoke she sprang from the rock: the men [watching, were] struck, with wonder and alarm by the sight. (Heliodorus 1997, 4)

But then quickly we return to Chariclea's image: "Her arrows rattled with her sudden movement; the inwoven gold of her dress glistened in the beams of the sun, and her hair, tossing below the wreath like the tresses of a bacchant, flowed widespread over her back" (5). We are told that the pirates are "filled with terror" (5) when they see her resemblance to a goddess and that they try but are unable "to form a true opinion" (5) about her identity. Eventually, they swoop down upon the two figures, and as before the narrator provides mostly visual and auditory information: "The noisy clatter of the men, and their shadows slanting across her view, caused the maiden to raise her head: she looked, then bent it down again . . . wholly engaged in tending the prostrate youth" (5). When Chariclea does speak—"If you are among the living, your life, it would seem, is one of brigandage; but your coming here is timely" (5)—interestingly, the pirates cannot understand her because she speaks a foreign tongue. But before they have time to contemplate this barrier, a *second* band of pirates appears on the horizon and scatters the first, who leave Chariclea and her beloved (Theagenes) to be taken prisoner. Thus ends the first episode of *The Ethiopian Story* with its mysteries pointedly unresolved.

Ancient romance, while experimental in its uses of temporal framing,[22] rarely strays far in its representations of *people* beyond the method of visual and auditory reportage that I have tried to capture here. Indeed, one can turn at random to almost any page of *The Ethiopian Story* and find the information constrained in this way: rich in sensory description and generous in dialogue but offering only minimal (if any) access to people's minds. This kind of narration still requires readers to interpret fictional mental functioning in the sense specified by Alan Palmer when he writes that "narrative is, in essence, the presentation of fictional minds" entailing *at least* the primary and enabling frame—what he calls "the continuing-consciousness frame" (175)—of a "cognitive relationship between the reader and the storyworld" (Palmer 2004, 184–85, 196). Evidence for the presence of this continuing-consciousness frame is the fact that Heliodorus's readers do basically assume that the people he describes possess minds as a given of their representations of humanness. However, there is rarely anything like a direct reference to their mental processing, let alone access to their inner speech or emotions.[23] Romance narrators report *that* people think such and such, or *that* they experience strong emotions; and parallel to this, people in romance often *announce* the content of their own minds, generally following up such announcements with physical expressions of their declared mental states. But readers tend to learn about the processing of interior experiences only *after* such processing has already taken place.

Palmer's continuing-consciousness model includes at least three subframes within which readers of fiction engage consciousness: the thought-action continuum, in which readers "decode . . . presentations of action" to infer what fictional people are thinking or feeling; "intermental" or group thought, in which readers track consciousness as it is exchanged between fictional people; and "intramental" or individual thought, in which readers and sometimes other fictional people (try to) gain access to other fictional people's private, interior speech (183, 205, 211, 218). Palmer convincingly demonstrates, in his analyses of texts like Jane Austen's *Emma* and Evelyn Waugh's *Vile Bodies*, that narratives may deploy all three subframes at once, rendering multiple representations of consciousness embedded within a single narrative.

But judging from a comparison between the post-eighteenth-century (mostly modern and postmodern) texts that Palmer discusses and the ancient romance, of which Heliodorus serves as a prototypical example,[24] it appears that such embedded multiplicities of consciousness were subject to historical development and furthermore that such embedded consciousness constitutes a relatively *recent* development in fiction as an art form. As the cognitive literary critic Lisa Zunshine (2006) has demonstrated, by the eighteenth century, writers' repertoires had noticeably expanded to include many more—and more direct—means of representing fictional people's mental lives—that is, Palmer's intermental and intramental subframes.

When did this change occur, and what exactly changed? It makes sense to suppose there to have been an intermediate phase in which techniques for representing mental processing actually began to emerge. Given the proliferation of Renaissance romance in the sixteenth and seventeenth centuries, it is not inconceivable that we should look for this intermediary stage starting with Sidney and his fellow emulators of the ancient fictions in prose, verse, and dramatic forms. Providing additional historical context for Palmer's account, my examples here explore developments associated with the transition from early romance to narratives with more complex intermental and intramental subframes. And I contend, speaking chronologically, that the first such development is the use of *direct reference*, which I would define as the moment when the narrator's focus zooms in on the head or mind of a represented human and thus objectifies it as a container of interiority. The second, probably following from the first, is *thought simulation*, the representation of inner speech. The latter seems highly unsophisticated, of course, compared to its descendant examples in the eighteenth-century novel; nonetheless, this method of figuring minds anticipates modern and even postmodern techniques for representing human interiority.

Direct Reference, Simulation, and the Birth of Character

By itself, the direct reference to fictional people's minds constitutes a significant shift in romance's strategies for representing human beings. Despite the fact that Heliodorus's people are constantly planning, remembering, loving, fearing, anticipating, and maintaining loyalty to one another, they somehow manage to do all this without the author drawing specific attention either to their heads or the brains/minds encased within them. Not so for Sidney or Greene, who are both self-consciously emulating *The Ethiopian Story* but *also* tentatively experimenting with treating fictional minds differently than does their model: as substantive, mysterious, even powerful entities worth making explicit in a variety of ways. Sidney is less experimental in this sense than Greene, but occasionally Sidney does offer a good example: such as the moment in *Arcadia*, Book 1, when Pyrocles slips away from Musidorus during a hunting party and secretly disguises himself as an Amazon warrior. Pyrocles's disguise does not fool Musidorus, who, once he finds him, berates his friend for having the poor judgment to take on a "womanish habit" (1987 [1577/1590], 133). In one of the speeches that follows, Musidorus uses terms that not only refer directly to Pyrocles's "mind" but assign that mind a noticeably independent and supervisory agency:

For likelier sure I would have thought it that any outward face might have been disguised than that the face of so excellent a mind could have been thus blemished. O sweet Pyrocles, separate yourself a little, if it be possible, from yourself, and let your own mind look upon your own proceedings. (130)

Greene similarly assigns such agency to "humane mindes" in *Pandosto*, beginning with the story's first line, in which the narrator contemplates how jealousy, as a state of "minde," is a formidable enough force to reduce a thriving kingdom to ruins (Greene 2005 [1588], 620). Unlike Sidney's very long, traditional, and highly episodic romance, Greene's romance is short, unusually unified in its narrative design, and frankly obsessed with its fictional people's fulminating minds, prominently showcasing the interior struggles of at least five different ones in sequence: Pandosto, Franion, Bellaria, Fawnia, Dorastus, and then back to Pandosto. At the center of these studies is the highly suspicious mind of King Pandosto, who has wrongly convinced himself that his queen Bellaria is being unfaithful to him. Greene notes how "a certaine melancholy passion entring the minde of *Pandosto*, drave him into sundry and doubtfull thoughts" (622) and that his "minde was so farre charged with Jealousy, that he did no longer doubt" (623). By the story's end, after Pandosto's "unwilling mynde" has led him to contemplate incest with—and even the murder of—his daughter Fawnia, he suffers from "desperate thoughts," then falls into "a melancholie fit," and finally commits suicide, leaving his kingdom to the "contented quiet" of his son-in-law Dorastus (656).[25]

But the second form of representation to emerge in the romance, the real-time simulation of thought processes, is even more radical than direct reference because of the way it invites readers' immersion into storyworlds to an extent that previous narratives' abstracts had not permitted. To get at why I might be justified in terming it radical, let me turn briefly to the increasingly familiar research on Theory of Mind and the aesthetic models that literary, theater, and performance scholars are now developing on its basis. Cognitive scientists curious about the mechanics of human sociability have discovered a complex of skills so basic to cognition as to seem invisible until defamiliarized by analysis. These skills may be summarized simply as a person's ability to infer the content of other people's minds based on the belief that other people in fact *have* minds (Baron-Cohen 1995; Gallese 2001).[26] Aesthetic models of fiction-reading (Palmer 2004; Zunshine 2006) and "theater-spectating" (McConachie 2008) based on this science have rendered provocative new analyses stressing the role that simulation and its cognate, empathy, play in our ability to construct and become immersed in the minds of imaginary agents. As Bruce McConachie describes this process, specifically with respect to theater-spectating:

> [Their] visuomotor representations . . . provide spectators with the ability to "read the minds" of actor/characters, to intuit their beliefs, intentions, and emotions by watching their motor actions. This mode of engagement, also known as empathy, extends to our understanding of actors' use of props and even their gestures and spoken language. Empathy is not an emotion, but it readily leads viewers to emotional engagements. In addition to experiencing [emotions] . . . , spectators often gain a conscious awareness of their emotional commitments, which encourages them to form sympathetic or antipathetic attachments to certain actor/characters. (McConachie 2008, 65)

Not unlike with live spectating, readers following interior self-talk, simulated over roughly the time that it would take a person to experience such thoughts, respond with empathy, which leads, in turn, to the reader's projection onto a fictional person the fuller range of his or her own cognitive functions (e.g., Herman's "projected environments"). These functions *gifted* to fictional people include emotions but also memory, attentiveness, concept-building, and even (in splendidly recursive fashion) the ability to infer the workings of the minds of others.

In general agreement with Palmer, I believe that our sense of a fictionalized psychology is more or less a function of how aggressively a given narrative works to generate gestalt- and mental-space-based three-dimensionality—that is, the mental topography that comes of layering one thing on top of another (consciousness upon consciousness) and from embedding virtual environments inside other virtual environments (fictional people's minds inside readers' minds). Because reading itself seems to mimic thought processing, the act of reading over an abstract character's thoughts doubles the effects of that mimicry, enabling a collapse of "selfness" between reader and character: a *re*-cognition. This may not seem like such a momentous conclusion—the gap between subject and object closes—until we remember that simulating consciousness is a relatively new strategy of fiction in the history of English literature. For some reason, whether gradually or relatively suddenly, storytellers themselves have had to become more conscious *about* consciousness in order to start experimenting with ways of representing it. I contend that Sidney is among the first—if not *the* first—such storyteller to try to capture the workings of consciousness in English prose fiction, having chosen the varied, episode-rich medium of the romance as his testing ground.

We catch sight of Sidney's attempts at simulation in the same moments from the *Arcadia* discussed earlier, just before Musidorus finds Pyrocles in his Amazon disguise. Musidorus reads a letter from Pyrocles, claiming that he has fallen in love and now wishes to be left alone. As is typical of fictional people in traditional romance, Sidney presents Musidorus's reaction in the form of strongly verbalized, already-experienced emotion: he cries out, "What have I deserved of thee to be thus banished of thy counsels?" (Sidney 1987 [1577/1590], 116). But then—and very atypically for romance—Sidney's narrator contracts the narrative *scope*, providing us suddenly with unusual access to Musidorus's nonverbalized interiority:

Then turned he his thoughts to all forms of guesses that might light upon the purpose and course of Pyrocles, for he was not sure by his words that it was love as he was doubtful where the love was. . . . But the more he thought, the more he knew not what to think, armies of objections rising against any accepted opinion. (117)

Whereas usually the cogitations of people in romance are only implied by the narrator, here the reader's ability to follow Sidney's plot—to know what happens next—is contingent upon his or her tracking of Musidorus's thoughts. This is a subtle and rare instance of thought simulation in the *Arcadia*. By contrast, Greene's *Pandosto* offers a plethora of such examples, to the point where it almost seems as if Greene had conceived of his entire story as a series of thought "arias," with each of the key represented people taking a turn at relating details of his or her innermost thoughts. Far more than mere references to minds, these moments in *Pandosto* resemble the medieval psychomachia except that the personae of Good and Evil have been fully absorbed into aspects of conflicted (but still relatively unitary) psyches. I have space here to quote from just one of these arias, that of Franion, a trusted counselor of Pandosto's whom Pandosto has asked to kill his friend and fellow monarch, Egistus, on the suspicion that Egistus has slept with Bellaria. Here is a truncated excerpt from Franion's lengthy debate with himself, which may give some sense of how his decision making is represented as a process unfolding in time (more so than the thoughts of Sidney's Musidorus in the previous example):

Ah Franion, *treason is loved of many, but the traitor hated of all: unjust offences may for a time escape without danger, but never without revenge, thou art servant to a king, and must obey at command. . . . What shalt thou do? . . . Egistus is a stranger, to thee, and* Pandosto *thy soveraigne. . . . Yea but* Franion, *conscience is a worme that ever biteth, but never ceaseth. . . . Preferre thy content before riches, and a cleare mind before dignitie: so being poore thou shalt have rich peace, or els rich, thou shalt enjoy disquiet.* (Greene 2005 [1588], 624)

In his attempt to determine the most prudent course of action—not to mention his longing for a "cleare mind"—Franion anticipates Shakespeare's Lancelot Gobbo and even Hamlet by about a decade.

Returning at last to Spenser's reading knights, let me end this chapter with a consideration of how the greatest of Renaissance poets engages in the simulation of consciousness, picking back up with my earlier discussion of how Spenser points to the relative newness of reading as a common experience and to the difference that literacy makes in terms of the experience of consciousness.

Recall that at the end of *The Faerie Queene's* Book 2, Canto 9, Arthur and Guyon had just sat down in the library of the Castle of Temperance to read through the hermit Eumnestes's history books. Canto 10 then begins with an address to the muses (Stanzas 1 and 2) and an encomium to Elizabeth I, citing specifically her descent from "mightie kings and conquerours in warre, / . . . fathers and great Grandfathers of old" (Stanzas 3 and 4, 4.6). Then a curious thing happens: Arthur has apparently physically opened the copy of *Briton moniments*, an exploration of the ancient Celts that begins with the "hideous [*Celticke*] Giants" (7.2) and ends in the time of Arthur's father, Uther Pendragon. In that transitional moment, when the Britons' history first begins to unfold in Arthur's mind, Spenser gives us only the barest trace of a frame through which to maneuver the shift of consciousness—the frame allowing us either to "shuttle back" to the storyworld of the knights (Canto 9) or "skip forward" into Arthur's storyworld (Canto 10). Spenser "dives" quite suddenly from the "enveloping" frame of Elizabeth's family heritage (Stanza 4) and "into" the "depths" of interiority of Arthur's storyworld-within-a-storyworld (Stanza 5). (For what it is worth, my last two sentences have included an attempt, using quotation marks, to acknowledge my own dependence on source/path/destination, up/down, and inside/outside image schemas and metaphoricity to capture rhetorically what I mean by Spenser's use of a narrative "frame.")

4
Thy name o soueraigne Queene, thy realme and race,
From this renowmed Prince deriued arre,
Who mightily vpheld that royall mace,
Which now thou bearst, to thee descended farre
From mightie kings and conquerours in warre,

Thy fathers and great Grandfathers of old,
Whose noble deedes aboue the Northerne starre
Immortall fame for euer hath enrold;
As in that old mans booke they were in order told.

5
The land, which warlike Britons now possesse,
And therein haue their mightie empire raysd,
In antique times was saluage wildernesse,
Vnpeopled, vnmanurd, vnprou'd, vnpraysd,
Ne was it Island then, ne was it paysd
Amid the Ocean *waues, ne was it sought*
Of marchants farre, for profits therein praysd,
But was all desolate, and of some thought
By sea to haue bene from the Celticke *mayn-land brought.*
(Spenser 1978 [1590], Canto 10, 329)

Spenser places the trace frame in the last line of Stanza 4: "As in that old mans booke they were in order told" (4.9), referring cryptically to Eumnestes. But this flickering signal is not sufficient to help us get fully oriented before we find ourselves deep in the interior of Briton land, accessed through the historical mindscape that Arthur now inhabits. The reader remains immersed inside Arthur's storyworld and consciousness—the two now synonymous—through the end of Stanza 68, over an impressive span of fifty-two stanzas. Poetically, this seamless enfolding of storyworlds achieves a complex cognitive blend of the heritages of Arthur and Elizabeth, a consistent trope throughout *The Faerie Queene* but one arrived at here specifically through the embedding of Arthur's consciousness within the storyworld of the Elizabethan Tudor dynasty.

Character Proper

This trick—this device—of fiction would not have been possible for the generation before Spenser, Greene, and Sidney, before the rise in reading literacy had reinforced all the many effects of printing in its aftermath. The result was an emergence of fresh qualities of mindedness, including a heightened sensitivity to the powers inherent in readers' creation and habitation of storyworlds. This sensitivity to *what goes on inside the human head* led in turn to the development of imaginary agents, fictional people who could embody and enact the conspicuously *cerebral* gifts of human agency. The moment represents nothing less than the premodern invention of the character proper.

Notes

1. *OED. Minde* and *braine* are not treated as evenly synonymous in the OED, but they both intersect with *faculty*, which includes memory, sense, thought, intentionality, imagination, and other properties commonly attributed to both minds and brains. Hamlet often cites "brains" when he is obviously referring to thought processes: "About, my brains! / Hum, I have heard / That guilty creatures, sitting at a play" (*Hamlet*, 2.2, ll. 588–90).

2. These authors' meditative works and others by both Reformist and Counter-Reformation spiritualists were hugely influential throughout the Renaissance, the Christian Platonists contributing to core curricula in grammar schools, universities, and princes' studies. Elizabeth I was said to have consulted Boethius's *Consolation of Philosophy* on a daily basis (by William Camden), and she famously produced her own translation in 1593.

3. See Stevens (1997, 270): "Though the heart is the seat of our life force and necessary for the continued existence of the body, it falls short of the brain in defining our selves. The brain, according to [Robert] Burton, 'is the most noble organ under heaven, the dwelling-house and seat of the soul, the habitation of wisdom, memory, and in which man is most like unto God.'" See also Crane (2001, 7) for a discussion of Stevens's findings in the context of contemporary cognitive literary and cultural theory.

4. Stevens (1997, 273) writes: "The heart was still discussed both as a muscle in material terms and the seat of the soul in what would be seen increasingly as metaphoric terms. Descartes's mechanistic conception of the body still contained mysteries, but it was increasingly obvious from Harvey's work onward that the heart was a muscle best understood as a pump. If the body offered a 'real' reification of the self it was to be found in the brain."

5. See Monika Fludernik's chapter in this volume.

6. See Shapiro (2005, 284–302). Shapiro offers a brief analysis of *Hamlet* as a striking innovation in the representation of consciousness on stage, seeing in Hamlet no less than Shakespeare's reconfiguration of the ontology of the tragic protagonist.

7. These observations show an obvious debt to two very different scholars, both groundbreaking in the field of early modern literacy studies: Elizabeth Eisenstein (1979) and Walter Ong (1982). Despite Eisenstein's controversial methods, with which historians still take issue, her thesis about the importance of printing has not been overturned and in fact has benefited from many subsequent studies. Ong's theories regarding orality, literacy, and particularly written literacy also provide important background. In his descriptive notes to *Orality and Literacy*, Ong claims, "Literacy, it is now clear, transforms consciousness, producing patterns of thought which to literates seem perfectly commonplace and 'natural' but which are possible only when the mind has devised and internalized, made its own, the technology of writing." Unlike Ong, I emphasize reading, not writing, and base my argument more on the quantity than the quality of early modern literacy.

8. It is very difficult to date Sidney's *Arcadia* because of the work's prolonged composition and revision dates (1578–84) and two "first" publications of different versions, one unfinished and published posthumously in 1590 (after Sidney's death in 1586), the other a revision overseen by his sister Mary and published in 1593 as *The Countess of Pembroke's Arcadia*. The latter edition adds Books 4 and 5 to what appeared in 1590, this "new" material apparently taken from Sidney's 1578–84 manuscripts, to which Mary Sidney presumably had access. The 1593 version then became the standard, popular reading text until the early twentieth century, when Sidney's 1578–84 manuscripts were rediscovered (and dubbed "old"). Although the date of publication is too complicated to allow for definitive judgments of direct influence, it seems safe to situate Book 1, the text on which my reading is based, among the manuscripts by Sidney that predate Greene's *Pandosto*; it also predates the publication of Spenser's *Faerie Queene* by some four to eight years. (This is to say nothing about the added complexities of manuscript circulation.) In any event, Book 1 was not among those added by Mary Sidney in 1593.

9. The studies of romance that I have found most compelling are Doody (1996), Mentz (2006), Newcomb (2002), and Salzman (1985). Questions about the class- and gender-based readership of romance have tended to dominate research on the genre (e.g., Newcomb 2002; Spufford 1981; and Watt 1991).

10. The survival of handwritten or hand-copied manuscripts alongside print in the late sixteenth century is something of a commonplace in English humanist studies (see Zwicker 2002, esp. 190).

11. There are a number of important discussions exploring the influence

of the ancient Greek novel on sixteenth-century romance or prose fiction. See Mentz (2006), Newcomb (2002), and especially Doody (1996).

12. The standard citation is still David Cressy's 1980 study *Literacy and the Social Order: Reading and Writing in Tudor and Stuart England*, which sought to measure literacy—or more properly illiteracy—on the basis of whether or not people could sign their names to documents. Cressy calculated that in 1500 only about 5 percent of men and 1 percent of women could sign their names. Although the rates rose slightly over the next century and a half—by Elizabeth's reign 20 percent of men and 5 percent of women could sign, and by 1642 it was 30 percent of men and 10 percent of women—such evidence still seems to indicate a significant majority of "illiterates" in the population.

13. "The poorer the family, the earlier the [child's] entry into the workforce" and the less likely that child would go on to grammar school to acquire the writing skills needed to sign documents (Charlton and Spufford 2002, 27, 43).

14. See also Charlton (1999); Charlton and Spufford (2002, 16–17); Fox (2000, esp. 13, 17, 18–19); Sanders (1998); and Spufford (1981).

15. These readers add to the numbers of aristocratic and merchant-class sons whose access to the humanist educational curriculum we can safely assume.

16. Donald makes an extensive argument for the role of intermediate memory—as distinct from short-term or long-term memory—in executive functioning (see Donald 2002, esp. 46–91).

17. Wolf (2007) describes how the executive functioning of a human child's brain is severely taxed when the child first begins reading, but once he or she has mastered reading, it becomes "rapid-fire and effortless" (15)—and I would add irreversible (try *not* reading that sign you pass on the freeway).

18. The lack of space breaks had once meant that texts generally needed to be read out loud in order for the reader and presumably an audience to *hear* discrete words.

19. Chartier (1995) does not claim that silent reading eliminated either reading aloud or public reading, but his work nevertheless presents a challenge to those who wish to demonstrate the continuities of older traditions of information sharing. Fox (2000) is one such response, a useful corrective to impressions that early modern reading practices simply replaced older habits, especially within the ranks of popular culture.

20. On the relative stability or "permanence" of written over spoken language, see Chafe (1994, esp. 42).

21. See Fauconnier (1994 [1985]) on the uses of gestalt theory to develop a concept of spaces in the mind. Fauconnier and Turner (2002) have since

elaborated on mental space theory in developing their model of "conceptual integration networks" or "cognitive blends."

22. As noted in my earlier discussion of Spenser's *Faerie Queene*.

23. We sense, for instance, both the pirates' and Chariclea's frustration when they try but fail to "form a true opinion" of one another and then stumble at communicating.

24. See Doody (1996) and Mentz (2006).

25. Shakespeare would use Greene's romance as the basis for *The Winter's Tale* (ca. 1612), modeling the jealousy-maddened Leontes directly on Pandosto and providing evidence that this shift in referentiality toward the mind was noticeable to contemporaries.

26. I say "simple" for the sake of description, but scientists consider the neuronal scaffolding supporting Theory of Mind to be staggeringly complex.

References

Baron-Cohen, Simon. 1995. *Mindblindness: An Essay on Autism and Theory of Mind*. Cambridge MA: MIT Press.

Burke, Peter. 1994. *Popular Culture in Early Modern Europe*. Rev. ed. Aldershot: Ashgate.

Cavallo, Guglielmo, and Roger Chartier. 1999. "Introduction." In *A History of Reading in the West*, ed. Guglielmo Cavallo and Roger Chartier, 1–36. Amherst: University of Massachusetts Press.

Chafe, Wallace. 1994. *Discourse, Consciousness, and Time: The Flow and Displacement of Conscious Experience in Speaking and Writing*. Chicago: University of Chicago Press.

Charlton, Kenneth. 1999. *Women, Religion and Education in Early Modern England*. London: Routledge.

Charlton, Kenneth, and Margaret Spufford. 2002. "Literacy, Society and Education." In *The Cambridge History of Early Modern English Literature*, ed. David Loewenstein and Janel Mueller, 15–54. Cambridge: Cambridge University Press.

Chartier, Roger. 1995. *Forms and Meanings: Texts, Performances, and Audiences from Codex to Computer*. Philadelphia: University of Pennsylvania Press.

Crane, Mary Thomas. 2001. *Shakespeare's Brain: Reading with Cognitive Theory*. Princeton: Princeton University Press.

Cressy, David. 1980. *Literacy and the Social Order: Reading and Writing in Tudor and Stuart England*. Cambridge: Cambridge University Press.

Donald, Merlin. 2001. *A Mind So Rare: The Evolution of Human Consciousness*. New York: W. W. Norton.

Doody, Margaret Ann. 1996. *The True Story of the Novel*. New Brunswick: Rutgers University Press.

Edelman, Gerald M. 1987. *Neural Darwinism: The Theory of Neuronal Group Selection*. New York: Basic Books.

Eisenstein, Elizabeth. 1979. *The Printing Press as an Agent of Change: Communications and Cultural Transformations in Early-Modern Europe*. 2 vols. Cambridge: Cambridge University Press.

Emmott, Catherine. 1997. *Narrative Comprehension: A Discourse Perspective*. Oxford: Clarendon Press.

Fauconnier, Gilles. 1994 [1985]. *Mental Spaces*. Cambridge: Cambridge University Press.

Fauconnier, Gilles, and Mark Turner. 2002. *The Way We Think: Conceptual Blending and the Mind's Hidden Complexities*. New York: Basic Books.

Fox, Adam. 2000. *Oral and Literate Culture in England 1500–1700*. Oxford: Clarendon Press.

Freeman, Walter. 2000. *How Brains Make Up Their Minds*. New York: Columbia University Press.

Gallese, Vittorio. 2001. "The 'Shared Manifold' Hypothesis: From Mirror Neurons to Empathy." *Journal of Consciousness Studies* 8.5–7: 33–50.

Gavins, Joanna. 2007. *Text World Theory: An Introduction*. Edinburgh: Edinburgh University Press.

Gerrig, Richard. 1993. *Experiencing Narrative World: On the Psychological Activities of Reading*. New Haven: Yale University Press.

Greene, Robert. 2005 [1588]. *Pandosto: The Triumph of Time*. [*The Historie of Dorastus and Fawnia*.] In *The New Variorum Edition of Shakespeare: The Winter's Tale*, ed. Robert Kean Turner and Virginia Westling Hass, 618–56. New York: Modern Language Association of America.

Hebb, Donald. 1949. *The Organization of Behavior*. New York: Wiley.

Heliodorus. 1997. *The Ethiopian Story*. Ed. J. R. Morgan. Trans. Sir Walter Lamb. London: J. M. Dent.

Herman, David. 2002. *Story Logic: Problems and Possibilities of Narrative*. Lincoln: University of Nebraska Press.

———. 2004. "Toward a Transmedial Narratology." In *Narrative across Media: The Languages of Storytelling*, ed. Marie-Laure Ryan, 47–75. Lincoln: University of Nebraska Press.

McConachie, Bruce. 2008. *Engaging Audiences: A Cognitive Approach to Spectating in the Theatre*. New York: Palgrave-MacMillan.

Mentz, Steve. 2006. *Romance for Sale in Early Modern England: The Rise of Prose Fiction*. Aldershot: Ashgate Publishing.

Newcomb, Lori Humphrey. 2002. *Reading Popular Romance in Early Modern England*. New York: Columbia University Press.

Olson, David R. 1994. *The World on Paper: The Conceptual and Cognitive Implications of Writing and Reading*. Cambridge: Cambridge University Press.

Ong, Walter. 1982. *Orality and Literacy: The Technologizing of the Word*. New York: Routledge.

Palmer, Alan. 2004. *Fictional Minds*. Lincoln: University of Nebraska Press.

Ryan, Marie-Laure. 1991. *Possible Worlds, Artificial Intelligence, and Narrative Theory*. Bloomington: Indiana University Press.

Salzman, Paul. 1985. *English Prose Fiction, 1558–1700: A Critical History*. Oxford: Clarendon Press.

Sanders, Eve Rachele. 1998. *Gender and Literacy on Stage in Early Modern England*. Cambridge: Cambridge University Press.

Semino, Elena. 1997. *Language and World Creation in Poems and Other Texts*. London: Longman.

Shapiro, James. 2005. *1599: A Year in the Life of William Shakespeare*. New York: HarperCollins.

Sidney, Sir Philip. 1987 [1577/1590]. *The Countess of Pembroke's Arcadia*. Ed. Maurice Evans. London: Penguin Books.

Spenser, Edmund. 1978 [1590]. *The Faerie Queene*. Ed. Thomas P. Roche Jr. London: Penguin Books.

Spufford, Margaret. 1981. *Small Books and Pleasant Histories: Popular Fiction and Its Readership in Seventeenth Century England*. Athens: University of Georgia Press.

Stevens, Scott Manning. 1997. "Sacred Heart and Secular Brain." In *The Body in Parts: Fantasies of Corporeality in Early Modern Europe*, ed. David Hillman and Carla Mazzio, 263–82. New York and London: Routledge.

Watt, Tessa. 1991. *Cheap Print and Popular Piety, 1550–1640*. Cambridge: Cambridge University Press.

Werth, Paul. 1999. *Text Worlds: Representing Conceptual Space in Discourse*. London: Longman.

Wolf, Maryanne. 2007. *Proust and the Squid: The Story and Science of the Reading Brain*. New York: HarperCollins.

Zunshine, Lisa. 2006. *Why We Read Fiction: Theory of Mind and the Novel*. Columbus: Ohio State University Press.

Zwicker, Steven N. 2002. "Habits of Reading and Early Modern Literary Culture." In *The Cambridge History of Early Modern English Literature*, ed. David Loewenstein and Janel Mueller, 170–98. Cambridge: Cambridge University Press.

4. 1620–1700
Mind on the Move

ELIZABETH BRADBURN

In the study of narrative discourse, the period 1620–1700 should be seen as a threshold because it immediately precedes the rise of the novel, the now-dominant form of narrative literature in English. Usually considered to have emerged as a distinct genre in the mid-eighteenth century, the novel developed out of several different literary forms widely used in the seventeenth. Some of these, such as romance, allegory and epic, have histories extending far back into the preceding centuries; others, such as travel narrative and spiritual autobiography, first rose to importance during the political, religious, and intellectual upheavals of the 1600s. The transitional nature of seventeenth-century narrative generally becomes important when one studies specific literary techniques, including those used to represent consciousness. Representations of mind in this period are especially diverse because older and emerging forms of narrative coexist, and because those forms are undergoing such dramatic changes.

One form this diversity takes is in the many ways authors use metaphor to represent consciousness. We may think of metaphorical representations of the mind primarily in terms of poetic language, as when Andrew Marvell writes of "The mind, that ocean where each kind / Does straight its own resemblance find" (1971, "The Garden," ll. 43–44). And indeed, the relative density of such language is one feature that traditionally differentiates poetry from prose narrative. But metaphor, and in particular metaphors for consciousness, can shape literary works at levels other than the local use of figurative language. At higher levels, metaphor can help to define genres and can interact creatively with other techniques of representation existent or being developed in a given culture.

In order to demonstrate the diversity of metaphorical representation during this transitional literary historical period, I will focus on a specific metaphor, THE MIND IS A BODY MOVING IN SPACE, so that we can see how it is manifested at different levels, both across the corpus of seventeenth-century narrative and within individual texts. The four narrative works that I have chosen range, in their representations of consciousness, from the relatively simple to the highly complex. John Bunyan's *Pilgrim's Progress* (1678) and Margaret Cavendish's *Blazing World* (1666) show how the representation of the mind as a moving body can shape narrative plots. In her protonovel *Oroonoko* (1688), Aphra Behn uses the metaphor of movement to begin developing distinctively novelistic techniques for representing consciousness. And, finally, we will see how the integrated use of metaphor at thematic, narrative, and linguistic levels creates the textual intricacy of the last great English prenovel narrative: John Milton's *Paradise Lost* (1674).[1]

Mind as Motion

In order to perceive the many ways in which metaphors shape literary works, we must understand metaphor as more than a literary device. The work of George Lakoff, Mark Johnson, and others in the field of cognitive linguistics is quite useful here. Lakoff and Johnson argue persuasively that metaphor is a cognitive mechanism, one that can generate abstract concepts from concrete experience and create mental imagery to help explain and draw inferences about internal and external data. They call this type of mechanism "conceptual metaphor" (Johnson 1987; Lakoff and Johnson 1999). Conceptual metaphor theory hypothesizes that all experience is embodied and that attempts to express abstract concepts are grounded in metaphor systems deriving from such embodied experience.[2] Here it should be stressed that conceptual metaphors are not figures of speech; rather, they indicate how thought itself is intrinsically metaphorical. Metaphors that exist in ordinary linguistic expressions are not random but form consistent patterns based on conceptual metaphors anchored in our experience as embodied beings situated in time and space.

Accordingly, we represent the mind, as a concept, in ways based on perceptual and kinetic experience. As Lakoff and Johnson (1999) put it, "It is virtually impossible to think or talk about the mind in any serious way without conceptualizing it metaphorically. Whenever we conceptualize aspects of mind in terms of grasping ideas, reaching conclusions, being unclear, or swallowing a claim, we are using metaphor to make sense of what we do with our minds" (235). In fact, they go on to note, we use many different metaphorical systems to conceptualize the mind, and these systems are not, and need not be, consistent with each other. It seems clear, however, that in folk psychology one of the dominant metaphorical systems figures the mind as a body moving through space. This conceptual metaphor (or system of metaphors) uses the physical experience of mobility as a model for what the mind does. Some of its entailments include THINKING IS MOVING, IDEAS AND EMOTIONS ARE LOCATIONS, REASON IS A FORCE, A LINE OF THOUGHT IS A PATH, and UNDERSTANDING IS FOLLOWING. When we say that our minds are "racing" or "wandering," that we are "forced to a conclusion" or "moved" by someone's story, we unconsciously express entailments of this conceptual metaphor in language.

An entailment of THE MIND IS A BODY MOVING THROUGH SPACE that will be especially important to my analysis is the metaphor MENTAL STATES ARE LOCATIONS. This second metaphor is a logical extension of the first. If mental processes are understood as motions, then the changes of state brought about by those processes can be understood as movements from one place to another, and thus the mental states themselves can be understood as locations. Consider the following sentences:

(a) *The group reached consensus.*
(b) *He passed from grief into anger.*

Both derive from the conceptual metaphor THE MIND IS A BODY; in both of these formulations, verbs of motion ("reached," "passed") refer to mental processes. They also turn the names of mental states ("consensus," "grief," "anger") into images of physical locations. These sentences use everyday expressions, not consciously literary ones. Yet they are metaphorical, manifestations of a conceptual system that imagines mental states as places toward which the mind moves.

Because we use conceptual metaphors unconsciously, we do not always notice the metaphorical status of expressions such as those in (a) and (b). Literary metaphors that derive from conceptual metaphors often create their aesthetic effects by calling attention to or formalizing the presence of metaphor in thought and language. Consider, for example, a passage from *Paradise Lost* in which Satan, having just escaped from Hell, is flying toward Paradise to take revenge on God by corrupting Adam and Eve. Watching the devil's flight from Heaven, God observes to the Son: "seest thou what rage / Transports our adversarie" (Milton 1998 [1674], Book 3, ll. 80–81). Christopher Ricks (1963, 59–60) has remarked on the special resonance of the word "transport" in these lines. The word's metaphorical sense is uppermost here—Satan is moved into an intense emotional state—but the rage is also the motivation for the flight itself—he is literally transported as well. The literary effect depends upon the double meaning of "transport," deriving from the conceptual metaphor THE MIND IS A BODY MOVING IN SPACE and its entailment MENTAL STATES ARE LOCATIONS.[3] Such effects pervade the representations of consciousness in *Paradise Lost*, and they exemplify what Mary Thomas Crane (2001, 28) has called "traces of cognitive process" in literary works.

Conceptual metaphors can shape literary texts at many levels. Perhaps the most familiar and obvious one is the local use of figurative language. As Lakoff and Mark Turner point out, literary metaphors often present versions of conceptual metaphors, extending them, drawing attention to them, combining them in complex ways, or using them to create vivid images (Lakoff and Turner 1989). For example, toward the beginning of *Paradise Lost*, we are told that some of the fallen angels

> *apart sat on a Hill retir'd,*
> *In thoughts more elevate, and reasoned high*
> *Of Providence, Foreknowledge, Will and Fate,*

Fixt Fate, free will, foreknowledge absolute,
And found no end, in wandring mazes lost.
(Book 2, ll. 556–61)

The notion that thinking and reasoning can be understood as wandering through a maze draws directly on the conceptual metaphor I have just described: THE MIND IS A BODY MOVING IN SPACE. But the image of the maze is Milton's extension of this metaphor into a vivid sensory correlate for the devils' particular mental experience. The passage incorporates a poetic device that both depends upon and evokes an unconscious cognitive mechanism.

At another level, literary works can take individual conceptual metaphors as themes. A writer interested in a particular domain of life may wish explicitly to examine the cognitive and cultural structures that organize experience in that domain. This is the case with *Paradise Lost*, which is concerned not only with representing the minds of its characters, but also with understanding and influencing how humans represent their minds to themselves. In a passage toward the end of the poem, for example, Adam receives some advice from the angel Michael that can also be read as Milton's advice to his reader. Adam says, "Henceforth I learne, that to obey is best, / And love with fear the onely God" (Book 12, ll. 561–62), to which Michael replies,

> *This having learnt, thou hast attaind the summe*
> *Of wisdom*
> ....
> *onely add*
> *Deeds to thy knowledge answerable, add Faith,*
> *Add vertue, Patience, Temperance, add Love,*
> *By name to come call'd Charitie, the soul*
> *Of all the rest: then wilt thou not be loath*
> *To leave this Paradise, but shalt possess*
> *A paradise within thee, happier farr.*
> (Book 12, ll. 575–76, 581–87)

Here Adam is explicitly instructed to create, as a step in his spiritual development, an inner representation of his physical experience. By having Michael refer first to a literal Paradise and then to a metaphorical one, Milton shows his awareness that metaphor can be used to structure mental experience, taking as his theme the conceptual metaphor MENTAL STATES ARE LOCATIONS, itself an entailment of THE MIND IS A BODY MOVING IN SPACE.

At a still higher level, conceptual metaphors can influence or even determine narrative structure. In Cavendish's *Blazing World*, for example, part of the plot involves platonic travel, in which certain characters' minds leave their bodies and move to others' bodies in geographically distant locations. This narrative image is comprehensible to readers only because they already have an unconscious understanding of the mind as a unified, bounded object that can move through space with integrity. To take another example: as an allegory, *The Pilgrim's Progress* derives its entire plot from a single metaphor: Christian's journey through the physical world represents the progress of his soul toward salvation. Because the logic of allegory demands consistent adherence to a central metaphor, Bunyan's story must contain the schematic elements of travel. Christian must be shown to move toward a destination, for instance, and he must relate to other characters primarily as fellow pilgrims, hindrances, or guides. The central metaphor of the mind as motion is, for Bunyan the author, a literary device, but the coherence of his text depends on his and his readers' unconscious knowledge of the conceptual metaphor from which the allegory derives. As Christian encounters the Slough of Despond, then the Hill of Difficulty, then Vanity Fair, the reader need devote no conscious effort to working out what type of experience these locations represent. We automatically recognize them as obstacles to progress and can focus on responding to the individual images and their meanings.

At the highest level, conceptual metaphors can help define genres, both shaping and responding to modes of representation. Consider the figuration, traditional in Western literature, of poetry as song. No doubt this image derives from oral tradition, but by the early modern period it has become entirely metaphorical. When Milton addresses his "Heav'nly Muse" by writing "I thence / Invoke thy aid to my adventrous song" (Book 1, ll. 12–13), we know that he is not literally singing, but we allow the image of song to stand for what is taking place between author and reader. The conceptual metaphor A POEM IS A SONG shapes Milton's representation of his authorship, and our experience of reading, throughout *Paradise Lost*. With the development of modern poetics, however, a different conceptual metaphor comes to affect the mode of communication between poets and readers. In modern and contemporary literature, a poem is no longer exclusively, or perhaps even primarily, thought of as a song, but as a *shared observation*. Ezra Pound's famously minimal imagist masterpiece, "In the Station of the Metro," for example, conjures not a bard, but a witness:

> The apparition of these faces in the crowd;
> Petals on a wet, black bough.

That the reader is being asked here to see an image, and not to hear a song, demonstrates that very different conceptual metaphors shape Milton's and Pound's poetic representations. Both of these metaphors are special cases of the more general metaphor THE MIND IS A BODY MOVING IN SPACE. In each, a mental activity—composing a poem—is conceptualized as a physical experience (looking) or action (singing).

Narrative forms, too, exhibit a reciprocal relationship between the structures of conceptual metaphor and techniques of representation. Just as poetry is often conceptualized as song, narrative is often conceptualized as travel. The metaphor NARRATIVE IS TRAVEL is also a special case of THE MIND IS A BODY MOVING IN SPACE. The sequence of developments that characterizes the mental activity of narration are thought of as the shifts in location that accompany the physical movement of travel. The importance of this conceptual metaphor is one reason that travel narratives such as Behn's *Oroonoko* played such an important role in the development of the novel. Travel narratives often partially or fully thematize the metaphor NARRATIVE IS TRAVEL in ways that both stimulate and respond to narrative techniques such as those for representing consciousness.[4] In the section on *Oroonoko* we will examine this dynamic relationship in greater detail. But first we will consider two simpler, but equally revealing, uses of conceptual metaphor to shape narrative structure in seventeenth-century works.

The Pilgrim's Progress

The Pilgrim's Progress is an allegory—that is, the narrative elaboration of a single complex metaphor. At the literal level it presents imagery from one domain that has one-to-one correspondence with meaning in another domain. The book's narrator falls asleep and dreams of a man named Christian, who, perceiving that he is condemned to die, receives instructions from another character, Evangelist, to "fly from the wrath to come" (Bunyan 1960 [1678], 10). Christian goes on a journey, beginning at the City of Destruction and ending at the Celestial City. Along the way he has adventures in locations such as the Slough of Despond and Vanity Fair. He also has encounters with other characters such as Evangelist, Hopeful, and Ignorance. Each element of Christian's journey has a specific nonliteral meaning, frequently signaled by a proper name. At one level it is the story of a physical journey; at a different level, it is the story of a progression toward spiritual salvation. Each level is self-coherent; they have the same morphology, but they do not mix. It should be fairly easy to see that the narrative is essentially the elaboration of a number of entailments of the conceptual metaphor THE MIND IS A BODY MOVING IN SPACE. The mind (soul) is represented as the body of Christian; psychological experiences such as despair, temptation, learning, and encouragement are represented as material locations, objects, and beings.

Christian's body functions as a mind at the beginning of the story, for example, when Christian begins to run from his home and hears the voices of his wife and children calling him back. He "put his fingers in his ears, and ran on crying, Life, Life, Eternal Life: so he looked not behind him, but fled towards the middle of the Plain" (10). Here open ears and looking back are meta-phors for mental states of receptivity to the persuasions of others and the demands of the past. Similarly, the physical process of traveling, along with corresponding features of the landscape that make traveling difficult, can represent internal states or experiences. For example, Christian encounters the Hill of Difficulty (41), whose height and steepness represent the difficulty of maintaining spiritual righteousness.

Some elements of the journey are realized as characters in the story, and so Bunyan must represent their consciousnesses alongside those of the dreamer/narrator and of Christian. These other characters are allegorical figures, not subjects, but the narrative demands that they be represented as having minds (usually very monotonous ones!) because they must interact with Christian. Some of the persons clearly represent aspects of Christian's own self in that they engage in prolonged debates with him; for example, Christian encounters a character named Mr. Worldly-Wiseman who persuades him to turn off the path to find a Mr. Legality who can help him remove the burden from his back. The allegorical meaning is that a devout man might be tempted to find loopholes for excusing his sinfulness rather than following the more difficult path to salvation. Other characters seem to represent other possible versions of Christian's self, things that he could have done had he gone wrong, because they take alternative physical actions instead of engaging in lengthy conversation. For example, two persons named Formalist and Hypocrisie travel toward the Hill of Difficulty with Christian, but they are rebuffed by its narrow and strenuous path, and each of them takes an alternate route. (As these two routes are called Danger and Destruction, the reader presumably can work out what happens to these characters.)

The simultaneously literal and allegorical nature of the characters can lead to oddly unrealistic representations of consciousness. For example, at one point Christian's friend Faithful recounts the story of his meeting with a man named Shame, who tries to persuade Faithful that religion is low and unmanly. Faithful has the physical response that Shame's name denotes: "I could not tell," Faithful reports, "what to say at the first. Yea, he put me so to it, that my blood came up in my face, even this *Shame* fetch'd it up, and had almost beat me quite off" (73). Faithful remembers in time that God, not worldly opinion, is the measure of the validity of religion, and realizes that "they that make themselves Fools for the Kingdom of Heaven, are wisest" (73). Remembering this, he tells Shame to depart. Here Shame seems to represent both the external provocateur and the internal feeling that someone like that can induce. What is especially interesting is that after Faithful tells Christian this story, they both agree that Shame is misnamed, because he himself is not ashamed but "audacious" (74). It is as though they are on the verge of questioning the allegory, or breaking the frame, because they implicitly acknowledge but do not consciously recognize that Shame is an aspect of themselves, even a potential one.

This conflict between the allegorical and literal levels can also make some representations of Christian's consciousness seem illogical. As Christian nears the mouth of Hell, for instance, he is approached by a group of fiends whom he is able to ward off by saying loudly, "I will walk in the strength of the Lord God" (63). But the narrator notes that "Now poor *Christian* was so confounded, that he did not know his own voice: and thus I perceived it: Just when he was come over against the mouth of the burning Pit, one of the wicked ones got behind him, and stept up softly to him, and whisperingly suggested many grievous blasphemies to him, which he verily thought had proceeded from his own mind" (63). Given that the journey itself, including the approach to the Pit, is itself a metaphor for Christian's conscious experience, it is difficult to determine the status of this represented event. Everything is proceeding from his mind, and so it does not make sense at the allegorical level for Christian to be confused about what is or is not his own mental experience. Here the story moves toward a realistic representation of consciousness, but at the expense of allegorical meaning.

Finally, the framework of the dream narrative often makes it difficult to separate representations of consciousness fully from other kinds of representations. The dreamer seems to have direct access to the mental states and processes of Christian and many of the other characters. Indeed, he presents these states not as though he is a literary narrator rendering them for the reader, but as though he is merely reporting events witnessed as a dream. The following passage captures the range of knowledge that the dreamer seems to have:

The path-way was here also exceeding narrow, and therefore good Christian *was the more put to it; for when he sought in the dark to shun the ditch on the one hand, he was ready to tip over into the mire on the other; also when he sought to escape the mire, without great carefulness he would be ready to fall into the ditch. Thus he went on, and I heard him here sigh bitterly: for, besides the dangers mentioned above, the path way was here so dark, that oft times when he lift up his foot to set forward, he knew not where, or upon what he should set it next.*

About the midst of this Valley, I perceived the mouth of Hell to be, and it stood also hard by the way side: Now thought Christian, *what shall I do?* (62–63)

Here we can see that the Christian's inner thought is presented exactly the same way that all the other elements of the dream are: the geography, the dark, the sigh, Christian's experience of trying to balance on the narrow pathway. The allegory is all of a piece, for everything in this scene has the status of allegory; the attempt to walk on the narrow path through the Valley of the Shadow of Death is a symbol for the spiritual state of every pilgrim, the mental state that he or she must pass through in order to attain Grace. Even if the reader believes literally in Hell, he or she does not believe that a person literally encounters Hell in his or her lifetime; the images merely indicate that a person is in spiritual danger of being damned. Because the object is not to render Christian's subjective experiences separately from anything else in the narrative, the text often fails to separate the dreamer's consciousness from Christian's even when it would be logical to do so. Such lapses in logic often occur when the necessity of depicting intersubjective conversation conflicts with the allegorical imperative.

The conceptual metaphor THE MIND IS A BODY MOVING IN SPACE affects *The Pilgrim's Progress* at a level higher than that of figurative language. The central image of travel partially determines the story's plot as well as its presentation of some other elements, such as characters and settings. Perhaps ironically, Bunyan's allegorical use of this metaphor for consciousness interacts rather awkwardly with the other techniques for representing consciousness that were available to him. We will consider how the techniques chosen by both Aphra Behn and John Milton express and extend the conceptual metaphor in different and more complex ways. In order to see these representational structures clearly, however, we must first consider another seventeenth-century journey of the mind.

The Blazing World

It is difficult to imagine two more different authors than the scantily educated nonconformist preacher John Bunyan and Margaret Cavendish, Duchess of Newcastle, monarchist and would-be member of the Royal Society (they did not admit women, though Cavendish managed to attend one meeting as a protest). Yet both writers began important works as forms of amusement, Bunyan to distract himself "from worser thoughts, which make me do amiss" (1960, 1) and Cavendish to "divert" the "studious thoughts" (2000, 153) that produced such scientific works as *Observations upon Experimental Philosophy* (1666). Where Bunyan's "Scribble" (1960, 1) quickly became the book-length sermon that is *The Pilgrim's Progress*, Cavendish sought in *The Blazing World* only to "delight the Reader with variety, which is always pleasing" (2000 [1666], 153). Although the fanciful travels narrated in Cavendish's romance have no allegorical significance, these travel scenarios are also shaped by the mind-as-travel metaphor and particularly by its entailment MENTAL STATES ARE LOCATIONS.

The book begins with an involuntary journey that profoundly restructures its heroine's psychology. In a "forreign Country," an unnamed "young Lady" (154) is kidnapped by a merchant who has fallen in love with her. The merchant forces her onto his ship, but a violent storm arises and blows the ship to the North

Pole. All the men in the ship freeze to death, but the Lady miraculously survives and passes with the ship through the pole and into another world, where she is rescued by creatures in animal shapes who walk upright like humans and live in humanlike cities. They escort her to the human emperor of their world, who almost immediately marries the lady and makes her an empress. The subjects of the kingdom worship her as a deity, and she begins a systematic program of scientific inquiry, questioning each type of creature to find out how the natural systems of the world work and eventually converting them to her own religion and building two chapels in which she regularly preaches sermons.

The Blazing World (so named because its night sky is filled with comets, or "blazing-stars") is not metaphorical in the same sense that a place such as Vanity Fair is. But just as Bunyan's town incorporates the abstract quality of vanity, the Blazing World embodies enhancements of human mental abilities. After the empress takes her throne in the Blazing World, she conducts systematic dialogues with her half human, half animal subjects, all of whom possess specific perceptual and cognitive talents. The Bird-men are excellent observers, while the Bear-men seem to operate with a group consciousness. The Worm-men can sense the "interior motions" (179) of vegetables and minerals. In fact, the empress collects a lengthy catalog of the natural properties of her new empire by using her subjects as a kind of extension of her own mind. Cavendish's narrative thus uses travel to a fanciful new location to suggest the acquisition of an imagined mental state or quality, a strategy that draws on the concept that mental states are analogous to physical locations.

Another element of The Blazing World that makes use of THE MIND IS A BODY MOVING IN SPACE is Cavendish's curious way of inserting herself into the story. Besides the animal men, the Blazing World contains "spirits of the air," one of whom offers to bring the empress the soul of any writer, living or dead, to be her scribe. When she asks for the soul of a "famous modern Writer," such as Descartes or Hobbes, the spirit suggests that a woman writer might be more appropriate, and he eventually transports the soul of Margaret Cavendish, the Duchess of Newcastle, to the Blazing World. The empress greets the soul of the duchess with a "spiritual kiss" (209); this visit and others "did produce such an intimate friendship between them, that they became Platonick Lovers, although they were both Females" (210). Later in the story the souls of the empress and the duchess travel together from the Blazing World to England, where they visit Cavendish's husband, the duke, by entering his body. There are then three souls in the duke's body. The duke's soul and the empress's soul become attracted to each through pleasant conversation. The duchess's soul feels jealous at first, but then, "considering that no Adultery could be committed amongst Platonick Lovers, and that Platonism was Divine, as being derived from Divine Plato, [she] cast forth of her mind that Idea of Jealousie" (223).

Clearly in this context "Platonick" means mainly disembodied, and adultery is defined as physical sex. The image of platonic love occurs frequently in seventeenth-century literature, perhaps most famously in John Donne's lyric "The Ecstasy," in which two lovers' souls leave their bodies and mingle together platonically. But platonic travel as Cavendish depicts it here literalizes the conceptual metaphor THE MIND IS A BODY MOVING IN SPACE. She and other writers can imagine the soul as a unified entity able to travel separately from the body because of the human experience of bodily coherence and mobility. Paradoxically, although conceptual metaphor in general is possible because the mind is embodied, specific conceptual metaphors can entail scenarios involving out-of-body transportation or travel, licensing platonic and other forms of dualism. Cavendish's text uses the conceptual metaphor and its entailment to generate both a plot device and a thematic exploration of mind-body relations.

Oroonoko

Like *The Blazing World*, *Oroonoko* resembles the travel writing—narratives of journeys to exotic (and often colonized) lands describing unfamiliar people, cultures, and natural phenomena—that was gaining popularity in seventeenth-century England. But whereas

Cavendish revels in her power to create a fictional world, Aphra Behn bills her tale as a "true history," using a discourse similar, Michael McKeon points out, to that of travel authors defending the veracity of their reports (1987, 111). "I do not pretend," Behn writes, "to entertain my Reader with the Adventures of a feign'd *Hero*, whose Life and Fortunes Fancy may manage at the Poet's Pleasure; nor in relating the Truth, design to adorn it with any Accidents, but such as arriv'd in earnest to him" (1997 [1688], 8). Behn's narrator had known the eponymous hero when she lived on a sugar plantation in the Surinam in the West Indies, where the novel is set. After describing the native West Indians, the narrator relates the story of Oroonoko's youth in the African nation of Coramantien (in modern-day Ghana), a tale she claims to have heard from Oroonoko himself. Eventually Oroonoko is captured as a slave and brought to Surinam, where the narrator befriends him. The second part of the book describes his life on the plantation, reunion with his African lover Imoinda (also a slave), attempted rebellion, and execution, all as witnessed by the narrator.

Oroonoko makes use of the conceptual metaphor THE MIND IS A BODY MOVING IN SPACE at two separate levels. At a lower or more local level, it uses the metaphor MENTAL STATES ARE LOCATIONS in its images of Surinam, the destination of both the narrator's and Oroonoko's journeys. Recently arrived herself in the West Indies, where "all things by Nature are Rare, Delightful and Wonderful" (44), the narrator at one point travels to visit a native Indian village, accompanied by her brother, her maid, and Oroonoko. (Because it is obvious to the white plantation owners that Oroonoko was a prince in his own country, he is not required to work and is treated as a kind of companion. This indulgent attitude changes dramatically, of course, when he begins to organize the other slaves for a revolt.) For Behn's narrator, the natives are "like our first Parents before the Fall" (9). They "represented to me an absolute *Idea* of the first State of Innocence, before Man knew how to sin: And 'tis most evident and plain, that Simple Nature is the most harmless, inoffensive and vertuous Mistress. . . . Religion woul'd here but destroy that Tranquillity, they possess by Ignorance; and Laws wou'd but teach 'em to know Offence, of which now they have no Notion" (10). This comparison evokes both a location (the Garden of Eden) and a state of consciousness (ignorance of good and evil); as Behn's narrator puts it, Surinam stands for an *"Idea."* The perception of native peoples as unfallen humans is hardly unique to Behn, but the concept is clearly shaped by the conceptual metaphor that analogizes places to psychological states. As we will see, Milton makes similar use of the topos of Paradise in his epic poem.

At a higher or more global level, conceptual metaphor provides a rationale for Behn's narrative technique. Reading *Oroonoko* as a literary instantiation of THE MIND IS A BODY MOVING IN SPACE illuminates how travel literature helped nurture the development of specifically novelistic modes of narration, in particular the way that novels with heterodiegetic narrators represent the consciousness of the characters whose actions they recount. Heterodiegetic narration, or third-person narration by a teller who does not participate directly in the events of which he or she gives an account, nonetheless creates the illusion of a witness to those events. In cases of extradiegetic-heterodiegetic narration, where the teller figure is a voice without character-like attributes, that voice is still embodied in that it perceives as though through human senses, sharing the physical and social space of the characters and scenes described.[5] Metaphorically, the mind of this kind of narrator is a body, a cohesive unit that "moves" in the sense that it retains its integrity across different physical locations depicted. Narration of this sort is something like the platonic travel experienced by the characters of Cavendish's *Blazing World*, except the narrator's mind never did occupy a physical body.

More generally, when the practice of fictional narration is framed in terms of the mind-as-motion metaphor, it becomes clear why travel narratives played an especially important role in the development of the novel. One purpose of a travel narrative is to report on people, societies, and landscapes that are foreign or exotic to the reader. The reporting traveler does literally what fictional narrators do metaphorically: moves among people and places, either directly witnessing scenes, events, and interactions or else conveying information about such happenings that has been obtained from other parties. Thus travel narratives provided a context in which writers could experiment with techniques for verbalizing types of witness.[6] *Oroonoko* serves as an especially illuminating example because Behn's homodiegetic narrator describes two different foreign places, one of which, Surinam, she has visited herself and one of which, Corimantien, she has only heard about from Oroonoko. In the section of the story set in Corimantien, we can see how the homodiegetic narrator begins to sound like a heterodiegetic one, and the travel narrative begins to feel more like a novel. This drift or slippage happens even though Behn's narrator is supposedly reporting events secondhand. Although she occasionally reminds the reader that she is retelling Oroonoko's story, more often her narration shifts into the mode of direct witness. Or, to put it in terms of the conceptual metaphor I have described, her mind travels to Corimantien.

Consider, for example, the following passage, in which the narrator describes Oroonoko's first encounter with Imoinda. Returning victorious from war, he visits her to report the death of her father, a general killed in battle.

When he [Oroonoko] came, attended by all the young Soldiers of any Merit, he was infinitely surpriz'd at the Beauty of this fair Queen of Night, whose Face and Person was so exceeding all he had ever beheld, that Lovely Modesty with which she receiv'd him, that softness in her Look, and Sighs, upon the melancholy Occasion of this Honour that was done by so great a Man as Oroonoko, and a Prince of whom she had heard such admirable things; the Awfulness wherewith she receiv'd him, and the Sweetness of her Words and Behaviour while he stay'd, gain'd a perfect Conquest over his fierce Heart, and made him feel, The Victor coul'd be subdu'd. (14)

This passage consistently creates the illusion that the narrator witnessed the meeting directly. It exemplifies the skillfully rendered "consciousness scene" that leads Fludernik to call Behn "the first practitioner of the novel" (1996, 131). Its success lies not only in Behn's specificity about Oroonoko's perceptions both external (Imoinda's face, sighs, demeanor) and internal (his memories, feelings, thoughts), but also in the seamless shifting between the two, so that the scene comes together as one complex but cohesive psychological experience.[7]

This quality stands out if we compare this passage with one describing a somewhat similar event in *The Blazing World*. Here is Cavendish's heterodiegetic narrator describing what happens when the Lady meets the emperor of the Blazing World:

No sooner was the Lady brought before the Emperor, but he conceived her to be some Goddess, and offered to worship her; which she refused, telling him, (for by that time she had pretty well learned their language) that although she came out of another world, yet was she but a mortal; at which the Emperor rejoycing, made her his Wife, and gave her an absolute power to rule and govern all that World as she pleased. (162)

Here subjective experience (conceiving, rejoicing) is labeled but not imagined in any detail; the narration is little more than a summary of events. Both passages refer to a character's acquired knowledge: one to the Lady's knowledge of the Emperor's language, and the other to Imoinda's acquaintance with Oroonoko's reputation. But whereas Cavendish refers to this knowledge through a parenthetical explanation, Behn integrates it into a fuller rendering of Imoinda's subjective sense of being honored; this sense is in turn simultaneously attributed to Imoinda and integrated into the larger scene, the whole "melancholy occasion." Behn also renders Oroonoko's emotional experience by transforming the image of conquest from literal and external to metaphorical and internal. Oroonoko begins the scene as a victorious warrior; by its end, he feels himself to have been conquered.

These elements strongly suggest a witnessing narratorial mind rather than a secondhand report. The most subtle, but also the most telling, sign of narratorial presence is in the phrase "this fair Queen of Night," which refers to Imoinda's blackness. Because the scene takes place in Africa among black Africans only, presumably Oroonoko himself would not feel the need to comment on the color of his lover's skin. But Behn's narrator certainly would, for one of the novel's central conceits is that both Oroonoko and Imoinda are beautiful and noble people by European standards even though their skin is black. This paradox receives much comment in the book and is the meaning of the phrase "Queen of Night." In context, the phrase further implies that, despite her actual distance from these events, the narrator is nonetheless present at the scene, because it describes a visually perceptible aspect of what is going on.

In passages such as these we can see how a convention of travel writing helps leads Behn to a specifically novelistic technique. As McKeon puts it, "no tension exists in her dual role as narrator and character, because both roles are dedicated to the single end of physically witnessing, and thereby authenticating, a central character whose personal history is distinct from her own" (112). A positive, if somewhat fanciful, way of stating the same idea would be to say that her character side shows her narrator side how to represent consciousness. The conceptual metaphor THE MIND IS A BODY MOVING IN SPACE shapes Behn's protonovel at the highest level, that of genre, and also at the lowest level, that of figurative language. The metaphor acts separately at each of these levels, however. In order to see the artistic complexity that results when an author uses a conceptual metaphor to create multiple internal connections in a narrative, we must turn to *Paradise Lost*.

Paradise Lost

Milton's epic poem, which tells the Christian myth of the fall of humankind based on the book of Genesis, centers on the consciousnesses of the three fallen creatures depicted: Satan, Adam, and Eve. It recounts how the Archangel Lucifer rebelled against God and was thrown into Hell along with his fellow rebels. Lucifer becomes Satan, and the fallen angels become devils. It also tells the story of the creation of Earth and the first humans, Adam and Eve. Satan sneaks into Paradise, where Adam and

Eve are living, and successfully tempts them to disobey the one order that God has left them, not to eat the fruit of the Tree of Knowledge. After they eat the forbidden fruit, they become sinful, and although they eventually repent and ask forgiveness, they are punished by being cast out of Paradise. Before departing they are given the knowledge that the Son of God will be incarnated on Earth at a later date so as to redeem their descendants from this original sin. Milton makes it explicit that his project is to "justifie the wayes of God to men" (Book 1, l. 26)—that is, he wants his audience to recognize the absolute justice of the providential plan within which these events took place. Satan and the humans had complete freedom of will, and their punishment is appropriate.

Again at a local level, Milton uses the conceptual metaphor THE MIND IS A BODY MOVING IN SPACE to create an architectonic image for Satan's consciousness by repeatedly figuring Satan's movement as an extension of his mental state. This technique originates when Satan lies paralyzed in amazement after his fall into Hell:

> So stretcht out huge in length the Arch-fiend lay
> Chain'd on the burning Lake, nor ever thence
> Had ris'n or heav'd his head, but that the will
> And high permission of all-ruling Heaven
> Left him at large to his own dark designs.
> (Book 1, ll. 209–13)

Here his "designs" are explicitly linked with his ability to move. God "permits" Satan both to move at this moment and, by design, to fly toward Earth to corrupt the humans. Later in Book 1 Satan states his intentions toward the Almighty in this way:

> If then his Providence
> Out of our evil seek to bring forth good,
> Our labour must be to pervert that end,
> And out of good still to find means of evil;
> Which oft times may succeed, so as perhaps

> *Shall grieve him, if I fail not, and disturb*
> *His inmost counsels from thir destind aim.*
>
> (Book 1, ll. 162–68)

The etymology of *pervert* ("turn aside") suggests that the intentions of both God and Satan take shape as a form of movement. The idea of movement turned aside, or gone wrong, continues later in the passage, as Satan seeks to "disturb his counsels from thir destind aim." The poem returns to this type of image many times, as when Satan finally approaches Eden to work his plan of evil and remarks "Revenge, at first though sweet, / Bittere ere long back on it self recoiles; / Let it; I reck not, so it light well aim'd" (Book 9, ll. 171–73).

At the same time, Milton explicitly links Satan's flight with the consciousness of the narrator/bard. Drawing on traditional analogies among poetry, flight, and song, he figures the narration itself as a flight that follows Satan's pilgrimage. As the scene of the story shifts from Hell to the region of Heaven and Earth, the epic bard pauses to address the reader, rejoicing that he, like Satan, has

> *Escap't the Stygian pool, though long detain'd*
> *In that obscure sojourn, while in my flight*
> *Through utter and through middle darkness borne*
> *With other notes then to th' Orphean Lyre*
> *I sung of Chaos and Eternal night.*
>
> (Book 3, ll. 14–18)

The "flight" undertaken by the epic bard is purely metaphorical, a journey of the mind. This is a version of the narratorial "platonic travel" I described earlier, but in the case of *Paradise Lost* it is explicitly developed for its literary effect. Milton links the conceptual metaphor NARRATIVE IS TRAVEL with the conceptual metaphor POETRY IS SONG. This connection is appropriate, of course, for the mixed genre of verse narrative. In combination with the image of Satanic movement as consciousness and other language in the poem, it creates a complex, integrated network of metaphors representing mental activity through motion.

This network in turn supports Milton's use of THE MIND IS A BODY MOVING IN SPACE at the thematic level. Unlike the other works I have discussed, *Paradise Lost* is explicitly concerned not only with the way that humans understand consciousness, but also with techniques for transforming consciousness. The passage I discussed earlier, in which Michael tells Adam how to acquire a "paradise within," culminates in a series of such textual moments. Milton punningly evokes the metaphorical entailment MENTAL STATES ARE LOCATIONS when Satan sees Adam and Eve "Imparadis't in one anothers arms" (Book 4, l. 506). In a well-known passage from Book 1, Satan, forced to accept that he has fallen from Heaven into Hell, delivers a monologue that in effect asserts the power of conceptual metaphor to change reality itself:

> Hail horrours, hail
> Infernal world, and thou profoundest Hell
> Receive they new Possessor: One who brings
> A mind not to be chang'd by Place or Time.
> The mind is its own place, and in it self
> Can make a Heav'n of Hell, a Hell of Heav'n.
> (Book 1, ll. 250–55)

Later, though, he discovers that the metaphor has more power over him than he over it. Tormented by the knowledge of all he has lost, he says, "which way I flie is Hell; my self am Hell; / And in the lowest deep a lower deep / Still threatning to devour me opens wide" (Book 4, ll. 75–77). Far from his mind's making Hell into Heaven, Hell itself has made his mind into Hell; it is a state of consciousness that travels with him wherever he goes.

The metaphorical connection between physical locations and mental states leads to internal suffering for Satan, but it provides a source of hope and redemption for Adam and Eve. Before being cast out of Paradise as punishment for their transgression, they receive a visit from the Archangel Michael meant to show them the consequences of their fall but also to reassure them about the ultimate fate of humanity: salvation through God's Son. They each receive this wisdom in a different way; Adam is given a narration of the future of humanity, and Eve is blessed with a healing dream while she sleeps. In both cases, though, Paradise becomes part of them. Thus, after Adam acknowledges Christ as his redeemer, Michael tells him only to add virtue to his wisdom and "then wilt thou not be loath / To leave this Paradise, but shalt possess / A Paradise within thee, happier farr" (Book 12, ll. 585–87). The physical location metaphorically becomes a mental state and suggests the possibility for a transformation of fallen consciousnesses into redeemed minds.

Eve's lesson is similar, although delivered by different means. When she wakes from her divine sleep, Eve reveals that she has received dreams "propitious, some great good / Presaging" (Book 12, ll. 612–13). She peacefully accepts their departure, saying to Adam,

> In mee is no delay; with thee to goe,
> Is to stay here; without thee here to stay,
> Is to go hence unwilling; thou to mee
> Art all things under Heav'n, all places thou.
> (Book 12, ll. 615–18)

For Eve, as for Adam, Paradise itself has become entirely metaphorical, the equivalent of an internal state. Just as Satan's continuing demise is represented by the assimilation of Hell itself into his consciousness, Adam's and Eve's redemption is represented by the assimilation of Paradise into their consciousnesses. Satan takes Hell with him everywhere he goes; Adam will take Paradise with him everywhere, and thus will himself be Paradise for Eve.

Milton's use of this system of metaphors in *Paradise Lost* provides an especially sophisticated example of the way that authors consciously elaborate and call attention to the conceptual metaphors that unconsciously structure our thinking. Earlier I pointed out that in the ordinary sentence *The group reached con-*

sensus, the verb of motion extends its metaphorical status to the word "consensus," so that it too becomes metaphorical, the image of a place. Milton's literary construction "Which way I flie is Hell; myself am Hell" does the same thing: it brings together an image of a location and a description of a mental state, but it does so as a conscious creative act. When Satan says "myself am Hell," the apparently static analogy actually contains, in very concise form, the set of connections implicit in the conceptual metaphor: *there is a place called Hell; being in that place induces certain psychological experiences; now, no matter where I am when I have those particular experiences, I feel as though I am in that physical place called Hell; but because the experiences are internal, I will say instead that the place called Hell is inside me.*

This sequence of inferences that I have attributed to Satan tells the story of an alteration in his mental state and also communicates his heightened awareness of that state. In other words, compressed within the metaphorical utterance "myself am Hell" is a narrative. This narrative elaborates on the structure of the conceptual metaphor. Satan invents a figurative name for a new inner state, and by speaking that name he also tells the story of how the state came about. The concision of the phrase embodies the unity of the experience: the immediate feelings of despair, the memories of Hell, and the sense of a changed consciousness form a single, if complex, psychological event. And yet describing the metaphorical structure as I have done reveals that this experience also contains a sequence of causally related occurrences—a sequence ending in the utterance itself. The words are really Milton's of course, not Satan's, but Milton succeeds in representing Satan's consciousness in two senses. He describes, by analogy, what kind of thing Satan's mind is (it is like a body), and he also tells the reader what Satan has consciously experienced (a steadily intensifying despair).

Both ways of representing consciousness, as I have tried to show in this chapter, depend on conceptual metaphor. The conceptual metaphor THE MIND IS A BODY MOVING IN SPACE gives us a way to understand what kind of thing the mind is, a way to conceptualize narrative (as a form of travel), and a grounding for the illusion of physical witness that structures fictional narration. While it is *Oroonoko*, and not *Paradise Lost*, that most fully anticipates the development of the novel, Milton's epic is distinctive for its complex and deliberate representations of consciousness. Both these narratives demonstrate how one cognitive mechanism through which we conceptualize our minds shaped narrative representations of consciousness during the transitional period of the late 1600s.

Notes

1. A few critics have suggested that *Paradise Lost* can be seen as a novel. Thomas N. Corns has argued that *Paradise Lost* could be considered "temporarily and provisionally dialogic" (1994, 289). Damrosch (1985) and Rappaport (1986) have drawn on Lukács's theory of the novel to argue that the representation of Adam and Eve as a domestic couple anticipates the representation of bourgeois consciousness that will arise as part of the development of the English novel.

2. For more on conceptual metaphors and issues of embodiment, see Leslie Lockett's contribution to the present volume. For a different approach to figurative language vis-à-vis representations of mind, see David Vallins's contribution. Finally, see Mandler (1992) for an explanation of how perceptual experience translates into the development of cognitive mechanisms in infancy.

3. For a more general account of the role of conceptual metaphor in polysemy, see Sweetser (1990).

4. A recent essay by Kai Mikkonen, which considers some of the theoretical implications and limitations of the conceptual metaphor NARRATIVE IS TRAVEL, focuses on a modern novel, Graham Greene's *Journey without Maps*, that deliberately foregrounds and ultimately questions the metaphor of narrative as travel (Mikkonen 2007). As is the case with Milton's *Paradise Lost*, *Journey without Maps* pays explicit attention to the cognitive and cultural structures that organize experience, giving the work a special complexity.

5. The witnessing narrator is one form taken by the "anthropomorphic experiencer" that Fludernik (1996, 13) says is essential to any narrative.

6. Mikkonen (2007) says something similar in his discussion of THE NARRATIVE IS TRAVEL metaphor. Although he is investigating not the representation of consciousness but the ways in which narrative itself is like travel, he observes that "the cognitive foundations and communicative

functions of the 'narrative is travel' metaphor are based, to a significant degree, on the representation of the human experience of space and movement" (299). In other words, NARRATIVE IS TRAVEL is a special case of THE MIND IS A BODY MOVING IN SPACE.

7. Behn was also a successful playwright, and her construction of such consciousness scenes owes something to her knowledge of the stage. The face-to-face encounter between Oroonoko and Imoinda has some of the structure of a dramatic scene (such as the reunion of Othello and Desdemona at Cyprus in *Othello*, 2.2), but the psychological experience is rendered indirectly through heterodiegetic narration rather than through direct dialogue (Fludernik 1996, 147). More broadly, although tracing the influence of dramatic technique on representations of consciousness in seventeenth-century verse and prose narratives is beyond the scope of this chapter, I would like to suggest here that metaphoric conceptions of the world as a theater, whose significance has been well documented in critical writings on Milton and Shakespeare, could be analyzed similarly to the way I have analyzed the metaphor NARRATIVE IS TRAVEL. A narrating consciousness could be imagined in terms of a soliloquizing character or of the internal audience so frequently found in Shakespeare's plays. In *Othello*, for instance, Iago performs both these functions, often developing in soliloquy a psychologically resonant image such as the one Behn's narrator presents in the passage from *Oroonoko*.

References

Behn, Aphra. 1997 [1688]. *Oroonoko*. Ed. Joanna Lipking. New York: W. W. Norton.

Bunyan, John. 1960 [1678]. *The Pilgrim's Progress from This World to That Which Is to Come*. Ed. James Blanton Wharey and Roger Sharrock. Oxford: Oxford University Press.

Cavendish, Margaret. 2000 [1666]. *A Description of a New World, Called the Blazing World*. In *Paper Bodies: A Margaret Cavendish Reader*, ed. Sylvia Bowerbank and Sara Mendelson, 151–251. Peterborough, Ontario: Broadview.

Corns, Thomas N. 1994. "'That Prerogative over Human': *Paradise Lost* and the Telling of Divine History." In *Contexts of Pre-Novel Narrative: The European Tradition*, ed. Roy Eriksen, 283–91. Berlin: Mouton de Gruyter.

Crane, Mary Thomas. 2001. *Shakespeare's Brain: Reading with Cognitive Theory*. Princeton: Princeton University Press.

Damrosch, Leopold, Jr. 1985. *God's Plot and Man's Stories: Studies in the Fictional Imagination from Milton to Fielding*. Chicago: University of Chicago Press.

Donne, John. 1967. *The Complete Poetry of John Donne*. Ed. John T. Shawcross. Garden City NY: Doubleday Anchor.

Fludernik, Monika. 1996. *Towards a "Natural" Narratology*. London: Routledge.

Johnson, Mark. 1987. *The Body in the Mind: The Bodily Basis of Meaning, Imagination, and Reason*. Chicago: University of Chicago Press.

Lakoff, George, and Mark Johnson. 1999. *Philosophy in the Flesh: The Embodied Mind and Its Challenge to Western Thought*. New York: Basic Books.

Lakoff, George, and Mark Turner. 1989. *More than Cool Reason: A Field Guide to Poetic Metaphor*. Chicago: University of Chicago Press.

Mandler, Jean M. 1992. "How to Build a Baby: II. Conceptual Primitives." *Psychological Review* 99:587–604.

Marvell, Andrew. 1971. "The Garden." In *The Poems and Letters of Andrew Marvell*, ed. H. M. Margoliouth, 1:48–49. 3rd ed. Oxford: Clarendon Press.

McKeon, Michael. 2002. *The Origins of the English Novel, 1600–1740*. 15th anniv. ed. Baltimore: Johns Hopkins University Press.

Mikkonen, Kai. 2007. "The 'Narrative Is Travel' Metaphor: Between Spatial Sequence and Open Consequence." *Narrative* 15:287–305.

Milton, John. 1998 [1674]. *Paradise Lost*. In *The Riverside Milton*, ed. Roy Flannagan. Boston: Houghton Mifflin.

Pound, Ezra. 1933. *Selected Poems*. Ed. T. S. Eliot. London: Faber and Faber.

Rappaport, Herman. 1986. "*Paradise Lost* and the Novel." In *Approaches to Teaching Milton's* Paradise Lost, ed. Galbraith M. Crump. New York: Modern Language Association.

Ricks, Christopher. 1963. *Milton's Grand Style*. Oxford: Oxford University Press.

Sweetser, Eve. 1990. *From Etymology to Pragmatics: Metaphorical and Cultural Aspects of Semantic Structure*. Cambridge: Cambridge University Press.

Part III

Contexts for Consciousness in the
Eighteenth and Nineteenth Centuries

5. 1700–1775
Theory of Mind, Social Hierarchy,
and the Emergence of Narrative Subjectivity
LISA ZUNSHINE

A peculiar sideline scenario plays itself out obsessively in one eighteenth-century novel after another: A protagonist responds to an apparently impoverished stranger's plea for assistance while being closely watched by an interested observer, such as a secret admirer, a parent, or a friend. For example, Laurence Sterne's *A Sentimental Journey through France and Italy* (1768) opens with Yorick in Calais, first rejecting the plea of a Franciscan monk begging on behalf of his convent, then feeling guilty and afraid that the monk has reported his uncharitable behavior to the attractive lady traveling next to Yorick, and finally making it up to the monk under the approving gaze of that increasingly attractive lady. Sarah Fielding's *The History of Ophelia* (1760) features a scene in which the rakish Lord Dorchester helps out the starving half-pay Captain Traverse, while Dorchester's beautiful young protégé, Ophelia, watches them both and describes their feelings. In Oliver Goldsmith's *The Citizen of the World* (1762), a series of essays written from the point of view of a fictitious Chinese philosopher living in London, the narrator first listens to his acquaintance, Mr. Drybone, inveighing against giving alms to beggars and then observes Mr. Drybone going against his own wise precepts and surreptitiously helping out several of them. In Anna Maria Bennett's *The Beggar Girl and Her Benefactors* (1797), Colonel Buhanun starts off by berating harshly a "little female mendicant" who begs him for "one halfpenny," but soon reveals his truer, gentler self, gives the girl money, and even fights to hide "an officious fluid, which sprang involuntarily to his eyes" at the sight of her distress (1:3). The exchange takes place under the attentive gaze of Buhanun's trusty servant—his occasional almoner and another crusty man with a heart of gold.

Similar scenes of observed benefaction occur in Samuel Richardson's *Clarissa* (1747–48), Henry Fielding's *Tom Jones* (1749), Tobias Smollett's *Peregrine Pickle* (1751), Eliza Haywood's *Jemmy and Jenny Jessamy* (1753), Frances Burney's *Cecilia* (1782), and Thomas Holcroft's *Anna St. Ives* (1792). In fact, it is difficult to think of an eighteenth-century novel, from *Clarissa* on, that does not contain one or several such scenes. And even before this pattern establishes itself in the novel, it is already present in Addison and Steele's *Spectator*, in which the narrator observes Sir Andrew Freeport giving money to a group of beggars in the street (1965 [1711], 2:405).

How do we account for the popularity of this scenario in eighteenth-century fiction? Traditional criticism offers two ways of approaching it. First, we can consider such scenes of observed charity in the context of the period's "sentimental" discourse. We can thus speculate that fictional accounts of induced empathy and shared benevolence struck a particular chord for a culture as invested in the representation of embodied sentiments as was the culture of the Enlightenment. Second, we can think of sociohistorical developments that challenged the established practices of giving alms and thus rendered philanthropy a newly fascinating and controversial topic. After all, Henry Fielding proclaimed charity "the very characteristic virtue [of his] time" (1988 [1752], 247), referring to such new forms of philanthropic association as hospitals (such as the Foundling Hospital, the Magdalene, the Lying-In Hospital, the Lock Hospital, and others) whose number rose from two before 1700 to thirty-one by 1800, a statistic that reflects deeper transformations in the social fabric of early modern England. Eighteenth-century men and women had to deal with such issues as the redefinition of the concept of the "deserving" poor, the secularization of philanthropy, and the changes in the relationship between private and public giving. Any one of these factors, as well as a combination of them, can be used to construct a plausible narrative about the interest that the scenes of observed charity elicited in eighteenth-century readers and writers.

To these explanations, which we could broadly characterize as historical, I want to add another explanation, which could be broadly characterized as cognitive. In what follows, I suggest that the pattern of mental embedment present in such scenes—a triangulation of minds fueled by different degrees of mutual awareness—makes these moments of observed benefaction particularly cognitively rewarding and as such may add to their narrative appeal. The real challenge—and potentially the most interesting part of the model that I develop here—lies in our ability to combine the historical and the cognitive explanations. That is, if we agree that the three-way mind reading implied by the scenes of observed benefaction feels rewarding to the evolved cognitive architecture that underlies our social functioning *and* that philanthropy was a hot topic in eighteenth-century public discourse, can we articulate a viable cognitive-historicist model (or several models) that can bring together and, by doing so, potentially transform both these explanations?

This is to say that a cognitive approach may eventually sharpen our historicist view: If, as I will argue below, readers are in principle *always* interested in the scenes featuring triangulations of minds, then we must inquire carefully into the specific cultural circumstances that made this particular pattern of fictional triangulation (the giver, the receiver, and the observer) so strikingly competitive in the eighteenth-century literary marketplace.

And, similarly, a historicist approach may eventually focus our cognitive view: If the concern about benefits and pitfalls of private philanthropy assumed such a prominent place in eighteenth-century mentality, then we must inquire into the ways in which the perceived importance of this topic may have enhanced the attractiveness of fictional narratives featuring mental triangulations. This is to say that the readers may have felt that by engaging in the distinctively structured attribution of mental states sponsored by such narratives, they also learned something about the politics of charitable giving. The perception of social relevance may have fueled the attractiveness of the cognitive work-out offered by the scenes of observed benefaction.

As you can see, I am anticipating my argument by presenting you with the two speculations that may follow from it. I am doing this on purpose. As you read my discussion of cognitive adaptations possibly underlying the eighteenth-century fascination with fictions of observed charity, I want you to think of the practical ways in which research in cognitive science can be used to further historicist inquiry. Underlying such interdisciplinary explorations is the assumption that specific social contexts engage our cognitive adaptations and by doing so shape the history of cultural representations and our subsequent thinking about this history.

The rest of this chapter is divided into four parts. Parts 1 and 2 introduce the concept of Theory of Mind to explore the cognitive underpinnings of the interest that scenes of triangulated mind reading elicit in readers of fictional narratives. Part 3 presents a cross section of such scenes in eighteenth-century fiction, focusing centrally on those triangulations that engaged the socioeconomic anxieties of contemporary readers. I return here to the representations of observed benefaction to speculate about the possibilities of an analysis that combines cognitive theory with historicist methods of studying literature. Specifically, I suggest that the fictional hierarchy of mental complexity involving the giver, the receiver, and the observer was co-implicated in eighteenth-century constructions of class boundaries and social mobility. Part 4, the conclusion, turns to an eighteenth-century philosophical treatise featuring numerous instances of three-way mind reading and considers whether contemporary writers might have been aware of the role played by such triangulations in the emergence of narrative subjectivity.

How Many Minds
Do We Want to Follow Around?

My main borrowing from cognitive sciences is the concept of Theory of Mind. "Theory of Mind" and "mind reading" are the terms used interchangeably to describe our ability to explain behavior in terms of underlying thoughts, feelings, desires, and intentions (Baron-Cohen 1995). We attribute states of mind to ourselves and others all the time; for example, we see somebody reaching for a cup of water, and we assume that she is thirsty. Our attributions are frequently incorrect (the person who reached for the cup of water might have done it for reasons other than being thirsty); still, making them is the default way by which we construct and navigate our social environment. When Theory of Mind is impaired, as it is in varying degrees in the case of autism and schizophrenia, communication breaks down.

An important assumption underlying my present argument is that our cognitive adaptations for mind reading are promiscuous, voracious, and proactive; these adaptations require, as a condition for their development and continued use, both direct interactions with other people and imaginary approximations of such interactions. In other words, so important is the mind-reading ability for our species, and so ready is our Theory of Mind to jump into action and to subject every behavior to "intense sociocognitive scrutiny" (Bering 2002, 12), that at least on some level we do not distinguish between attributing states of mind to real people and attributing them to fictional characters. Figuring out what the attractive lady is thinking as she observes Yorick's interaction with the Franciscan monk feels almost as important as figuring out what a real-life attractive stranger is thinking as she looks us in the eye and holds forth on how she enjoyed reading the book that we currently have in our hands. Hence the pleasure afforded by following various minds in fictional narratives is to a significant degree a *social* pleasure—an illusive but satisfying confirmation that we remain competent players in the social game that is our life.

Which brings us to the question about the *number* of minds that we enjoy following both in real life and in fictional narratives. As a starting point for this discussion, consider the studies of "size and structure of freely formed conversational groups" by R. I. M. Dunbar, N. D. C. Duncan, and Daniel Nettle, which have shown that "in spontaneous interaction, social groups of any size usually fragment into smaller conversational cliques.

Such cliques are typically of 4 or fewer individuals, only exceeding this limit in infrequent formal contexts" (Stiller, Nettle, and Dunbar 2004, 401). Thus when four people are talking together at a cocktail party and the fifth person joins the conversation, the group soon splits into two relatively independent conversational units consisting of two and three people. This observation implies that we have a difficult time tracking more than four minds (including our own) at the same time, and, if left to our own devices, we try to rearrange the social contexts that require us to go over that limit.

In related studies, Dunbar and his colleagues have demonstrated that when we are faced with short narrative vignettes that force us to process multiply embedded minds (along the lines of, "I believe that you think that he wants you to understand that . . . ," only, of course, appropriately contextualized), our understanding plummets 60 percent when we move beyond the fourth level of embedment. The recursive mental embedment of the fourth level and above thus seems to place high demands on our cognitive processing, both in real-life conversations and in the context of narrative. Cognitive psychology offers a series of fascinating speculations about why this might be so, but for the purpose of this discussion, I focus not on the possible evolutionary origins of this cognitive pattern but on its implications for our study of fictional narrative.

For example, we may want to take a fresh look at the novelistic construction of crowds and ask how writers get around the problem of representing the number of minds—fifty, a hundred, a thousand—that clearly take us outside our zone of cognitive comfort. It seems that authors deal with this challenge in several ways. Sometimes they represent a crowd through three or four distinct personalities—the spokespeople who capture various points of view held by the multitude. Sometimes they depict a crowd as being of one mind, shouting or grumbling in unison, which, in turn, allows them to have this unified "mob mind" interact with two or three other distinct individuals, who respond to the mob's concerns, so that the cumulative number of minds still stays within the comfortable range of four.[1]

Third-Level Mind Reading in Fiction

We can now be aware of the special challenges faced by authors who want to pack four or more recursive mental states into one scene (as in, "A was observing B while B was observing C while C was following the interaction between D and E," or "A was thinking about what B was thinking about what A was thinking about what B was thinking," and so forth).[2] To prevent such a representation from appearing odd or unintelligible, a writer has to construct a compelling social context, within which this complicated pattern of mind reading feels natural and does not draw attention to itself (unless the writer *wants* to draw our attention to it).

Thus it would be wrong to take the research of Dunbar and his colleagues as an indication that fiction writers cannot or should not build frames that embed more than four subjectivities. In fact, the opposite is the case. Fictional narratives endlessly *experiment with* rather than *automatically execute* our evolved cognitive adaptations. When cognitive scientists succeed in isolating a certain regularity of our information processing (such as an apparent constraint on the number of levels of embedded subjectivity that we can process with ease), we can take that constraint and see how it plays itself out in a fictional narrative. What we discover is that where there is a cognitive constraint, there is a guarantee that writers will intuitively experiment in the direction of challenging that constraint, probing and poking it and getting around it. The exact forms of such probing and poking will depend on specific cultural circumstances. The culturally enmeshed cognitive limits thus present us with creative openings rather than with a promise of stagnation and endless replication of the established forms.

Elsewhere I have discussed examples of such experimentation in Restoration comedy (e.g., in the last scene of Etherege's *The Man of Mode* [Zunshine 2007]), in the eighteenth-century sentimental novel (e.g., in the "Miss Partington" episode of Richardson's *Clarissa* [Zunshine 2005]), in modernist fiction (e.g., in the "Lady Bruton" scene of Woolf's *Mrs Dalloway*), and in a handful of narratives that emphasize the comic incomprehensibility of the "I know that you know that she knows that we know" situations (Zunshine 2006). Here, however, I want to focus on what goes on within our zone of cognitive comfort—on the third level and the cusp of the fourth level of mental embedment—before we cross over to the challenging fifth ("I know that you think that he wants you to believe that she was angry at him") but certainly above the commonsensical second ("I know that she is hungry").

Fascinating things happen on that third (or third-to-fourth) level. This is where the attractive lady observes Yorick's dealings with the Franciscan monk; where the psyche splits into id, ego, and superego;[3] where moments of "deep intersubjectivity" unfold (to use the term from George Butte's study, *I Know That You Know That I Know*); and where eavesdropping and overhearing, so beloved by authors since antiquity, occur. In other words, this is the level at which much of our culture happens, for it seems that the interplay of three subjectivities (however many physical bodies it may actually involve) is the staple of our philosophy, representational art, and fictional narratives.

In fact, according to cognitive literary critic Blakey Vermeule (2010, 214) moments in fiction that engage third-order Theory of Mind are the "moments that we consider especially literary, and that have therefore attracted intense critical scrutiny." You can test this suggestive claim by taking a random sample of your favorite works of literary scholarship and seeing what passages critics typically select for closer analysis, or by going over the passages that you choose for exercises in close reading that you conduct with your students. Moreover, in thinking of our critical and classroom discussions of the moments of triangulated mind reading, we may also consider the possibility that we like focusing on such moments not just because they embed three minds but also because when we analyze them we start generating triangulated mind readings of our own.

Which, in turn, makes one wonder just what it is about generating such moments that may feel so intrinsically rewarding to us. At present, cognitive evolutionary psychology and anthropology are the fields most prepared to address this question, however tentative their answers might be. One possible explanation, which speculates about the social rewards of situations in our evolutionary past in which three-way mind readings naturally occurred, has been offered by Daniel Nettle. As he puts it,

> [The] natural situation in which we have three-way mind-reading going on is one that might be rewarding for several reasons. First, if we know what person A is thinking about person B but person B does not know this, then we are in a position of privilege and power. Either person A had taken us into their confidence, which would mean we were a valued coalition partner, or we are very clever, and/or we now have some leverage over person B because we know something important that they do not. If we feel well-disposed to B we may want to warn them, and gain their gratitude and reciprocity; if we are ill-disposed to B we may wish to use it against them or withhold it spitefully. In any event, this is a very significant situation in which we, although a spectator, are now part of a social triangle. This would not be so true if we knew what person A thought about B and B also knew this.[4]

One issue that any such explanation—whether emerging from cognitive evolutionary psychology or from cognitive literary criticism—would have to tackle has to do with the relationship between the *ultimate* and *proximate* causes of the cognitive satisfaction that we apparently experience in encountering and generating the moments of three-way mind reading. Starting with the ultimate causality, it may be that our present-day preferences can be traced back to our evolutionary past. For example, it is possible that negotiating three-way mind-reading situations was a must for our social survival in the Pleistocene. As a recurrent cognitive challenge it thus impacted the evolution of our mind-reading adaptations, which means that today we may feel particularly good about ourselves whenever we are intuitively aware that we are operating smoothly on the third level of mental embedment (e.g., "I know what he wants her to think!"), even when the social situation in question is completely contrived (e.g., when "he" is the Big Bad Wolf and she is Red Riding Hood).

If we turn to proximate causes, we may suggest that imaginary representations of three-way mind-reading model a variety of social challenges that we face in our daily lives. As such they may feel particularly attention-worthy, especially because fictional narratives present us with cleaned-up versions of real-life mind-reading instabilities. That is, in a work of fiction, you actually get to know what *X* thought about *Y*, whereas in real life you have to settle for your imperfect guesses of other people's mental states (Palmer 2006). But whichever explanation we consider, proximate-level causes will have to be integrated with ultimate-level causes. This is to say that our broader interest in fictional mind reading—of which our interest in the three-way mind reading is an important subset—builds both on our evolutionary history and on our everyday exercise of our Theory of Mind adaptations.

Historicizing Fictional Representations of Three-Way Mind Reading

Given these two factors—the importance of triangulated mind reading to our social life and the deep engagement of fictional narratives with our Theory of Mind—we must expect scenes featuring three interacting minds to be present in all cultures and historical periods. And so they are. Stories that do not triangulate minds can, of course, also be found in any culture, but they indicate something about their intended audience and genre rather than about that period's overall narrative engagement with three-way mind reading. For instance, early twenty-first-century books for toddlers often feature only two interacting minds, but that tells us something interesting about their authors' intuitive perception of their audience's mind-reading capacities rather than about the dominant pattern of mind reading in our culture.

But if representations of mental triangulation constitute a narrative universal, can we historicize it? Specifically, given this volume's goal of tracing the emergence of the mind in narrative discourse in English from its beginnings to the present day, can we say that eighteenth-century writers developed particular, historically contingent ways of triangulating fictional minds? I submit that the answer is yes, but with the following proviso.

As my example of books for toddlers shows, different narrative patterns of mind-reading triangulation can comfortably coexist. The same historical period can produce fictional stories that contain few or no triangulations, formulaic triangulations, and triangulations that strike a nerve for readers immersed in that particular historical moment but not for those outside it. So when we discuss three-way mind reading in the fiction of a specific period, we must avoid treating a certain pattern of mental triangulation as dominant simply because it happens to predominate in our present selection of case studies.

Hence in the rest of this section I present a sample of patterns of triangulated mind reading in eighteenth-century fiction, discussing texts that pointedly do not contain any triangulations; those that feature conventional, non-period-specific triangulations; and those that construct triangulations responsive to their readers' concerns about philanthropic giving. Although I am primarily interested in the latter—given their compelling connection to the specific historical moment—I cannot claim that they represent a dominant pattern of mind-reading triangulations in eighteenth-century fiction. Instead, I advance a more functionally specific argument that fictional narratives frequently use mental triangulations to support or question existing social hierarchies. Hence the scenes of observed benefaction represent one instance of such ongoing literary participation in the cultural construction of the category of social class.

No Connected Story—No Triangulation

One striking example of an eighteenth-century narrative that does not feature triangulated mind reading is a religious treatise aimed at very young children. Generously illustrated and occasionally catechistic, Anna Laetitia Barbauld's *Hymns in Prose for Children* (1866 [1781]) consists of fifteen vignettes describing various aspects of God's close involvement with the natural and social world. Approaching this text from the perspective of the cognitive theory of mind reading, one is struck by how thoroughly Barbauld interdicts the possibility of reading more than two minds into any given passage. The overwhelming majority of the hymns focus on just one mind (e.g., "I will praise God with my voice; for I may praise him, though I am but a little child" [3]); several allow for two minds (e.g., "You may sleep, for He never sleeps" [25]), and none allow for three.[5]

It is difficult to say whether Barbauld intentionally precluded the possibility of reading three interacting consciousnesses into her *Hymns*. We know that she wanted to write a book radically different from the "multitude of books professedly written for children" and yet "not adapted to the comprehension of a young child" (Ellis 1874, 101–2; Barbauld 1866 [1781], vi). In the preface to *Hymns*, she criticizes religious literature for children for the unnecessary artfulness of story lines. As she saw it, a "connected story, however simple, is above [the] capacity . . . of a child from two to three years old" and only interferes with the grand project of impressing upon the child's mind the "full force of the idea of God" (Ellis 1874, 101–2). As I see it, a "connected story" contains triangulations of minds, so avoiding one allows writers to avoid the other. In other words, in a way that anticipates subsequent research by developmental psychologists, which posits the age of four as an important threshold in the maturation of Theory of Mind, Barbauld refrained from creating story lines that involve cognitive complexity attendant on a three-way mind reading.

Formulaic Triangulations

The most traditional pattern of mental triangulation found in all national literatures involves a person observing two people who are in love or falling in love. We get access to the mind of the observer and, through it, to the mutually reflecting minds of the two lovers. Eighteenth-century writers heavily rely on this pattern; indeed, it seems to constitute the majority of the three-way fictional mind readings of the period.

As a paradigmatic example of this pattern harkening back to the earliest days of the novel, consider a scene from Heliodorus's *An Ethiopian Romance* (third century A D), in which an Egyptian priest, Calasiris, tells the story of the first meeting between the protagonists, Chariclea and Theagenis.[6] In this highly reflexive passage, the account of the young people's subjectivities responding to each other is filtered through Calasiris's perception:

At first they stood in silent amazement, and then, very slowly, she handed him the torch. He received it, and they fixed each other with a rigid gaze, as if they had sometime known one another or had seen each other before and were now calling each other to mind. Then they gave each other a slight, and furtive smile, marked only by the spreading of the eyes. Then, as if ashamed of what they had done, they blushed, and again, when the passion, as I think, suffused their hearts, they turned pale. In a single moment, in short, their countenances betrayed a thousand shades of feeling; their various changes of color and expression revealed the commotion of their souls. These emotions escaped the crowd and Charicles. . . . But I occupied myself with nothing else than observing these young people. (73)

Note the obliviousness of Charicles, Chariclea's adoptive father. His might have been the fourth mind added to this scene. That is, Calasiris could have been aware of Charicles's noticing the young people's reaction to each other, in which case the subsequent story would have been quite different. Charicles, however, remains preoccupied with something else, and so the scene merely hints at the possibility of the four-way mind reading without committing to it. We encounter exactly the same representational strategy in Henry Fielding's novel *Tom Jones* (1749), in which the narrator of the novel functions as an observer, reporting on the erotic mutual awareness of Tom Jones and Sophia Western, while Sophia's father, Squire Western, who should have noticed that his only daughter is falling in love (which, again, would have changed the course of the story), remains blind to what is going on.

One important difference between the ways Heliodorus and Fielding treat these scenes has to do with the figure of the observer. Whereas in *An Ethiopian Romance* the observer is a flesh-and-blood character (so to speak), in *Tom Jones* it is the nebulous narrator, omnipresent but invisible to the characters in the story. I will return to this point later, in my discussion of Adam Smith,

so let me say now only that using fewer than three physically present characters to construct a mental triangulation is a strategy
frequently deployed—though certainly not invented—by eighteenth-century writers. (Think, for example, of Richardson's
Lovelace presenting himself as an observer of his and Clarissa's
wordless exchange of loving looks in the scene in which he imagines her breastfeeding his illegitimate twins.)

The tradition of constructing mental triangulations by exploring the feelings of two lovers as caught by the watchful eye of a
third party continues in later fiction. In Lev Tolstoi's *Anna Karenina* (1877), Kitty observes Anna and Vronsky's growing mutual
infatuation at the ball. Her own love for Vronsky seems to render her an inordinately astute observer: she can read the couple's emotions in a way that other people around them cannot.
Helen Fielding's *Bridget Jones: The Edge of Reason* (1999) features a
similar scene, in which the brokenhearted observer grows strikingly perceptive about the feelings of would-be lovers. As Bridget
muses, there "are sometimes those relationships that once you
see them starting you just know, click: that's it, it's perfect, it's
going to work, they'll go for the long haul—usually the sort of
relationships you see starting between your immediate ex, who
you were hoping to get back with, and somebody else" (323).

Note that whereas Tolstoi uses physically present characters
to construct his scene of three-way mind reading, Fielding eschews physical bodies and goes for the hypothetical "you," "your
ex," and "somebody else." This is not to say that Tolstoi generally
prefers to embody his mental triangulations while Fielding favors
disembodied exchanges. *Anna Karenina* and *Bridget Jones* contain
generous helpings of both, demonstrating that the combination
of embodied and disembodied triangulations constitutes one of
the essential features of the novel as a genre, even if some novels feature more triangulations of one kind than another.

I call the mental triangulation involving two lovers and an observer formulaic because it seems not to have changed significantly
since *An Ethiopian Romance*. At the same time, even though it is
omnipresent in the eighteenth-century novel, from Aphra Behn's
Oroonoko (1688) to Jane Austen's *Emma* (1816), I hesitate to call it

dominant. Again, the cognitive profile of the eighteenth-century fictional narrative is too variegated to designate any of its mind-reading triangulations as either dominant or essential.

If we insist on making a larger claim about some essential feature of the eighteenth-century pattern of narrative triangulation, perhaps that feature should be precisely this variety—that is, the coexistence of texts that use formulaic triangulations, those that resist triangulations (like Barbauld's *Hymns*), those that build their triangulations around topical issues, such as philanthropy, and those that deploy triangulations to increase the rhetorical appeal of their philosophic, theologic, and aesthetic arguments. Cultural historians have commented extensively on the unprecedented expansion of the market for the print media throughout the eighteenth century (Hunter 1990; McDowell 1998; Warner 1998). What this expansion may have indicated—to translate it into specifically cognitive terms—is that a rapidly developing capitalist economy offers its consumers increasingly diverse ways of engaging their mind-reading adaptations. Topical constructions of fictional representations of mind-reading triangulations emerge all the time, but they do not replace formulaic constructions; instead they engage different aesthetic and ideological concerns and explore different pathways within the same genre. The legacy of the eighteenth-century literary marketplace is thus the legacy of mind-reading diversity, in which formulaic and topical triangulations codeveloped sometimes in different narratives and sometimes on the pages of the same book.

Topical Triangulations

We can now rethink our initial analysis of the genealogy and effects of eighteenth-century fictional scenes of observed benefaction. First, we may say, quoting Vermeule's work on three-way mind reading, that such scenes "sponsor the experience of what we think of as literariness—the special buzzing thickness, the strange harmony of the faculties that Kant described when he found himself in the presence of serious art" (2010, 221). Or, to take the same cognitive-evolutionary argument and frame it in social rather than aesthetic terms: The depiction of an observer, who registers the feelings of a benefactor, who, in turn, registers the feelings of a beggar, presents a reader—*any* reader—with an immediately appealing possibility of triangulated mind attribution, appealing, that is, because it arguably makes the reader feel good about her own mind-reading prowess or social acumen.

Second, we may suggest that there was at least one reason the eighteenth-century middle-class reader—in contrast, that is, to just *any* reader—would be particularly interested in following such a three-way exchange. The problem faced by the fictional giver—the need to decide on the spot that an apparently impoverished stranger was not a professional mendicant aiming to impose on her good will—was the problem that the reader herself faced daily. Commenting on the "cataclysmic" growth of the urban population in eighteenth-century London and in "newer industrial centers," historian David Owen points out that "it would be out of the question to translate to an urban environment the network of relationships, personal and professional, that made rural England an ordered society. . . . Direct almsgiving and neighborhood charity, which in a village could be carried on without fear of being unduly imposed upon, now served to encourage the professional mendicant" (1964, 91–92).

The problem of telling the deserving poor from the professional mendicant was somewhat palliated for people who could afford to spend time and money on researching and planning out their charitable activities. As Donna T. Andrew (1995) has demonstrated, eighteenth-century philanthropists with substantial resources evolved investigative strategies that allowed them to discriminate between deserving and fraudulent objects of charity, such as sponsoring a network of local agents who could check the claims of people asking for assistance. Those strategies, however, were not available to middle-class men and women—who constituted the majority of contemporary readers—when strangers begging for immediate relief accosted them.

One may thus speculate that for such readers a fictional story featuring a character encountering a claimant to her charity might have provided a pleasant compensatory fantasy. Even if that character herself ended up duped by the crafty stranger, readers still had what felt like privileged access to that stranger's real intentions, an advantage rarely available to them in their everyday social interactions.[7]

Of course, we have no way of proving this, and I, personally, would not press the compensatory fantasy argument too far. However, I would suggest that the obvious topicality of such scenes—their palpable relevance to readers' everyday dilemma—might have further enhanced the appeal created by these scenes' pattern of triangulated mind reading. The impression of personal/social relevance might have corroborated the impression of personal/social mind-reading prowess. At present we largely lack a conceptual framework to describe the exact workings of such a process of mutual enhancement. Still, if we are to evolve a cognitive-historicist analysis of literature, we have to find ways of charting this new conceptual territory.

Social Class and Theory of Mind in Scenes of Observed Benefaction

As one example of such a cognitive-historicist analysis of fictional scenes of observed benefaction, consider the novel's treatment of the mentality of the recipient of charity, who is typically presented as having no other narrative function besides putting the protagonist on the spot and forcing her to decide whether this stranger deserves her assistance. In what follows, I demonstrate that this construction of the recipient was implicated both with the pattern of triadic mind reading and with eighteenth-century views of social class and social mobility.

I start by turning once more to the work of Vermeule, who has brilliantly resituated the traditional literary-critical distinction between flat and round characters in the context of research on mind reading. As Vermeule (2010, 219) puts it,

Flat characters may not be especially psychologically realistic but they can be extremely psychologically compelling. When flat characters interact with round characters, they mine a rich vein of Theory of Mind. In literary narratives from ancient to modern times, some version of the following pattern repeats itself over and over again: a flat or minor character provokes a fit of reflection in a round or major character. The fit of reflection enlarges the scene and the minds of the people in it, who engage in elaborate rituals of shared attention and eye contact. The scene itself becomes soaked in mindfulness, increasing the sense of self-consciousness all around.

If we look at eighteenth-century scenes of observed benefaction we realize that the people who receive assistance are what we can call flat characters. Typically (though with some interesting exceptions to be discussed shortly) they seem to have no qualities besides embodying extreme need. The suspicion that they may fake that need complicates them somewhat, but not so far as to actually render them round. Their function is still exclusively to "provoke a fit of reflection in a round or major character" (Vermeule 2010, 219), that is, to put the protagonist in a quandary, as she is trying to decide whether to assist the apparently needy stranger or to ignore his entreaties. Moreover, to continue quoting Vermeule, the protagonist's "fit of reflection enlarges the scene and the minds of the people in it"—that is, the observers of the charitable action—"who engage in elaborate rituals of shared attention and eye contact." This is how that "special buzzing thickness" is created and the scene increases "the sense of self-consciousness all around."

Note now how the considerations of social class inform this emergent sense of narrative self-consciousness. Cultural historian Matthew O. Grenby has observed that in eighteenth-century fictional representations of charitable encounters, "charity was a process to be understood entirely from the point of view of the donor, not the recipient" (2002, 190). Grenby's argument focuses on children's books, but it seems that the assumption that the psychological processes of the donor are more fascinating than those of the recipient applied to the period's literature for grown-ups as well.

What is important here is that the objects of charity in such stories always belong to a lower, and sometimes significantly lower, social class than their benefactors. Scenes of observed benefaction thus build on, legitimate, and reinforce the existing class hierarchies. People of lower social class are naturalized by these scenes as *less interesting* and *less emotionally complex*—deserving of readers' consideration only so far as they can provoke complex feelings in the main characters, who typically come from the upper middle class. The mental processes of the observer can be mapped along the lines of, "I can see that she (i.e., the giver) doesn't know what he (the beggar) is really thinking"; and the mental processes of the donor can be mapped along the lines of, "I don't know what he (the beggar) is really thinking, and I also know that you (the observer) are watching me trying to figure out what he is really thinking." Both of these are rich, multilevel reflections, whereas the mental processes of the recipient are typically limited to the simple: "I need help now," or, "I want her to think that I need help now."

The cognitive informs the social and vice versa. To the extent to which triadic mind reading calls for a hierarchization of mental complexity, writers have to decide, not necessarily consciously, which characters will carry on complex mind-reading reflections and which will have to settle for simpler ones. This decision could be informed by considerations of social class, of gender or race, or of any other parameter reflecting current ideological investments of the society. (Of course the ability to reflect other people's mental states does not automatically translate into superior ethics: as Vermeule observers, crafty villains can be "masterminds" carrying on triple or even quadruple mental embedments.)

Note too that in the scenes of observed benefaction, some flat characters are slightly rounder than others, and the difference between the two is directly proportionate to their class standing and social aspirations. For example, the impoverished Henrietta Belfield (Burney, *Cecilia*)—who nevertheless retains some of her gentility and is destined to marry up at the end of the book—is allowed to actively respond to the perceived mental states of both her benefactress (Cecilia) and the observer (Albany). Miserable about being perceived as an object of charity, she tries to turn down Cecilia's benevolent offering. Similarly, the "Fair Stranger" (Haywood, *Jemmy and Jenny Jessamy*), who is relieved in her distress by Lady Speck and Mr. Lovegrove under the watchful eye of Jenny, is shown "blushing" (2005, 197) as she accepts their money and later trying to turn down Jenny's own offerings. It is important that this young woman, who is thus somewhat capable of seeing herself as reflected in the minds of others, also comes from an impoverished genteel family and at the end of the novel marries the son of the rich Sir Thomas Welby and is established as part of her former benefactors' social circle.

By contrast, the anonymous beggars of Goldsmith's *The Citizen of the World* seem to barely register the presence of the benefactor much less that of the observer. They occupy the lowest rung of the social hierarchy and their striking flatness or (to put it in cognitive terms) their inability to reflect any state of mind, including, apparently, their own, assures the reader that this is where they "naturally" belong.

Fictional constructions of mental embedment thus actively engage current ideologies. Although at present we are very far from having mapped the rich variety of the emotional and narrative effects of such engagements, it is clear that the combination of historicism with research in Theory of Mind represents one fruitful area of interdisciplinary analysis of fictional consciousness. In seeking to understand how the eighteenth-century novel engaged its readers' mind-reading adaptations, we thus continue to build on the rich tradition of inquiry into the political, economic, and social contexts of the British Enlightenment.

Effects of Triangulation beyond the Novel

I have argued throughout this chapter that a charitable encounter—as observed by an interested third party—presented an eighteenth-century writer with a handy social context for building up a cognitively enjoyable scenario of triangulated mind reading. Now I want to ask how far we can take this argument. Can we say that writers are always on the lookout—even if they do not think about it this way—for compelling social contexts that would allow them to embroil several minds in action? That a writer may care passionately about philanthropy in her private life (and many eighteenth-century writers did!), yet when it comes to writing about it, philanthropy becomes a means to an end—a pretext for constructing a compelling context for a three-way mind reading?

And if this is so, should we look at a wide range of social contexts with this particular yardstick in mind? Should we ask if certain genres at certain points in their development tend to rely more heavily on specific social dilemmas to get their readers' Theory of Mind racing?[8] And should we ask if some writers are more prone than others to take advantage of such dilemmas? It is already arguable that moments of observed benefaction are a staple of sentimental novels; perhaps we should take a closer look at such novels and see what other cultural contexts they repeatedly conscript to construct their moments of triangulated mind reading.

Here then are the questions with which we can approach a broad selection of fictional and nonfictional texts. What goes into a given construction of a mind-reading triangulation? What cultural scripts are relied on—or subverted—to bring this triangulation into existence? What historically specific contexts are used to make it more compelling, and, in turn, what historically specific ideological agendas are rendered more compelling because they foster a three-way mind reading in their audience? What religious, aesthetic, and philosophical arguments derive at least part of their appeal from mind-reading triangulation?

Does it matter, for example, that Adam Smith's *The Theory of Moral Sentiments* (1759) is chock full of vignettes featuring three minds in action? To demonstrate that we cannot empathize with the "contemptible" man who takes insults lightly, Smith conjures up a scene that features the minds of two adversaries and the collective mind of the "mob" (I.II.23). To specify what constitutes a proper emotional reaction to a trying event, Smith imagines two people, one of whom observes another's behavior and compares the feelings apparently underlying it to those he himself would have on the same occasion. The three mental states here are those of the observer as he watches the man in front of him, of that man as he responds emotionally to something that happened to him, and of the observer as he imagines his own emotional reaction had the same bad or good luck befallen him (I.I.28).

In another vignette, dealing with our response to madness, Smith begins with his typical pattern—two bodies and three mental states—and then transforms it into something more interesting. First, the spectator compares the feelings of the person whom he observes to those he himself would feel in his place. Soon after that, however, the spectator alone becomes the source of three mental states:

Of all the calamities to which the condition of mortality exposes mankind, the loss of reason appears, to those who have the least spark of humanity, by far the most dreadful, and they behold that last stage of human wretchedness with deeper commiseration than any other. But the poor wretch, who is in it, laughs and sings perhaps, and is altogether insensible of his own misery. The anguish which humanity feels, therefore, at the sight of such an object, cannot be the reflection of any sentiment of the sufferer. The compassion of the spectator must arise altogether from the consideration of what he himself would feel if he was reduced to the same unhappy situation, and, what perhaps is impossible, was at the same time able to regard it with his present reason and judgment. (I.I.11)

Look at that last sentence again. The spectator feels anguish (that's a representation of one mind) at the sight of a mad person because he imagines himself being mad and feels pity for that mad self (another mind) even more so because that mad self would apparently not feel any pity for himself (third mind).

And so forth. If you are familiar with Smith's oeuvre, you know that the treatise with a somewhat daunting title *The Theory of Moral Sentiments* is a surprisingly enjoyable read. Its complex discussion of the psychological foundation of human ethics apparently insinuates itself into the reader's mind by "pretending" to be a bunch of stories built on the pattern of a particularly pleasing social-cognitive complexity.

It thus might be worth our while to look at other nonfictional discourses and see whether their arguments are constructed as a series of triangulated mind readings. For example, we can safely predict that works of literary criticism will be found triangulating minds all the time. This is not to say that such works are necessarily convincing and well written, but that the degree to which they are considered convincing and well written may correlate in interesting ways with the degree to which they engage in this kind of triple mind attribution.

Note, meanwhile, how my view of Smith's novelistic rhetorical strategies supports an argument proposed before the advance of cognitive literary studies—by John Bender in his influential study *Imagining the Penitentiary: Fiction and the Architecture of the Mind in Eighteenth-Century England*. (I generally think that it is a sign of a cognitive approach's strength when it turns out to be compatible with—yet offer new insights into—the claims of established literary criticism.) Bender suggests that, "while Smith's metaphor for consciousness is theatrical [that is, it constantly conjures the image of a spectator observing the action] its mode of representation is entirely mental. [Smith] considers spectatordom as the fundamental condition ordering social life, but the state of being he characterizes as theatrical must always be staged in a non-theatrical mental field that much more resembles the transparency of the *realist novel* than the non-narrative fictions of theater" (1987, 227; emphasis added).

This brings me to my concluding question: How much awareness of the role played by three interacting consciousnesses in the construction of fictional subjectivity can we ascribe to eighteenth-century authors? I could not find any explicit references to the narrative possibilities opened by three-way mind reading in contemporary public discourse. I looked for something more specific than various theological meditations responding, directly or not, to St. Augustine's *On the Trinity*—that is, for something along the lines of Josiah Royce's early 1910s assertion that the "relations of minds are essentially social; so that a world without at least three minds in it—one to be interpreted, one the interpreter, and the third the one for whom or to whom the first is interpreted—would be a world without any real mind in it at all" (Royce 1951, 174).

Of course, this does not mean that such references do not exist. It does mean, however, that at this point we can only speculate about eighteenth-century writers' understanding of the relationship between mental triangulations and narrativity. Hence if we think that exploring the fringes of fictionality increases one's awareness of the sociocognitive underpinnings of narrative imagination, we can ascribe such an awareness to Smith, whose narratives encourage novelistic thinking without being novels, and to Barbauld, whose narratives discourage the construction of connected stories. They must have known that a fictional world emerges out of three interacting minds.

Notes

1. For an important related analysis, see Palmer (2006, 2010).

2. We need to differentiate between the overall number of minds populating a given work of fiction—which could be quite large—and the number of minds we deal with within one particular scene. Of particular use here are James Stiller's concept of "time slice" (Stiller, Nettle, and Dunbar 2004, 399), Catherine Emmott's work on "frames of reference and contextual monitoring" (1994, 158–63), David Herman's work on "hypothetical focalizers" (2002, 311–21), and David Miall's analysis of "episode structures in literary narratives" (2006, 119–41).

3. Freud's theory of ego, superego, and id is a classical example of three mental states driving the actions of *one* body. From a cognitive perspective, one reason that this theory has been so influential is that it makes possible numerous interpretations that impose a three-minds model onto a variety of cultural contexts. As such, it is literally "good to think with."

4. Daniel Nettle, e-mail, June 28, 2006. Also, see Herman's suggestive argument about "thinking about thinking—or intelligence about intelligence" (2006, 372).

5. Arguably, however, a phrase such as, "When we could not think of him, he thought of us; before we could ask him to bless us, he had already given us many blessings" (38) presupposes three minds: God's, the young children's, and the older children as they reflect back on their younger selves. To me, this indicates the difficulty faced by an author who tries to avoid the three-way mind reading: the third mind worms its way in.

6. See F. Elizabeth Hart's discussion of Heliodorus's narrative, in a different context, in her contribution to the present volume.

7. For a related discussion, see Grenby (2002, 190).

8. For example, can we speculate about the relationship between certain recurrent plot turns in Sophocles and Aeschylus and their innovative introduction of a third actor into tragedy? For a discussion of Aeschylus's and Sophocles's innovation and Aristotle's view of this, see Kaufmann (1968, 34–35). As Kaufmann puts it, "Aristotle clearly thought that with the addition of the third actor and the emergence of Sophoclean tragedy, familiar to us from seven surviving examples, tragedy 'found its true nature.'"

References

Addison, Joseph, and Richard Steel. 1965 [1711]. "Number 232, Monday, November 26." In *The Spectator*, ed. Donald F. Bond. 5 vols. Oxford: Clarendon Press.

Andrew, Donna T. 1995. "*Noblesse oblige*: Female Charity in an Age of Sentiment." In *Early Modern Conceptions of Property*, ed. John Brewer and Susan Staves, 275–300. London: Routledge.

Barbauld, Anna Laetitia. 1866 [1781]. *Hymns in Prose for Children*. London: John Murray.

Baron-Cohen, Simon. 1995. *Mindblindness: An Essay on Autism and Theory of Mind*. Cambridge MA: MIT Press.

Bender, John. 1987. *Imagining the Penitentiary: Fiction and the Architecture of Mind in Eighteenth-Century England*. Chicago: University of Chicago Press.

Bennett, Agnes [Anna] Maria. 1813. *The Beggar Girl and Her Benefactors*. 5 vols. 3rd ed. London: Printed at the Minerva Press, for A. K. Newman and Co.

Bering, Jesse M. 2002. "The Existential Theory of Mind." *Review of General Psychology* 6 (1): 3–24.

Dunbar, R. I. M., N. Duncan, and Daniel Nettle. 1994. "Size and Structure of Freely-Forming Conversational Groups." *Human Nature* 6:67–78.

Ellis, Grace A. 1874. *A Memoir of Mrs. Anna Laetitia Barbauld, with Many of Her Letters*. Boston: James R. Osgood and Co.

Emmott, Catherine. 1994. "Frames of Reference: Contextual Monitoring and the Interpretation of Narrative Discourse." In *Advances in Written Text Analysis*, ed. Malcolm Coulthard, 157–66. London: Routledge.

Fielding, Henry. 1988 [1752]. *The Covent-Garden Journal and a Plan of the Universal Register-Office*. Ed. Bertrand A. Colgar. Middletown CT: Wesleyan University Press.

Grenby, Matthew O. 2002. "'Real Charity Makes Distinctions': Schooling the Charitable Impulse in Early British Children's Literature." *British Journal for Eighteenth-Century Studies* 25:185–202.

Haywood, Eliza. 2005. *The History of Jemmy and Jenny Jessamy*. Ed. John Richetti. Lexington: University Press of Kentucky.

Herman, David. 2002. *Story Logic: Problems and Possibilities of Narrative*. Lincoln: University of Nebraska Press.

———. 2006. "Genette Meets Vygotsky: Narrative Embedding and Distributed Intelligence." *Language and Literature* 15 (4): 357–80.

Hunter, J. Paul. 1990. *Before Novels: The Cultural Contexts of Eighteenth-Century English Fiction*. New York: W. W. Norton.

Kaufmann, Walter. 1968. *Tragedy and Philosophy*. New York: Doubleday.

McDowell, Paula. 1998. *The Women of Grub Street: Press, Politics, and Gender in the London Literary Marketplace 1678–1730*. Oxford: Clarendon Press.

Miall, David S. 2006. *Literary Reading: Empirical and Theoretical Studies*. New York: Peter Lang.

Owen, David. 1964. *English Philanthropy, 1660–1960*. Cambridge MA: Harvard University Press.

Palmer, Alan. 2006. "The Middlemarch Mind: Intermental Thought in the Novel." *Style* 39 (4): 427–39.

———. 2010. "Storyworlds and Groups." In *Introduction to Cognitive Cultural Studies*, ed. Lisa Zunshine, 176–92. Baltimore: Johns Hopkins University Press.

Royce, Josiah. 1951. "Mind." In *Royce's Logical Essays: Collected Logical Essays of Josiah Royce*, ed. Daniel S. Robinson, 146–78. Dubuque: William Brown. See also http://www.brocku.ca/MeadProject/Royce/Royce_1913b.html.

Smith, Adam. 1790 [1759]. *The Theory of Moral Sentiments*. 6th ed. London: A. Millar.

Stiller, James, Daniel Nettle, and Robin Dunbar. 2004. "The Small World of Shakespeare's Plays." *Human Nature* 14:397–408.

Vermeule, Blakey. 2010. "Machiavellian Narratives." In *Introduction to Cognitive Cultural Studies*, ed. Lisa Zunshine, 214–30. Baltimore: Johns Hopkins University.

Warner, William B. 1998. *Licensing Entertainment: The Elevation of Novel Reading in Britain, 1684–1750*. Berkeley: University of California Press.

Zunshine, Lisa. 2005. "Can We Teach the 'Deep Intersubjectivity' of Richardson's *Clarissa*?" *New Windows on a Woman's World: A Festschrift for Jocelyn Harris. Otago Studies in English* 9:88–99.

———. 2006. *Why We Read Fiction: Theory of Mind and the Novel*. Columbus: Ohio State University Press.

———. 2007. "Why Jane Austen Was Different, and Why We May Need Cognitive Science to See It." *Style* 41 (3): 273–97.

6. 1775–1825
Affective Landscapes
and Romantic Consciousness

DAVID VALLINS

In this chapter I will argue that the most distinctive aspect of the representation of consciousness in Romantic-period narrative is its expression of subjectivity through metaphorical spaces (whether in the form of landscape, architecture, or the visionary space of dreams), which differ fundamentally from the quasi-literal landscapes of eighteenth- or nineteenth-century realism. Rather than shaping the subjectivity of the characters in a practical or psychological sense, or indeed being colored by their moods or emotions, the spaces or landscapes of Romantic-period fiction often evoke a form of pure affect that is implied to be inexpressible except through these metaphorical forms, existing for the reader only as an aspect or reflection of such fictional spaces.[1] The mutual determination of objective and subjective factors described by theorists of space such as Bachelard and Lefebvre is thus removed in Romantic narrative to new levels both of unity and of fictionality.[2]

Whereas Jane Austen's characters, for example, are primarily concerned with the practical significances of space as property or as a mark of social status, in Ann Radcliffe or Mary Shelley the mountains, castles, caverns, or laboratories—or, indeed, Frankenstein's premonitory dream of the death of his adoptive sister, Elizabeth—give us direct access to states of mind—whether involving sublimity, oppression, horror, or terror—familiarly and customarily associated with such images or spatial forms. As I will show, however, the domestic emphasis of Shelley's ideology often inverts the aesthetic value systems of Radcliffe and most other Romantic writers, associating mountains (for example) with states of transgression, isolation, and horror more closely resembling Burke's description of the sublimely "terrible" than a Kantian vision of transcendence. In Wordsworth, on the other hand, the affective significance of landscape resembles the more familiar and spontaneous variety familiar from Radcliffe's fiction. In his autobiographical narrative, *The Prelude*, for example, landscape is often a metaphor of subjective elements that seem impossible to envisage in its absence, such as the "correspondent breeze" of the poet's returning creativity in Book 1, which echoes that of nature's revival in spring, or the "dim and undetermined sense / Of unknown forms of being" which, in the same book, arises from his perception of a mysterious mountain crag appearing to pursue him across a lake. Precisely because their subjective meanings are so spontaneously apparent, yet also so inseparable from the images themselves, however, the dramatic spaces of Radcliffe's or Wordsworth's narratives seem to express similarly formalized types of affective content, often involving the dualistic extremes of emotion that are familiar from Gothic fiction. This form of unity or inseparableness of image and affect, I argue, is interestingly connected with the characteristically Romantic theme of the unity of mind and nature, or (more philosophically) of the physical world as merely one of the modes in which a transcendent unity of subject and object expresses itself, alongside the more obvious forms of (mental) creativity. Hence the metaphorical structure of Romantic narrative can be described as a form of dialectic, in which the synthesis of landscape and consciousness parallels their theoretical unification in Romantic philosophy.

This integrated, self-contained relation of tenor and vehicle on several levels of meaning at once unifies consciousness with the landscapes depicted in the narrative and makes that consciousness an aspect of the text or of the metaphor to a far more obvious extent than any form of subjectivity that arises more freely and randomly from an encounter with society or the physical world. This difference between the consciousness depicted in Romantic narratives and that described in realist narrative, which characterizes the physical world as fundamentally shaping experience, emerges particularly clearly from comparing either Radcliffe's or Wordsworth's modes of representation with those of Jane Austen. In Austen's works, the Gothic or Romantic union of subjectivity with physical and metaphorical contexts is specifically depicted as a form of self-indulgent delusion and contrasted with a world of more mundane surroundings and emotions, tending less toward revolutionary visions either of a political or of a philosophical nature. Moreover, as Edward Said, among others, has noted, not only the landscapes of Jane Austen's fiction, but also the remoter scenes of the Napoleonic wars and of plantations in the Caribbean that inhabit their imaginative hinterlands, are relevant and of interest to her characters primarily as tokens of wealth, social status, and the security they may offer to potential brides or suitors.[3] Byron's ironic comparison of the "sweet[ness]" of "first and passionate love" with that of "prize-money to seamen" (a phrase referring to the rewards received by British naval officers on capturing enemy ships) quite accurately evokes the affective significance of war for many of Austen's characters—however much virtue, in her novels, is equated with a transcendence of such purely pecuniary interests.[4] The virtue of Anne Elliot in *Persuasion*, for example, is primarily an abstract quality of endurance, persistence, and the preservation of humane values or ideals alongside a practical awareness of the dynamics of wealth and fortune; and though Austen's characters are often described as experiencing intense emotions of shock, anxiety, or joy, her reliance on emphatic phrasing to evoke these (often unexpressed) emotions arising from familiar social situations involves an obvious contrast with the Romantic experiences of oppression, despair, terror, hope, or liberation that authors such as Radcliffe or Wordsworth express in their varied (yet also familiar and well-defined) registers of landscape and ancient ruin.[5] We know of Anne Elliot's emotions primarily through direct description of them rather than through any metaphoricity in her surroundings. In this sense, I would argue, emotion in Austen's fiction, however much emphasized descriptively, remains less prominent than in Radcliffe or Wordsworth—except in the case of *Northanger Abbey*, where the literature-derived ex-

tremes of Catherine Morland's self-indulgent terror are specifically satirized as having nothing to do with the mundane facts
of "greedy speculation" that surround her developing relationship with Henry Tilney.[6] The fact that the emotions of Austen's
characters are often concealed behind a reserved and decorous
appearance, indeed, not only reflects the greater emphasis on
rational control in her fiction, but is also closely related to the
fact that she rarely seeks to expand the "core" of individual emotion into the kind of expressive landscape that, I have suggested,
tends in Romantic narrative paradoxically to restrict and define
that inner core, rendering it perhaps scarcely less distinctively
literary, less rooted in the play of the imagination, than Austen
herself ironically suggested.

The relation between Romantic modes of representing consciousness and Romantic philosophy and psychology—the interplay between concepts of the unity of mind and matter and
narrative uses of space to express subjectivity—is prominent in
slightly different ways in Shelley's *Frankenstein*. The dream visions (such as that of the "grave-worms" in his mother's shroud)
that Frankenstein experiences just after his initial rejection of
the creature, for example, are at once metaphorical or symbolic
externalizations of subjective intuition and expressions of a Romantic fascination with dreams as tending to reveal the connections between conscious and unconscious aspects of the mind
(see Shelley 1994 [1818], 57). The distinctly pre-Freudian nature
of Romantic concepts of the unconscious, moreover, frequently
involves the connection of such intuitive or imaginative visions
with a more fundamental creative or productive power than that
of the individual mind—a movement beyond phenomena not
merely toward a psychological essence, but also toward powers
and insights associated with the divine.[7] Hence *Frankenstein* portrays dreams revealing a moral insight suppressed by the overreaching desire for knowledge, power, or (as many critics have
suggested) the broader liberation associated in the period with
scientific enlightenment. This portrayal combines a relatively new
form of psychological theory with moral and religious elements
while also using the dream to express subjective or intuitive con-

sciousness in ways analogous to the widespread Romantic use of spatial representations to evoke subjectivity. As this example suggests, the spaces of Frankenstein are filled with substantially different forms of moral significance from those of Radcliffe's fiction. Radcliffe's mountains primarily evoke the ideal of liberty from or transcendence of oppressive forms of aristocratic and religious institution (depicted primarily through the Gothic structures they inhabit).[8] By contrast, the mountains in Frankenstein variously symbolize the isolation or exclusion of the creature and the overreaching of his creator, thus acquiring a distinctly negative significance in comparison with the domestic scenes that Frankenstein's experiment has disrupted. Shelley thus distinctively shifts the significances of mountain landscapes from those of sublimity, liberty, and hope evoked by contemporaries such as Wordsworth and Coleridge, as well as Radcliffe, to those of hubris, excess, isolation, exclusion, and negation, by continually stressing the value of domesticity in opposition to that of transcendence and the early Romantic ideals of enlightenment and liberation.

Several critics have argued that this distinctive quality of Frankenstein (and of several of Shelley's later novels) expresses a distinctively female or feminine value system in contrast with the masculinist politics and aesthetics of many Romantics (see Mellor 1988, 79–82, 111–12; Poovey 1980, 332–36). It is, indeed, notable how Shelley inverts not only the value system but also the psychological significance that, in Radcliffe, Wordsworth, Coleridge, and (to a significant extent) Percy Shelley, emerge almost as given or necessary aspects of the relation between space and mood. Whether or not we choose to define Mary Shelley's form of the Gothic as distinctively feminine, however, her use of landscape to express affect or emotion as well as moral ideas is scarcely less prominent than Radcliffe's. Yet Frankenstein's prolonged internal conflict between the quest for power or knowledge and the attempt to preserve domestic values often entails an opposition between his predominant mood or perception and the moral significances that Shelley intimates. The relation between space and affect in Radcliffe is thus more direct than it is in Shelley, in the sense of allowing less distinction between subjectivity and the spaces in or through which it is evoked. At the same time, however, Shelley's psychology is clearly more sophisticated, foregrounding the duality of conscious and unconscious explored by contemporary psychological theorists such as Coleridge, and similarly associating intuitions derived from the unconscious with deeper forms of moral, metaphysical, or religious insight. In contrast, Radcliffe's moral and psychological vision is distinctly more two dimensional, even if the subterranean passageways penetrated by her heroes and heroines may be seen either as connoting a passage to the unconscious mind or as subconsciously expressing a suppressed sexual content (see, for example, Millbank's introduction to *A Sicilian Romance* in Radcliffe 1993 [1790], xxii–xxvii). This very two-dimensionality, however—which, I would argue, is no less evident in these ambiguous and heavily signifying subterranean regions—is perhaps what gives Radcliffe's fiction its striking degree of force or vividness, in that signifier and signified are allowed by her to be so patently inseparable. The spaces she depicts are immediately and obviously spaces of the mind as well as of the landscapes or surroundings her characters experience, suggesting the simultaneously subjective and objective nature of perceptual objects described in a contemporary context by Kant, and also by later theorists of space such as Bachelard and Lefebvre.[9]

Wordsworthian Space and the Unity of Mind and Nature

Although the relation between landscape and consciousness is often no less direct and unambiguous in Wordsworth than it is in Radcliffe, Wordsworth subjects that relation to a form of interpretation or critical analysis that constitutes the central philosophical content of poems such as *The Prelude*. A central theme of the poem is the power of nature to awaken in the poet an awareness of how nature—informed by a divine influence—can produce both insight and virtue in the individual. Thus, Wordsworth engages in a quasi-philosophical restatement of the relation between landscape and mood that the poem also employs as its principal method of expressing consciousness or subjectivity. I say *quasi*-philosophical because the moods or states of mind Wordsworth describes as being engendered by landscape are also defined primarily through and in terms of landscape. Hence what is supposed to be caused or explained by the inwardly divine landscape of the Lake District has—at least as a literary phenomenon—little existence apart from the physical forms or images by which it is evoked. In this sense, the philosophical content of *The Prelude* cannot be disentangled from its metaphors, at least to the extent that these are regarded as more than metaphors—that is, as causes of the states of mind that they also express.

Book 1 of *The Prelude* provides many good examples of the relation not only between landscape and affect, but also between Wordsworth's metaphors of consciousness and his philosophy. Immediately after describing the difficulties he sometimes experienced in composition, for example, Wordsworth famously writes:

> *Was it for this*
> *That one, the fairest of all rivers, loved*
> *To blend his murmurs with my nurse's song,*
> *And, from his alder shades and rocky falls,*
> *And from his fords and shallows, sent a voice*
> *That flowed along my dreams? For this, didst thou,*
> *O Derwent! winding among grassy holms*
> *Where I was looking on, a babe in arms,*
> *Make ceaseless music that composed my thoughts*
> *To more than infant softness, giving me*
> *Amid the fretful dwellings of mankind*
> *A foretaste, a dim earnest, of the calm*
> *That Nature breathes among the hills and groves.*
> (Wordsworth 1979, 43–45, ll. 269–81)

The seemingly egotistical nature of Wordsworth's rhetorical questions in this passage—questions concerning whether God or Nature (to use a Spinozistic formulation with which he was undoubtedly familiar) really intended him to be ineffective in evoking its morally and spiritually enlightening power, particularly as manifested in his own creative vision—is interestingly combined with precisely the kinds of spatial metaphors I have described as characteristic of Romantic narrative.[10] Just as Wordsworth's intuition, or "dim earnest," of the (implicitly inner) calm of nature depends on, and indeed seems largely to consist in, the quiet and musical flow of the shallow river Derwent, so our knowledge of this intuition and of the larger, more metaphysical calm that it suggests to him depends on the landscape imagery he uses. Further, this image of a consciousness so imbued with the calming qualities of nature as to intuit the deeper, metaphysical calm that underlies it connects the metaphorical or spatial evocation of subjectivity or affect so closely with philosophical argument as to render them almost indistinguishable. Whether the theory of a certain unity of mind with nature engenders this particular metaphoricity in Wordsworth's (or other Romantic) writing, or whether (conversely) this mode of portraying or apprehending consciousness gives rise to such a theory, is perhaps impossible to determine. In this as in many other contexts, the metaphoricity and the philosophy seem almost as deeply co-implied as the mood and the landscape. The difference from Radcliffe's mode of writing is primarily that Wordsworth makes an interpretative step beyond the pure expression of affect through evocations of visual or spatial forms and colors. The latter do, of course, have certain political connotations in Radcliffe's dramas of oppression and liberation; yet these overtones of Enlightenment idealism (as well as, occasionally, of nationalistic anti-Catholic dogma) are not overtly theorized in any political or philosophical sense, and indeed depend for their appeal on a certain intuitive recognition by the reader of shades of meaning that, if made explicit, would often seem both banal and contradictory.[11]

As noted earlier, however, Wordsworth's philosophy—at once materialist (and more specifically Hartleian) in its emphasis on the power of environment to shape the affective experience and moral character of the individual, and idealist (though in this, again echoing the paradoxes of Hartley) in describing those forms as products of a divine power—is so integrated with the nature of his metaphors as to acquire a quality almost of necessity—another respect, perhaps, in which Romanticism developed its particular persuasive power.[12] Thus the mood of calm is at once the character of the landscape, the feeling or emotion it produces, and the metaphorical meaning of both; but it is only enabled to combine this complex of meanings by the philosophical analysis through which Wordsworth half highlights, and at the same time half conceals the intrinsically metaphorical nature of both mood and meaning. The deeper significance of the scene and his emotion is only revealed to the narrator and thus the reader through a "dim earnest"; the passage thus underscores the way in which the tenor of his metaphor is subtly projected by Wordsworth into an inevitably hazy intuition of that larger "flow" or "river" that, like Coleridge, he envisaged as underlying and generating all forms of consciousness. A similar process accounts for the centrality of the sublime in much Romantic writing—that is, of an intuition that is at once beyond and inaccessible through mere subjectivity or visual forms, yet at the same time is suggested by them, its key distinctive quality being that it cannot be separately or distinctively envisaged. The liminality of the sublime (or its association with that which is just beyond the threshold of direct experience) has much to do with such a subtle extension of metaphor into the realm of the imperceptible and incomprehensible. The sublime power underlying nature and human consciousness, in other words, must at once be known and unknown—at once the same as perceptual forms and utterly distinct from them. Hence the "river" of Coleridge's "Kubla Khan" is, in only a slightly more detached and nonphysical sense, inevitably a "Vision in a Dream." The river is emphatically physical, and even sexual, in its motions and connotations, yet at the same time otherworldly, seeming to reveal at once the unconscious mind of the poet and the nature of creative "imagination" in the broad, Coleridgean and Schellingian sense of a power underlying but never to be identified with the alternating worlds of sensuous intuition and of thought or intellection (see Coleridge 1912, 1:295–98; Vallins 2000, 21–23; and Wheeler 1982, 17–41).

Hence a distinctively Romantic form of dialectic emerges from both Wordsworth's and Coleridge's evocations of the relation between perceptions, emotions, and whatever dimly intuited power it is that brings them into relation with each other.

This close connection of the sublime with the simultaneous identity and differentness of space and affect that characterizes Wordsworth's philosophized metaphors of subjectivity is no less evident in the famous description, slightly later in Book 1 of *The Prelude*, of his encounter, while rowing on a lake, with a mysteriously looming peak that filled his mind (or "brain," as Wordsworth interestingly puts it) "with a dim and undetermined sense / Of unknown modes of being" (see Wordsworth 1979, 49–51, ll. 357–400). Even the quasi-philosophical passage that immediately precedes this narrative highlights the centrality of figurative images to Wordsworth's evocations of mood and also of the infinite or divine power he describes as underlying both mind and matter. "Dust as we are," he writes,

> . . . the immortal spirit grows
> Like harmony in music; there is a dark
> Inscrutable workmanship that reconciles
> Discordant elements, makes them cling together
> In one society.
> (Wordsworth 1979, 47, ll. 340–44)

Though not exactly landscape metaphors, the figurative images in this passage are the only means by which we know not only the qualities of the musical phenomenon that Wordsworth is describing, but also the dimly intuited force or activity itself. The metaphors of apparent discord and evolving, underlying harmony quite vividly recall the dichotomous "optimistic" vision of, for example, Joseph Priestley, who in his *The Doctrine of Philosophical Necessity Illustrated* describes how, in the final fulfillment of God's design, "all seeming *discord* is real *harmony*, and all apparent *evil*, ultimate *good*" (Priestley 1777, viii–ix). Hartley's analogous description of the inherent tendency of associative processes in the brain to convert all "pains" into "pleasures," however, is perhaps still more pertinent to Wordsworth's description of the "Inscrutable workmanship" through which the deity enables all illusions of pain or discord to be ultimately beneficial or enlightening (see Hartley 1749, 1, 82–83). Hence, in this passage, relatively abstract conceptions of pleasure and displeasure replace landscape as the vehicle of Wordsworth's metaphor, the tenor being a still more sublime abstraction that has no name, because it is what shapes all our ideas and perceptions—and hence, implicitly, what enables metaphors in general to have meaning or be comprehended.

A closely related form of sublimity, however, also characterizes the mood or emotion that Wordsworth describes as having been produced in him by the mountain that appears to pursue him as he rows across the lake. "After I had seen / That spectacle," he writes,

> . . . for many days, my brain
> Worked with a dim and undetermined sense
> Of unknown modes of being; o'er my thoughts
> There hung a darkness, call it solitude
> Or blank desertion. No familiar shapes
> Remained, no pleasant images of trees,
> Of sea or sky, no colours of green fields;
> But huge and mighty forms, that do not live
> Like living men, moved slowly through the mind
> By day, and were a trouble to my dreams.
> (Wordsworth 1979, 51, ll. 390–400)

The mood or state of consciousness described here seems interestingly to be almost without content apart from the force or power of which it *seems* to be an intuition. Affect, in this passage, is thus largely reduced to a correlative of metaphysics, albeit of a kind which, Wordsworth implies, reflects the mood of sublimity through which he became conscious of it. This mood, however, does have a physical or spatial cause or correlative as well; and as with Priestley's dualism of harmony and discord noted above, its character is distinctly binary, contrasting "pleasant images of trees / Of sea and sky" and "colours of green fields" with "huge and mighty forms, that do not live / Like living men" (Wordsworth 1979, 51, ll. 396–99). In the simultaneous starkness and blandness of this contrast, which seems largely to lack the modulations of actual subjectivity, there is a close parallel to the contrasting scenes of domesticity and oppression that characterize Radcliffe's fiction. Yet what in Radcliffe would be primarily a negative and menacing phenomenon—and what in Wordsworth at first appeared (he says) to be so—is depicted in *The Prelude* as the source of an intuition of the divine, substantially following Kant's two models of the sublime. One model characterizes the sublime as "mathematical," in which the inability of comprehension to keep pace with apprehension in our perception of objects of great size produces the sense of "a supersensible substrate (underlying both nature and our faculty of thought) which is great beyond every standard of sense." The other model characterizes the sublime as "dynamic," in which the perception of threatening natural forces from which we are in fact secure produces a sense of our own unity with whatever transcends the visible world (Kant 1952 [1790], 99–104, 109–12).[13] The problem, however, is that in reading Wordsworth's text it seems difficult to say whether the experience or the interpretation comes first, or rather, as in Radcliffe, these two phases or moments can be construed to be (as Coleridge said of the contrasting theses of "realism" and "idealism") "co-inherent and identical" (Coleridge 1983 [1817], 1:285). The states of mind that Wordsworth describes confirm his philosophy as much as the latter is an interpretation of them; and both are presented to us through such well-defined contrasts of harmony with discord, beauty with menace, and the domestic with the sublime. Where Radcliffe most notably differs from this model is in associating transcendence not with a perception of the incomprehensible or the potentially terrifying, but rather with liberation from both terror and incomprehension into a freedom that is at once domestic and associated with the untrammelled vastness of nature. Radcliffe's dichotomous landscapes thus signify more directly and intuitively than Wordsworth's, since Wordsworth's use of language to figure consciousness depends on a philosophical content that transforms the significance of "darkness" and "blank desertion" into an intuition of Kantian sublimity. Yet in both cases the landscapes and the moods they evoke are, so to speak, imbued with each other rather than existing separately as perception and affect—a pattern which, I would argue, notably distinguishes the relation between landscape and emotion in Romantic narrative from that which characterizes its "realist" others, in which physical environments are most often depicted as shaping subjectivity.

A slightly later passage of Book 1 provides further important illustrations both of the patterns of spatial metaphoricity and of the philosophical and psychological ideas I have been describing. Following his quasi-animistic apostrophe to the "Presences of Nature in the sky / And on the earth," and to the "Visions of the hills / And Souls of lonely places,"[14] Wordsworth asks them the following rhetorical question:

> . . . can I think
> A vulgar hope was yours when ye employed
> Such ministry, when ye through many a year
> Haunting me thus among my boyish sports,
> On caves and trees, upon the woods and hills,
> Impressed upon all forms the characters
> Of danger or desire; and thus did make
> The surface of the universal earth
> With triumph and delight, with hope and fear,
> Work like a sea?
> (Wordsworth 1979, 55, ll. 464–75)

The "Presences of Nature" that connect perceptual space ("caves and trees . . . woods and hills") with affect ("danger or desire") thus again seem to constitute the "third term," which, like Schelling's "imagination," mysteriously breaks the deadlocked antithesis of mind and matter, and at the same time enables the latter metaphorically to represent and be identified with consciousness or subjectivity (see Schelling 1978 [1800], 229–30). The mystery which Wordsworth is describing here, indeed, is precisely that of how those "characters / Of danger or desire" came to be "impressed" on visible "forms," or in other words of how certain kinds of space acquired affective significance. To what extent that significance might be regarded as existing outside the literary context in which it is presented to us is, of course, impossible to determine; and in an important sense that particular relation of space and affect cannot exist outside the literary framework of metaphor, the "mystery" of whose functioning seems almost to be self-referentially invoked by the dramatic apostrophe through which Wordsworth seeks to externalize that sublimely incomprehensible shaping force.

Thus both the problem and its resolution, the antitheses and their synthesis, are largely of Wordsworth's creation; yet the relation of space and affect can only acquire the meaning which he gives it through this hypostatization of an unnameable origin, toward which he seems to reach through his obscure and contradictory references to "Presences," "Visions," and "Souls." His description of how the latter force (or forces) made "The surface of the universal earth / With triumph and delight, with hope and fear / Work like a sea" further highlights both the literary device and the conceptual structure through which space is made to express or coincide with emotion. The fictional Wordsworth's own emotions here seem to be retrojected, so to speak, into the landscape that supposedly infused them into him under the benevolent and ultimately enlightening influence of those unnameable "Presences." Hence what he earlier calls the "Wisdom and Spirit of the universe" or "Soul that art the eternity of thought, / That givest to forms and images a breath / And everlasting motion" (Wordsworth 1979, 51, ll. 401–4) emerges as being, very largely, Wordsworth himself, whose thought is lent a quality of eternity and externality by its obfuscating hypostatization. And by the same token, what "intertwine[d] for me / The passions that build up our human soul . . . / With life and nature," leading him to "recognize / A grandeur in the beatings of the heart" (Wordsworth 1979, 51, ll. 404–14), can be interpreted as the poet's own metaphorizing imagination, alternately portraying emotion as a product of space and as its origin or the determinant of its meaning. As noted earlier, experiential space does of course partake of such a mutual influence of subjective and objective elements; and the grandeur of mountains is perhaps so universal a sentiment as to reduce any impression of Wordsworth's distinctively shaping vision. Yet in moving from that grandeur—the fusion of space with affect that emerges with such seeming spontaneity in Radcliffe's fiction—to diverse evocations of the dimly transcendent, Wordsworth repeatedly objectifies, while also distancing, the third term in this metaphorical dialectic of high Romanticism—a Romanticism whose elevated status depends precisely on this self-reflexive and philosophizing strategy.

Mary Shelley and the Disruption of Unity

By contrast, Mary Shelley's *Frankenstein* substantially inverts the affective meanings that emerge, as if spontaneously, from both Radcliffe's and Wordsworth's representations of landscape or perceptual space. In particular, Frankenstein's encounter with his forsaken creature on the Mer de Glace beneath Mont Blanc portrays the sublimity of nature as a place of exclusion, desertion, abandonment, and destructive excess, rather than of elevating faith or enlightenment. The solitude in which nature becomes for Wordsworth an expression of the "beatings" of his own heart, revealing its unity with the origin of the visible world, becomes in Shelley an exclusion from social or domestic forms of meaning and value, a place of mutual despair and loathing—emotions that recur in similarly bleak surroundings until the conclusion of the novel on the arctic ice flows. The pattern of Frankenstein's encounter with the creature thus inverts those Romantic expectations regarding the sublimity of mountainous landscapes that had arisen from the work of earlier Romantics, including Wordsworth. Having described the vastness and grandeur of the scene in what, despite its vividness, is almost a textbook recitation of the classic contexts of both the "mathematical" and the "dynamical" sublime (in Kant's theory), Frankenstein continues: "These sublime and magnificent scenes afforded me the greatest consolation that I was capable of receiving. They elevated me from all littleness of feeling, and though they did not remove my grief [over the deaths of his brother and the family's servant, Justine], they subdued and tranquillized it" (Shelley 1994 [1818], 93).

When Frankenstein ascends to the edge of the glacier at Montenvers, however, it rapidly becomes apparent that this is merely a respite from the disastrous consequences of Romantic ambition, rather than a liberation into a Wordsworthian form of transcendence in which the landscape's simultaneous production of and transformation by sublime emotion focuses attention on either the author's or the character's creative imagination.[15] The "solitary grandeur of the scene," which he seeks to preserve by going "without a guide," is clearly a product of Frankenstein's own solitary contemplation of it, highlighting—in Kantian manner—the "supersensible substrate (underlying both nature and our faculty of thought)," whose contrasting infinitude underlies his elevating emotions (see Shelley 1994 [1818], 94, and Kant 1952 [1790], 104). This "grandeur" arising from a sense of the transforming power of his solitary contemplation, however, is precisely what Shelley seeks to undermine by suddenly reminding Frankenstein of the social world beyond the dialectic of mind and matter that he wishes to protect from such disturbance. Her emphasis on Frankenstein's "surmount[ing] the perpendicularity of the mountain," on his fascination with the "terrific" desolation of the scene, and on his seemingly somewhat disingenuous (if ultimately valid) reflection on the powerlessness of man compared with the cloud-capped mountains (Shelley 1994 [1818], 94–95), seems again to highlight the paradox of celebrating a "grandeur" in nature whose value to the observer depends on its indication of his own reflective or imaginative power.[16] The irony of this reflection, however, turns to more direct satire when Frankenstein's Wordsworthian apostrophe to the "Wandering spirits" he envisages as underlying his own relation to the "awful majesty" of Mont Blanc is immediately followed by the appearance of "the wretch whom I had created," "advancing towards me with superhuman speed" (Shelley 1994 [1818], 95). In this passage, as in many others in the novel, this "horrible" creature appears to be Frankenstein's alter ego, representing what

Shelley sees as the negative aspects or effects of his attempt to take control of everything outside the self and transform it into a reflection of his own creative or imaginative power.[17] The "disdain and malignity" he associates with the "spirit" or "daemon" (as he revealingly calls it in other passages) are ultimately the qualities Shelley associates with this Romantic quest for a consciousness of imaginative power or transcendence, while his "bitter anguish" implies the consequences—whether for himself or others—of such indifference to society as Frankenstein notably demonstrates.[18]

The "Wisdom and spirit of the universe" that Wordsworth intuits when sensing his own unity with a greater power than that of nature is thus transformed, in Mary Shelley, into a horrifying image of Romantic "overreaching," revealing the intensity of Shelley's rejection of the aesthetic and philosophy underlying high Romanticism. Indeed, Frankenstein's subsequent modes of addressing the creature go still further in highlighting this transformation of values:

"Devil," I exclaimed, "do you dare approach me? And do not you fear the fierce vengeance of my arm wreaked on your miserable head? Begone, vile insect! Or rather, stay, that I may trample you to dust! And, oh! That I could, with the extinction of your miserable existence, restore those victims whom you have so diabolically murdered." (Shelley 1994 [1818], 96)

These epithets and accusations may seem to distance the creature from any metaphorical representations of the evils of Frankenstein's own hubris. However, Shelley is quick to remind us not only of the creature's relation to the spiritual power Frankenstein envisages as underlying nature itself, but also of its inseparableness from the mind or spirit that transcendently envisages that power.

"I expected this reception," said the daemon. "All men hate the wretched. . . . Yet you, my creator, detest and spurn me, thy creature, to whom thou art bound by ties only dissoluble by the annihilation of one of us." (Shelley 1994 [1818], 96)

The metaphorical representation of Frankenstein's quest for mental or imaginative power over nature—a power capable of excluding or dominating the power of other minds—again comes into play in this passage. Yet even this ironic representation of Romantic transcendence has a literal as well as a metaphorical aspect, evoking the child's dependence on its parent in a way that simultaneously stresses Frankenstein's indifference to the social world he seeks to "surmount" through his experimental conquest of nature.[19]

Hence, the space in which these figures meet and address each other is one imbued with Shelley's own ideological purpose, despite the critique of Romantic spiritualizations of nature which that very purpose involves. This space, however, ultimately signifies the hopelessness of Frankenstein's efforts to surmount both nature and all other living creatures, implying an ideology substantially opposite to Wordsworth's and stressing the natural rather than the ideal, and the other in opposition to the ambitions of the self. Accordingly, the desolateness of the mountain scenery comes to be associated in *Frankenstein* with horror rather than delight or liberation, primarily because Frankenstein's attempts to see his own greatness reflected in it ultimately fail, as his long struggle to control its spirit or "daemon" is defeated. The self and nature ultimately split apart, because the creature refuses to play the role intended for it, and insists on reintroducing the natural into the ideal while also forcing Frankenstein to recognize the falsity of his own imaginative impositions on the natural world.

Shelley's rejection of the Kantian and Wordsworthian sublimity associated with the sense of a common infinitude underlying both the incomprehensible vastness of mountains and the mind of the observer is again highlighted when Frankenstein and his friend, Henry Clerval, are travelling down the Rhine from Strasbourg on their way to England, where Frankenstein plans to consult an eminent scientist before attempting the creation of a second, female creature to act as a companion to the first. Clerval's distaste for the mountains of Switzerland, whose steep descents he describes as casting "black and impenetrable shades" over the lakes, threatening to cause "a gloomy and mournful appearance," is contrasted with his enthusiasm for the more human and domestic "chasm" of the valley of the Rhine—an enthusiasm that Frankenstein, however, mistakenly interprets in terms of Wordsworthian sublimity, thus failing to appreciate the lessons of Clerval's insight. "Look at that castle which overhangs yon precipice," Clerval exclaims,

"and that also on the island, almost concealed amongst the foliage of those lovely trees; and now that group of labourers coming from among their vines; and that village half hid in the recess of the mountain. Oh, surely the spirit that inhabits and guards this place has a soul more in harmony with man than those who pile the glacier, or retire to the inaccessible peaks of the mountains of our own country." (Shelley 1994 [1818], 150–51)

The passage thus draws a contrast between the unity of the spirits who inhabit the glacier with Frankenstein and his creature, on the one hand, and human fellowship with a domesticated nature, on the other hand. Such fellowship, despite resembling that evoked by Wordsworth in his celebration (in "Tintern Abbey") of "farms, / Green to the very door," notably eschews the idea of a metaphysical unity (Wordsworth 1940–49, 2:259, ll. 16–17). Yet the passage from "Tintern Abbey" that Frankenstein chooses to express Clerval's imaginativeness suggests a failure to appreciate this distinction.

> *The sounding cataract*
> *Haunted him [sic] like a passion: the tall rock,*
> *The mountain, and the deep and gloomy wood,*
> *Their colours and their forms, were then to him [sic]*
> *An appetite, a feeling, and a love,*
> *That had no need of a remoter charm,*
> *By thought supplied, or any interest*
> *Unborrowed from the eye.*
> (Shelley 1994 [1818], 151;
> cf. Wordsworth 1940–49, 2:261, ll. 76–83)

By replacing Wordsworth's autobiographical "me" with "him," Frankenstein transforms Wordsworth's narrative of his own introduction to the sublime into a misapprehension of Clerval's mentality and values that merely transfers onto his friend his own limited apprehension of humankind's relation to nature. Frankenstein thus takes Wordsworthian or Kantian sublimity to an extreme, wishing only "to view . . . mountains and streams, and all the wondrous works with which Nature adorns her chosen dwelling-places"; but as a result he becomes (as—ironically—he describes the eventually murdered Clerval) only "a blasted tree . . . a miserable spectacle of wrecked humanity," destroyed for seeking to control nature, to become "a free and lofty spirit" through his philosophizing imagination (Shelley 1994 [1818], 154–55).

Perhaps the novel's most striking transformation of sublime into destructive spaces, emotions, and significations, however, is its description of the afternoon and evening following the wedding of Frankenstein to his adoptive sister, Elizabeth Lavenza. Victor and Elizabeth's journey across Lake Geneva to Evian, during which they enjoy distant views of Mont Blanc and the surrounding mountains in calm and sunny weather, is followed by a dark and stormy night during which the creature murders Frankenstein's bride. The obvious correlations of weather, mood, and meaning are, by this stage of the novel, so familiar and predictable as to move beyond the radical inversions of the sublime that characterize the earlier passages I have discussed, into a form of cliché that is at the same time a summation or *reprise* of the novel's distinctive themes. By highlighting the increased familiarity of these elements, however, this passage underscores the cumulative effect of Shelley's insistent critique of Kantian and Wordsworthian aesthetics. Shelley transforms her own unorthodox viewpoint into a vision whose spatially defined emotions and values seem almost as familiar as the liberating and transcendent qualities that Radcliffe and Wordsworth associate with the perception of mountain ranges. The way in which Shelley achieves this effect is to present her own ideology or value system in the form of a repeated succession of perceptions and events, in which the seemingly natural associations of landscape and imagery are effectively denaturalized, so that the sublime becomes an obvious harbinger of horror, terror, and destruction.

Elizabeth's comments on the landscape observed from Lake Geneva, for example, combine this implied anticipation of disaster with a quality of artificiality (as if blending the style of a Wordsworthian poem with that of a contemporary guide book), which further distances the narrative and its meanings from the familiar ones she still repeats:

"Be happy, my dear Victor," replied Elizabeth; "there is, I hope, nothing to distress you; and be assured that if a lively joy is not painted in my face, my heart is contented. Something whispers to me not to depend too much on the prospect that is opened before us, but I will not listen to such a sinister voice. Observe how fast we move along, and how the clouds, which sometimes obscure and sometimes rise above the dome of Mont Blanc, render this scene of beauty still more interesting. . . . What a divine day! How happy and serene all nature appears!" (Shelley 1994 [1818], 186–87)

The "prospect that is opened before" Elizabeth and the reader is thus not only the obvious anticipation of disaster, but at the same time the familiar scene of the sunlit Alps. Shelley's intervention in the aesthetics of Romantic space, in other words, is so forceful as to make the vanishing of the light—as clouds obscure the moon "swifter than the flight of the vulture" (Shelley 1994 [1818], 188)—almost as necessary or inevitable as the unity of Wordsworth's mood and spirit with the invisible power underlying the grandeur of the natural world. The difference lies not only in the deliberateness with which Shelley reshapes or negates the familiar meanings of such spaces, but also in the resulting disjuncture between the shaping spirit of her own imagination and the relations between humanity and nature or the physical world she envisages. In Wordsworth, the functioning of the imagination in unifying physical spaces with emotions and ideas is paralleled by the forms of unity of nature and spirit that the imagining consciousness depicts. In Mary Shelley, by contrast, the imaginative vision of nature and human consciousness is in itself perhaps no less vividly unified or persuasive; yet she also depicts a disjuncture or conflict between certain forms of human aspiration and the constraints of nature or the physical. This disjuncture between the unifying function of the author's imagination and its portrayal of disunity or conflict can in turn be seen in two quite different lights. On the one hand, the disjuncture can be viewed as weakening the work of art through its separation of visions and creative processes that in Wordsworth (and substantially in Radcliffe) are firmly integrated with each other. On the other hand, it can be viewed as freeing the reader and the narration itself from an element of cliché or deception—namely, that which is involved in claiming to discover a unity in experience, or in the actual relations of mind and matter, which in fact exists only in the work of art. Hence, despite the artifice involved in her inversions of Romantic space and signification, Shelley could be seen as more honest in her portrayal of the relation between consciousness and the concrete, or between aspiration and the actual, regardless of whether her pessimistic vision of disunity, contradiction, and limitation is accepted. Indeed, to assert the greater accuracy of either Wordsworth's or Shelley's visions would be to presume a knowledge of the relations between subjective and objective transcending all particularity, historicity, and textuality.

Shifting Landscapes of the Mind in Romantic-Period Narrative

As the foregoing discussion shows, the emphasis in eighteenth-century narrative either on a subjectivity shaped by external circumstances or on a rational response to and interpretation of the latter is replaced in Romantic-period narrative by a merging of landscape and mood in which both rationality and ideas of causation become relatively unimportant. As landscape becomes more directly expressive of subjectivity, the moods or ideas it expresses are often difficult to separate from the landscapes themselves, sharing both their dramatic contrasts and their subtle suggestions of the infinite or sublime. This distinctive relation between physical space and subjectivity, moreover, interestingly parallels Romantic theories of the unity of mind and nature. Indeed, Romantic narratives themselves sometimes depict their authors' imaginative unification of subjectivity with physical landscapes as analogous to the quasi-divine spirit that several Romantic philosophers describe as unifying subject and object. The rational consciousness of Jane Austen's characters is thus replaced not only by forms of subjectivity reflecting and reflected in landscape imagery, but also by an intuitive knowledge of supersensible truths, implicitly arising from a pre-Freudian unconscious having partial access to the infinite or divine.

In later Romantic narratives such as those of Mary Shelley, however, such self-conscious intuitions of the relation between mind and nature are replaced by a more modern distinction between the protagonists' quests for transcendence and a narrative that indirectly highlights their delusive nature. Yet this latter, more politicized and critical form of Romantic narrative still uses landscapes and other forms of visual imagery in ways analogous to earlier Gothic novelists such as Radcliffe, though distinctively imbuing them with contrasting forms of meaning. Hence the earlier and the later forms of Gothic narrative I have discussed, together with the more philosophical narratives of Wordsworth, all make use of a distinctively Romantic unification of landscape imagery with moods and ideas while adapting those states of mind to express contrasting forms of ideology.

Notes

1. For other perspectives on the role of metaphor in narrative representations of mind, see Leslie Lockett's and Elizabeth Bradburn's contributions to this volume.

2. See, for example, Bachelard (1964 [1958], xxii–xxiv) on how "space which has been seized upon by the imagination . . . has been lived in, not in its positivity, but with all the partiality of the imagination," so that our images of houses "move in both directions: they are in us as much as we are in them." See also Lefebvre (1991 [1974], 11–12).

3. In addition to the examples from *Mansfield Park* discussed by Said (1995), Captain Wentworth's assistance of Anne Elliot's friend Mrs. Smith at the end of *Persuasion*, whereby he puts her "in the way of recovering her husband's property in the West Indies" (Austen 1985 [1818], 253), highlights

the extent to which Austen sometimes reduces landscapes, and even entire regions of the world, to the social and economic functions they serve for the English upper classes.

4. See Byron, *Don Juan*, Canto I, ll. 991–1011 (1986–93, 5:48–49). Apart from the newly rich Admiral Croft's replacing Sir Walter Elliot at Kellynch Hall, the most important respect in which the Napoleonic wars feature in *Persuasion*, for example, is in enabling Captain Wentworth to return to England from the navy, first "in the year eight, with a few thousand pounds," and then, in 1814, "with five-and-twenty thousand pounds," thus enabling him to overcome Lady Russell's objections to his marrying Anne Elliot (Austen 1985 [1818], 248–50).

5. In chapter 23 of *Persuasion*, Anne reflects that if she had agreed to marry her cousin William Elliot in preference to the young Captain Wentworth, "all risk would have been incurred, and all duty violated" (Austen 1985 [1818], 246), thus demonstrating a loyalty and genuineness of affection that Austen depicts as transcending purely practical or financial concerns. See also the evocations of emotion in Austen (1985 [1818], 103, 111, 129–32, 178, 240, 242).

6. See especially the pseudo-Radcliffean conclusion of Catherine's explorations of the mysteries of Northanger Abbey and Austen's reference to General Tilney's "greedy speculation" on her inheritance (Austen 2003 [1818], 139–46, 186).

7. See my discussions of this point in Vallins (2000, 1–2) and Vallins (2001, 54–56).

8. Alison Milbank comments that Radcliffe's omission, in *A Sicilian Romance*, of "any but the briefest mention of Mount Etna" implies a wish "to revise the location of the sublime in the purely vertical, and the purely powerful. . . . It is experience of the feminine situation of confinement and powerlessness, whether in mansion or cave, that allows a movement to the transcendent" (Radcliffe 1993 [1790], xxvii). A similar pattern is evident in *The Mysteries of Udolpho*, in the contrast between Radcliffe's description of the immediate surroundings of the Castle of Udolpho, home of the exploitative Montoni ("a vista . . . that exhibited the Appenines in their darkest horrors"), and Emily St. Aubert's earlier perceptions of the Alps, whose "scenes of sublimity . . . brought to her recollection the prospects among the Pyrenees, which [she] had earlier experienced together" with her suitor, Valancourt (Radcliffe 1966 [1794], 226, 163). Radcliffe thus contrasts the Burkeian sublime of terror with a sublimity of liberation that also differs strikingly from the Kantian model of the sublime as identification with the infinite

forces underlying the natural world (see Burke 1970 [1759], 58–60, 95–98, and Kant 1952 [1790], 98–112).

9. See, for example, Caygill (1995, 379) and Bachelard (1964 [1958], xxxi–xxxv). Despite his critique of the poststructuralist "sophistry whereby the philosophico-epistemological notion of space is fetishized and the mental realm comes to envelop the social and physical ones," Lefebvre (1991 [1974]) emphasizes the importance of explaining "logico-epistemological space, the space of social practice, the space occupied by sensory phenomena, including products of the imagination such as projects and projections, symbols and utopias" by connecting "the physical—nature, the Cosmos"—with "the mental, including logical and formal abstractions," and "the social" (5, 11–12).

10. On Spinoza's conception of "God or Nature" (*Deus sive Natura*) and Coleridge's attitudes toward it, see Vallins (1995, 111–17). In *Biographia Literaria*, Coleridge mentions his early discussions of Spinoza with Wordsworth (Coleridge 1983 [1817], 1:194).

11. In *A Sicilian Romance*, for example, the abbey in which Julia Mazzini takes refuge from her father—a "proud monument of monkish superstitions and princely magnificence," whose "high-arched windows" are "stained with the colouring of monkish fictions"—evokes the forms of (Catholic) oppression that "civilization" and enlightenment progressively dissolve (Radcliffe 1993 [1794], 116–17). This implicit association of Catholic tradition with oppression is consistent with the contemporary values of revolutionary France, yet in the context of Radcliffe's novel it also implies an element of Protestant nationalism.

12. For more on how Hartley combines empiricist theories of knowledge with Platonic philosophy, anchoring his account of the spiritual nature of consciousness in the association of ideas derived in turn from sensory impressions, see Fairchild (1947, 1017–18) and Vallins (2000, 112–13).

13. Hamilton (1986) interprets Wordsworth's troubled intuition of "unknown modes of being" as connoting an imaginary "rebuke" or "adult censorship of his presumption" at having "stolen" the boat in which he rows across the lake (85–87). Though Wordsworth does mention the "stealth" with which he loosed the boat from its moorings, this passage also strikingly recalls Kant's classic analysis of the sublime effects of landscape, with which Wordsworth may already have been familiar by 1797, when this passage was written (see Wu 1993, 80–81). See also Grob's (1973) comment that the sense of fear Wordsworth describes himself as experiencing "does not mean . . . that the pursuing mountain is to be taken, as it so often is, as an illustration of the incipient workings of conscience" (84–87).

14. See Grob (1973, 79–83) on "the animistically characterized 'Presences of Nature,'" which the early Wordsworth describes as "operating through sense phenomena."

15. I use the modern spelling to refer to this well-known viewpoint over the "Mer de Glace" near Chamonix. Shelley, however, uses the spelling "Montanvert."

16. On this paradox, see especially Kant (1952 [1790], 104–5, 110–11).

17. On the way in which Frankenstein and the creature resemble "fragments of a mind in conflict with itself, extremes unreconciled, striving to make themselves whole," see Levine (1979, 14–16).

18. See Shelley (1994 [1818], 95–96, 161). The OED notes that the spelling "daemon" (as against "demon") is often used to distinguish the sense of "a supernatural being of a nature intermediate between that of gods and men" or "an attendant, ministering, or indwelling spirit; a genius," from that of "an evil spirit." Frankenstein's reference to his creature as "the daemon" thus highlights the extent to which the creature represents the diverse implications of the Romantic spirit with which Frankenstein himself has endued the natural world.

19. On the way in which *"Frankenstein* portrays the consequences of the failure of the family, the damage wrought when the mother—or a nurturant parental love—is absent," see Mellor (1988, 39–47).

References

Austen, Jane. 1985 [1818]. *Persuasion*. Ed. D. W. Harding. Harmondsworth: Penguin.

———. 2003. *Northanger Abbey* [1818], *Lady Susan* [1871], *The Watsons* [1871], *Sanditon* [1925]. Ed. James Kinsley and John Davie. Oxford: Oxford University Press.

Bachelard, Gaston. 1964 [1958]. *The Poetics of Space*. Trans. Maria Jolas. Boston: Beacon Press.

Burke, Edmund. 1970 [1759]. *A Philosophical Enquiry into the Origins of Our Ideas of the Sublime and Beautiful*. Menston: Scolar Press.

Byron, George Gordon (Lord). 1986–93. *The Complete Poetical Works of Lord Byron*. Ed. Jerome J. McGann. 7 vols. Oxford: Clarendon Press.

Caygill, Howard. 1995. *A Kant Dictionary*. Oxford: Blackwell.

Coleridge, S. T. 1912. *Poetical Works*. Ed. E. H. Coleridge. 2 vols. Oxford: Oxford University Press.

———. 1983 [1817]. *Biographia Literaria*. Ed. James Engell and W. Jackson Bate. 2 vols. Princeton NJ: Princeton University Press.

Fairchild, H. N. 1947. "Hartley, Pistorius, and Coleridge." *PMLA* 62:1010–21.

Grob, Alan. 1973. *The Philosophic Mind: A Study of Wordsworth's Poetry and Thought, 1797–1805*. Columbus: Ohio State University Press.

Hamilton, Paul. 1986. *Wordsworth*. Brighton: Harvester.

Hartley, David. 1749. *Observations on Man: His Frame, His Duty, and His Expectations*. 2 vols. London: Samuel Richardson.

Kant, Immanuel. 1952 [1790]. *The Critique of Judgement*. Trans. J. C. Meredith. Oxford: Clarendon Press.

Lefebvre, Henri. 1991 [1974]. *The Production of Space*. Trans. Donald Nicholson-Smith. Oxford: Blackwell.

Levine, George. 1979. "The Ambiguous Heritage of Frankenstein." In *The Endurance of 'Frankenstein': Essays on Mary Shelley's Novel*, ed. George Levine and U. C. Knoepflmacher, 3–30. Berkeley: University of California Press.

Mellor, Anne K. 1988. *Mary Shelley: Her Life, Her Fiction, Her Monsters*. New York: Routledge.

Poovey, Mary. 1980. "My Hideous Progeny: Mary Shelley and the Feminization of Romanticism." *PMLA* 95:332–47.

Priestley, Joseph. 1777. *The Doctrine of Philosophical Necessity Illustrated*. London: J. Johnson.

Radcliffe, Ann. 1966 [1794]. *The Mysteries of Udolpho*. Ed. Bonamy Dobrée and Frederick Garber. Oxford: Oxford University Press.

———. 1993 [1790]. *A Sicilian Romance*. Ed. Alison Milbank. Oxford: Oxford University Press.

Said, Edward. 1995. "Jane Austen and Empire." In *Romanticism: A Critical Reader*, ed. Duncan Wu, 417–33. Oxford: Blackwell.

Schelling, F. W. J. 1978 [1800]. *System of Transcendental Idealism*. Trans. Peter Heath. Charlottesville: University Press of Virginia.

Shelley, Mary. 1985 [1826]. *The Last Man*. Ed. Brian Aldiss. London: Hogarth Press.

———. 1994 [1818]. *Frankenstein: or, the Modern Prometheus*. Ed. Maurice Hindle. Harmondsworth: Penguin.

Shelley, Percy Bysshe. 1977. *Shelley's Poetry and Prose*. Ed. Donald H. Reiman and Sharon B. Powers. New York: W. W. Norton.

Vallins, David. 1995. "Production and Existence: Coleridge's Unification of Nature." *Journal of the History of Ideas* 56:107–24.

———. 2000. *Coleridge and the Psychology of Romanticism: Feeling and Thought*. Basingstoke: Macmillan, 2000.

———. 2001. "Self Reliance: Individualism in Emerson and Coleridge." *Symbiosis* 5:51–68.

Wheeler, Kathleen. 1982. *The Creative Mind in Coleridge's Poetry*. Cambridge M A: Harvard University Press.

Wordsworth, William. 1940–49. *The Poetical Works of William Wordsworth*. Ed. E. de Selincourt and Helen Darbishire. 5 vols. Oxford: Clarendon.

———. 1979. *The Prelude 1799, 1805, 1850: Authoritative Texts, Context and Reception, Recent Critical Essays*. Ed. Jonathan Wordsworth, M. H. Abrams, Stephen Gill. New York: W. W. Norton.

Wu, Duncan. 1993. *Wordsworth's Reading, 1770–1799*. Cambridge: Cambridge University Press.

7. 1825–1880
The Network of Nerves
NICHOLAS DAMES

Is there an ur-scene of the Victorian depiction of consciousness? One could do worse than begin with one of the Victorian novel's most famously shocking moments: Walter Hartright, one of the central narrators of Wilkie Collins's 1859–60 *The Woman in White*, meeting the eponymous apparition on a moonlit Hampstead Heath:

I had now arrived at that particular point of my walk where four roads met—the road to Hampstead, along which I had returned, the road to Finchley, the road to West End, and the road back to London. I had mechanically turned in this latter direction, and was strolling along the lonely high-road—idly wondering, I remember, what the Cumberland young ladies would look like—when, in one moment, every drop of blood in my body was brought to a stop by the touch of a hand laid lightly and suddenly on my shoulder from behind me.

I turned on the instant, with my fingers tightening round the handle of my stick.

There, in the middle of the broad bright high-road—there, as if it had that moment sprung out of the earth or dropped from the heaven—stood the figure of a solitary Woman, dressed from head to foot in white garments, her face bent in grave inquiry on mine, her hand pointing to the dark cloud over London, as I faced her.

I was far too seriously startled by the suddenness with which this extraordinary apparition stood before me, in the dead of night and in that lonely place, to ask what she wanted. The strange woman spoke first.

"Is that the road to London?" she said. (Collins 1973 [1860], 15)

The scandal of the passage, at least as far as a history of the depiction of consciousness might go, is that it scarcely seems to evoke consciousness at all—at least what conventionally goes under the umbrella of such a term. The complicated by-play of memory, desire, and inner negotiation, the standard basis for novelistic analysis since Richardson, at least, is replaced here by a series of sudden, and automatic, physical responses. Hartright's blood is "brought to a stop" in a vivid, if now rather clichéd, image for the physiological response of fear; his hand (involuntarily?) clenches; his powers of speech desert him. All but visual acuity is removed, and what presents itself to Hartright's vision is oddly still, as if his sensorium can only process a frozen image. Furthermore, the scene is literally momentary, dotted with reminders of a speed—"in one moment," "on the instant"—that is closer to the speed of neural operations than to fully conscious deliberation. Lest we imagine this sudden seizure of fright and shock as an interruption of a fully self-aware process of thought, we are told that Hartright had been previously walking "mechanically," engaged in a half-formed reverie, his mind proceeding numbly on the rails of mental drift. In the terms of, say, Jane Austen's alert and continually ratiocinative protagonists, Hartright is, we might say, not all there. Hartright himself seems to confirm it shortly thereafter: "Was I Walter Hartright? Was this the well-known, uneventful road, where holiday people strolled on Sundays? Had I really left, little more than an hour since, the quiet, decent, conventionally-domestic atmosphere of my mother's cottage?" (Collins 1973 [1860], 18).

Neither is it anachronistic to point to the various psychic automatisms on display in this scene. In her acute and aesthetically conservative 1862 attack on the sensation novel, Margaret Oliphant mounted a full-scale close reading of this scene, and one other from *The Woman in White* much like it, to demonstrate its odd dependence on nerves rather than conscious thought. "It is a simple physical effect, if one may use such an expression," Oliphant claims. "It is totally independent of character, and involves no particular issue, so far as can be foreseen at this point of the story . . . these two startling points of this story do not take their power from character, or from passion, or any intellectual or emotional influence. The effect is pure sensation, neither more nor less" (Oliphant 1862, 572). "Pure" sensation, "simple" physicality: Oliphant is reaching for a language adequate to what seems like Collins's discovery of a mental response reduced to nothing but its own transmissibility, an electrical pulse alone. She is careful to praise the technique that can produce such a pulse, and conscious of its primary effectiveness, that of immediate impact upon a reader. "The reader's nerves are affected like the hero's. He feels the thrill of the untoward resemblance, an ominous painful mystery. He, too, is chilled by a confused and unexplainable alarm" (Oliphant 1862, 572).

Oliphant's reading offers the following analysis: what might seem like a thematic concern of sensation fiction (with instantaneous, physiological/mental shocks) becomes its formal principle (insofar as it is interested in producing these shocks)—a principle of great, if troubling, potency, given the inherent contagiousness of the "nervous." Collins, Oliphant argues, is responsible for dissolving the usual cognitive boundaries of individuals by appealing to the commonest aspect of human response: the rhythms and susceptibilities of the nervous system. Oliphant understood this technique as a radically new one, suited to the rapid expansion of a mass reading public for whom "response" would mean *reaction* rather than judgment or even affect. Like Hartright, the reader of a sensation novel would feel blood halt and muscles tighten, but would not have higher-order mental functions addressed at all. The analysis was echoed, with more asperity and less admiration, by subsequent critics. Henry Mansel's 1863 omnibus review of the sensation fad proclaimed that "it would almost seem as if the paradox of Cabanis, *les nerfs, voilà tout l'homme,* had been banished from the realm of philosophy only to claim a wider empire in the domain of fiction—at least if we may judge by the very large class of writers who seem to acknowledge no other element in human nature to which they can appeal." Mansel's conclusion was that such fiction was evidence of "morbid phenomena of literature—indications of a wide-spread corruption, of which they are in part both the effect and the cause; called into existence to supply the cravings of a diseased appetite, and contributing themselves to foster the disease, and to stimulate the want which they supply" (Mansel 1863, 482).

Such readings vividly remind us that the line between mind and brain—put another way, between the functions of the cortex and the spinal ganglia—was a live topic of British psychology in the nineteenth century, so much so that it could leak into the discourses of periodical criticism and serial fiction. The argument that I make in what follows, however, is to suggest that what Oliphant and Mansel identified in sensation fiction was not limited to that particular subgenre. It is more accurate to say that sensation fiction made visible, and even schematic, a dynamic that mainstream Victorian fiction grappled with in its own ways: the developing sense that consciousness was at least partly comprised of, and possibly even dominated by, the formerly debased realm of automatic, nervous functions. "Mind" and "brain," in the increasingly materialist psychologies of the period, were if not one and the same then at least too intimately related to separate easily. This physiological understanding of psychology, which came to dominate British theories of mind in the middle decades of the century, had consequences for the form of the period's fiction, given that fiction's traditional interest in matters of motive, interiority, self-development, and intimacy. Sensation fiction emerged as a consequence of mainstream realist fiction's interest in embodied minds rather than the reverse; its dramatically successful (if, in market terms, short-lived) appeals to the reading public simply took an explicit position in regard to the question domestic fiction had come to negotiate: what is the mind if not body?[1]

In our contemporary moment, when neuroscience offers a fully confident promise that all psychological questions are finally questions of neural chemistry, the challenge that physiological notions of consciousness posed to the Victorians is not an entirely foreign one. In terms recently supplied by the neurologist Antonio Damasio, we can describe the conflict faced by Victorian psychologists and novelists as that between an "autobiographical self," composed of a unique set of individually distinct memories and habits, and a "core consciousness," something like the organism's sense of its own basic functioning, its recognition of any disturbances to its homeostasis. Damasio describes this "core consciousness" as "the very thought of you—the very feeling of you—as an individual being involved in the process of knowing of your own existence and of the existence of others" (Damasio 2000, 127). The core consciousness, or in Victorian terms the physiological self, is a new property of nineteenth-century narration that disturbs any stable sense of how the narrative representation of consciousness might function. Hartright's encounter with the Woman in White both is, and is not, a depiction of interiority; it depicts an interior consciousness in wholly new terms and with a newly precise temporality, a core rather than an autobiography. It is consciousness only in a specifically physiological context, one which had a crucial—and not yet fully understood—role to play in even more normative Victorian fictions.

The Age of Physiological Psychology

The student of physiological psychology, the dominant model of psychological theory of the mid-Victorian period, is immediately confronted with an interesting and unique disciplinary muddle: many of the most well-known names in physiological psychology were also practicing literary critics, often in close connection with novelists themselves, who brought the data of physiological psychology to bear upon their understanding and assessment of contemporary fiction. Their names are more or less obscure today: G. H. Lewes (1817–78), George Eliot's partner; E. S. Dallas (1828–79), one of the *Times*'s major critics and a psychological theorist of some repute; Alexander Bain (1818–1903), the period's most influential mental theorist, who also attempted literary theory within his celebrated psychological textbooks; and, later, Vernon Lee, née Violet Paget (1856–1935), who remained dedicated to the insights of physiological psychology long after that methodology had been supplanted by psychoanalytic approaches. The presence of serious science within widely disseminated literary criticism is, to say the least, an unusual one from today's perspective, so unusual that it has mostly been overlooked.[2]

Physiological psychology was at its core a materialist theory of mental processing that remained somewhat hesitant about its own materialism. It attempted a more or less cautious correction of associationist and faculty psychology by insisting that associations—considered the primary mechanism of mental functioning since the Scottish school of the eighteenth-century—and faculties were mere terms of art with no grounding in biological reality. Lewes's pivotal 1860 work, *The Physiology of Common Life*, was in this respect paradigmatic: it was far more cautious in its overall claims than in its actual details, which tended to undermine faculty psychology at every turn. The book began with a lengthy and mutedly controversial claim:

Psychology is the science of Mind; Physiology is the science of Life. All who recognize the former as a science, declare its aim to be the elucidation of the laws of Thought, the nature of the Soul, and its prerogatives. This science may seek—and I follow those who think it ought to seek—important means of investigation in the laws of Physiology; just as Physiology itself must seek important aids in Chemistry and Physics. But as an independent branch of inquiry, its results cannot be held amenable to physiological canons; their validity cannot be decided by agreement with physiological laws. To cite an example: Psychology announces that the mind has different faculties, and that each of these faculties may have a temporary exaltation, or a temporary suspension. This fact seems established on ample evidence, and is valid in Psychology, although no corresponding fact in Physiology has been discovered—neither the anatomy of the brain, nor any knowledge of the brain's action, can be adduced as furnishing the evidence; and if Psychology were absolutely amenable to the conclusions of Physiology, we should here have to doubt one of the most indisputable of psychological facts. (Lewes 1860, 2:2–3)

The argument for the importance of physiological work—for the empirical, vivisectionist, experimental study of the nervous system and its functions—rests on a curious paradox: that it is entirely separate from psychology (the distinction between "Mind" and "Life"), while psychology is nonetheless urged to consider the evidence physiology has discovered; evidence, moreover, that

Lewes suggests will not necessarily bear out the cherished tenets of psychology. The very term "physiological psychology," then, encapsulates an uneasy truce between mentalist theories dating back to the previous century and more up-to-date materialist data. In many ways physiological psychology represented a final stage of collaboration between hard neuroscience and soft psychological theory before their decisive split in the late nineteenth and early twentieth centuries. If today mind-brain research seems to have healed that split, such healing comes at the cost of a decisive privileging of hard neurophysiological evidence; the fMRI scanning techniques of the present are treated by some analysts as a bedrock layer of dispositive evidence.[3]

Much of the procedure of these Victorian theorists was devoted to an unpacking of various nomenclatural ambiguities inherent to psychology as it then stood. A primary ambiguity was that associated with the word "consciousness." Alexander Bain, in his massively influential *The Emotions and the Will*, devoted several pages simply to marking out the various meanings and usages of the term, most of which contradicted the others (Bain 1865, 599). Lewes was similarly attentive to these ambiguities, which seemed rooted in a desire to maintain for consciousness some nonbiological origin. Here Lewes offered a seemingly inoffensive redefinition of the term: "Every excitement of a nerve-centre produces a sensation; the sum total of such excitements forms the general Consciousness, or sense of existence" (Lewes 1860, 2:65). Consciousness, therefore, is the background mental hum of the constant combination and recombination of simple neural sensations "exciting and modifying each other"; as a result, it is something of an illusion, similar, to use a more modern analogy, to the illusion of motion pictures, whereby single frames run at a certain speed seem to be a single stream of images (Lewes 1860, 2:73). *The Physiology of Common Life* was the text that first coined the phrase "stream of consciousness," but it is important to recognize that this stream was for Lewes merely epiphenomenal, rooted in a series of interweaving neural impulses. The physiological definition of consciousness seemed neutral enough, or at least inarguable on its face, but in fact contained a controversial presupposition: that all mental operations are, in actuality, results of biological (and noncognitive) pulses. This materialist core was often disguised by the plethora of metaphors physiological psychologists used to describe the play of consciousness: Lewes used images of mental chemistry, in which simple elements form complex compounds; the color spectrum; overlapping and merging ripples in a pond formed by multiple stones dropped into its surface (Lewes 1879, 180).[4]

More crucially, perhaps, such a definition of consciousness made nonsense of the concept of an unconscious. Strictly speaking, for physiological psychologists no sensation can be unconscious, since every sensation feeds into consciousness, even if we are often hard pressed to analyze consciousness into its separate elements. Insofar as Victorian theorists retained some use of the unconscious, they retained it in a specific form: as a shorthand term for sensations that are not distinguishable from the general hum of consciousness. In Bain's *Emotions and the Will*, this approach resulted in a clear formula that prefigures twentieth-century gestalt theory: the unconscious is the set of sensations that intellect does not distinguish separately, such as the several sensations making up Walter Hartright's inattentive reverie prior to the Woman in White's sudden appearance. Another word for "intellect" is, in fact, "attention": the act of fixing upon a passing wavelike consciousness and isolating one element from the rest (Bain 1865, 566). Continental European work in the field of psychophysics, or the measurement of neural sensations, provided a term that lingers today; with the help of this approach, the unconscious could be described as sensations that fall below threshold, or below the powers of attentive analysis. Bain's work here borrowed from Gustav Fechner's 1860 *Elemente der Psychophysik* in determining that the threshold between the conscious and the unconscious—insofar as that distinction was considered to have any meaning—was merely that of attention.

The Victorian unconscious, therefore, was not the residue of some process of repression. It was simply the large mass of biological, neural inputs that pass without explicit notice. Contemporary cognitive science uses other terms, from the "psychophysical complex" (Varela, Thompson, and Rosch 1991) to the "non-conscious" (Palmer 2004), in an explicit attempt to eliminate the psychoanalytic overtones of unconsciousness, although the roots of these later terms are present in Victorian notions of the unconscious. It was the body's ongoing register of experience, capable at any moment of being activated into something at the center of one's attention. The arrival of a sensation (or set of related sensations) at the forefront of attention was not necessarily a process of repression and return, as twentieth-century psychoanalytic critics so often claim; it might be simply a gradual process of additive, minute bodily impulses that—with the addition of one more sensation, the proverbial straw that breaks the camel's back—finally are noticed by the intellect. An excellent example of such reasoning is provided by a climactic moment from George Meredith's 1879 *The Egoist*, in which Clara Middleton, engaged to the Egoist Sir Willoughby, describes the process of her disillusionment to the outraged Mrs. Mountstuart Jenkinson:

"*I have found that I do not . . .*"
 "*What?*"
 "*Love him.*"
 Mrs Mountstuart grimaced transiently. "*That is no answer. The cause!*" *she said.* "*What has he done?*"
 "*Nothing.*"
 "*And when did you discover this nothing?*"
 "*By degrees; unknown to myself; suddenly.*" (Meredith 1968 [1879], 424)

This is not the temporality of repression; it is, more properly, the temporality of physiological consciousness, in which a gradual process of addition (unknown to the intellect) is finally, and suddenly, discovered by an act of attention. It is a set of below-the-threshold sensations bursting through the threshold of mental concentration. As Mrs. Mountstuart Jenkinson angrily characterizes it, "*gradually* you *suddenly* discovered" a mental fact: revulsion for Sir Willoughby (Meredith 1968 [1879], 429). This is not a war between unconscious desire and conscious repression but instead a winnowing process, whereby sensations compete for the limelight of conscious awareness.

This does not mean that nonconscious phenomena were not occasionally described in more mythopoeic ways. E. S. Dallas's 1866 aesthetic treatise *The Gay Science* devoted much analysis to what Dallas called "the hidden soul": the field of mental operations that are automatic rather than willed. Dallas, in an orthodox physiological phrase, insisted that "in almost every mental operation there are several distinct wheels going, though we may be conscious of only one" (Dallas 1866, 1:223). Dallas argued for the aesthetic importance of these unnoticed mental operations or, put another way, for the superior effectiveness of the automatic; his examples included the unconscious ease a superior pianist feels during performance, as opposed to the anxious attention of a beginner. The lesson of Dallas's "hidden soul" is that "many lines of action which when first attempted require to be carried on by distinct efforts of volition become through practice mechanical, involuntary movements of which we are wholly unaware" (Dallas 1866, 1:223–24). Art, for Dallas, springs from and appeals to this "mechanical, involuntary" neural life; its task is to bypass the selectivity of conscious attention and gain access to the bodily routines and stimuli that help constitute the mind's scope and power. The "hidden soul" is not the repressed, simply the constitutively unnoticed. A route to its secrets is *a relaxation of the intensity of conscious attention*—a state akin to meditative trance.

Dallas here offers a clue to one of the oddities of physiological psychology: its denigration of attentiveness. Lewes's *Physiology of Common Life* consisted of prolonged and detailed descriptions of the relations of mental functioning to basic biological functions, such as eating and digestion, the circulation of the blood, respiration, sleep, and dreaming. These fundamental components of mental life are obscured by approaches that foreground states of conscious awareness. In a very real sense, physiological psychology posited a theory of consciousness according to which attention distorts our sense of self; the more one concentrates on the autobiographical self of Damasio's theory, the less that core consciousness can be appreciated, and the less, therefore, that the whole self can be known. The conscious selectivity of attentive thought is as likely to be deceptive as to be illuminating. Physiological psychologists generated a set of anecdotes and tales to demonstrate that operations carried out mechanically are done more efficiently, more adeptly, and more *truly*, than operations carried out by the force of will. The body, that is, remains the final court of appeal. Mental processes separated from the automatism of the body are unmoored from physiological "truth"; in some sense, they remain phantasms.

These findings were by no means esoteric or specialized. They were disseminated throughout Victorian culture—particularly the culture of Victorian fiction—by the close working relationship between physiologists and novelists, and via their shared venue, the weekly or monthly periodical, where results of recent physiological experiment could be found alongside lengthy critical work written by practicing physiologists. Lewes, for instance, was primarily known as a literary critic and editor, a major force in the London world of metropolitan intellectuals; his periodical criticism, with its constant appeal to physiological concepts, was more widely known than his book-length scientific studies. One might even say that physiological psychology was most culturally pervasive *as a language for aesthetic assessment*. Take, for example, one of Lewes's most influential critical pieces, an 1872 reassessment of Dickens published in the *Fortnightly Review*:

When one thinks of Micawber always presenting himself in the same situations, moved with the same springs, and uttering the same sounds . . . one is reminded of the frogs whose brains have been taken out for physiological purposes, and whose actions henceforth want the distinctive peculiarity of organic action, that of fluctuating spontaneity. . . . It is this complexity of the organism which Dickens wholly fails to conceive; his characters have nothing fluctuating and incalculable in them, even when they embody true observations; and very often they are creations so fantastic that one is at a loss to understand how he could, without hallucination, believe them to be like reality. (Lewes 1872, 149)

Here the veracity of fictional portrayal—the central question of the reality of Dickens—is assessed through the category of the organic or lifelike, which is in turn defined with reference to physiological experiment. Vivisection tells the physiologist what the organic is; in this case, the organic consists of the fluctuating spontaneity of consciousness, a species of incalculability that Lewes finds lacking in Dickens's characters. Critical work like this did much to cement physiological psychology and novelistic discourse into a temporarily seamless whole. Yet the combination was not without its challenges, particularly for novelists. How to represent consciousness when attention was not a route to self-understanding? How to get past the autobiographical self to core consciousness? How does one narrate a thoroughly embodied, material, nervous self?

Victorian Narration and the Nervous Self

Not, as it turns out, through introspection, which physiology routinely disdained. The difference of texture between mid-Victorian domestic realism and its close predecessors in late eighteenth-century and Regency fiction is the much greater weight given to introspection in the latter. Jane Austen might usefully stand as an example of the pre-physiological mode of fictional consciousness, which featured fully alert minds, in solitary conditions, engaged in a virtually forensic examination of their own motives, particularly by reassessing the data of memory. Elizabeth Bennet's reported inner speech, on concluding a critical examination of Fitzwilliam Darcy's explanatory letter, is paradigmatic: "How despicably I have acted! . . . I, who have prided myself on my discernment!—I, who have valued myself on my abilities! . . . I have courted prepossession and ignorance, and driven reason away, where either were concerned. Till this moment, I never knew myself" (Austen 1982 [1813], 208). The self in Austen is capable of this kind of linguistic and temporal self-alienation, in which a faculty of judgment looks at past behavior and attaches abstract terms (ignorance, reason, discernment) in order to arrive at a stable, and potentially consensual, self-knowledge. Where this kind of Socratic self-knowledge is for some reason blocked or temporarily not possible, as with the more self-deluded heroines of *Northanger Abbey* or *Emma*, free indirect discourse acts as a kind of proxy for self-knowledge, demonstrating an alienation between a character's own language and a more accurate, less deluded language possessed by the narrative voice.

Physiological psychology, in its cautious but nonetheless thorough dismantling of the introspective procedures of associationism and faculty psychology, presupposed instead a form of consciousness in which alert attention (of the kind Elizabeth Bennet excels at above) is more of a ruse than a path to truth. The springs of action for physiologically grounded consciousness are neural combinations and recombinations—bodily inputs morphed, in an impossibly complicated process, into ideas and movements that can never be entirely retraced to their source. The result, as far as novelistic character is concerned, was a new emphasis on unknowability. The Victorian fictional narrator has ever more work to do given the necessary self-ignorance of even the most emotionally acute characters. Much of the tone and leisurely length of Victorian narrative is owed to this new epistemological split between a knowing narrator and characters who are constitutively, perhaps even ontologically, unaware of the basis of their motives. Free indirect style, which had been such a valuable tool for Austen and which would flourish in writers like Flaubert and Joyce, and as a result became foregrounded in theories of the novel influenced by modernist practice, is a much less marked presence within mid-Victorian fiction.[5] Instead, loquacious, chatty, discursive narrative voices abound, albeit with different affective colorations, such as Thackeray's melancholic cynicism, Trollope's generous equanimity, or Eliot's high-secular forgiving wisdom. Their different tones obscure their remarkably similar functions vis-à-vis their characters: to elucidate what the characters themselves cannot, or at least to point out the mysteries of self-knowledge their characters are incapable of solving. This is so common an aspect of Victorian narration that it might virtually be called an interiority function: fictional selves are signaled as psychologically real to the extent that they are incapable of accurate introspection.

Take, for instance, an entirely typical moment from Trollope's 1862–64 *The Small House at Allington*. Here Trollope gestures to the motives that lead Lucy Dale to openly avow her engagement to the decidedly more reluctant Adolphus Crosbie, who, we are told, would rather that Lucy be more reticent. Crosbie's desire is itself an act of self-deception, since what passes for him as a preference for female modesty is in fact a wish to break off the engagement, a wish that becomes ever more problematic with each public proclamation Lucy makes. As for Lucy, she is scarcely more aware of the sources of her openness:

Why should she be ashamed of that which, to her thinking was so great an honour to her? She had heard of girls who would not speak of their love, arguing to themselves cannily that there may be many a slip between the cup and the lip. There could be no need of any such caution with her. There could surely be no such slip! Should there be such a fall, —should any such fate, either by falseness or misfortune, come upon her, —no such caution could be of service to save her. The cup would have been so shattered in its fall that no further piecing of its parts would be in any way possible. So much as this she did not exactly say to herself; but she felt it all, and went bravely forward, —bold in her love, and careful to hide it from none who chanced to see it. (Trollope 1980 [1864], 93)

The (entirely Trollopian) ingenuity of the passage is its use of what we might call *false free indirect style*: although the language of this analysis presents itself as Lily's own (the cup, its shattering), as if seen in the typical double-perspective of Austenian narration, we are then told, remarkably, that "so much as this she did not exactly say to herself," as if in fact the Trollopian narrator needs to supply the very linguistic terms in which to evoke a character's much more formless inner resolutions. Unlike the inner language-world of Elizabeth Bennet, Lily Dale can only feel a need to publicly proclaim her engagement; she cannot articulate it, even in self-deluded terms. The need is less psychological in nature (i.e., accessible to Lily's conscious introspection) than it is a kind of nervous impulse—an impulse to press "bravely forward," to possibly even anticipate the public ruin that she already obscurely knows will occur. It is not that the narrator possesses an epistemologically superior vantage point from which to assess a character's own self-conversation; it is, rather, that the narrator needs to elaborate upon a character's deep, and wordless, impulses.

The result is the talky, garrulous texture of Victorian fiction: the sign of an ontological split between the knowing voice of narration, which cannot properly possess a psychology at all, and the psychologies of characters, which are continually belied by their words. Lily's eventual refusal to move on from Crosbie, who jilts her in a famously cruel manner, cannot be explained in Austenian terms. It is instead a nervous stubbornness, a constitutional inability to forsake a cherished cathexis, which seems finally more physical than cerebral. Even in the terms of Trollope's narration it *makes no sense*; but that is, paradoxically, the sign of its authenticity, the sign of Lily's personhood. That this should be so in the novels of Trollope, whose interests were far from the world of physiological psychology, and whose narratives were similarly far from the explicitly physiological shocks of sensation fiction, shows us the extent to which the presuppositions of the physiological approach to mind were literally formative—that is, form-producing—for Victorian fiction.

Those same presuppositions are also evident in novels that do without third-person explanatory narration. One of the more remarkable documents of Victorian psychological portrayal, Charlotte Brontë's 1853 *Villette*, is devoted to its narrator's inscrutability. That this inscrutability is underwritten by a nervous breakdown is both obvious and beside the point; at all moments Lucy Snowe engages in a complicated narratorial game of hide-and-seek, in which characters and reader alike are castigated for their inability to penetrate a forbidding exterior, while the suggestion remains that perhaps nothing lies behind the exterior—nothing, that is, but a repetition of exterior signs. Actions are taken without explanation; emotions are cited but not traced to a source. Surfaces threaten to reveal interiors, then darken. Lucy Snowe is a reader of surfaces, and her readings yield what is essentially a mirror image, as in this glimpse, across a concert hall, of the King of Labaseecour:

I had never read, never been told anything of his nature or his habits; and at first the strong hieroglyphics graven as with iron stylet on his brow, round his eyes, beside his mouth, puzzled and baffled instinct. Ere long, however, if I did not know, *at least I* felt, *the meaning of those characters written without hand. There sat a silent sufferer—a nervous, melancholy man. Those eyes had looked on the visits of a certain ghost—had long waited the comings and goings of that strangest spectre, Hypochondria.* (Brontë 1979 [1853], 290)

Nervous maladies abound, and while they are legible on the surface of the body, they are described in the language of Gothic hauntings, as if any more particular source—such as, for instance, autobiography, the facts of a personal past—were beside the point. This elision of Damasio's autobiographical self is particularly striking in what is, after all, a fictional autobiography. Brontë and her narrator seem committed to the notion, common to physiological psychology as well as the more specific theories of mind that Brontë knew well, that interiority is constitutional rather than developmental, that the core self supersedes and renders merely accidental the facts of personal history.[6] In some very strange fashion, even narrative itself—the succession of incidents in a given story, the events that make up a reader's experience—is powerless to plumb the wordless depths of the mind's neural substrate. *Villette* is an extreme instance, but it is nonetheless representative of one of the strongest paradoxes of Victorian prose: the great age of autobiography was also the age most openly skeptical of the truths autobiography might yield.

George Eliot and the Scarcely Perceptible

With George Eliot, we have the nineteenth-century novelist most explicitly engaged with physiological psychology and its study of consciousness. As Lewes's partner and occasional scientific collaborator, Eliot was immersed firsthand in the experimental procedures of physiology—Lewes conducted many experiments on frogs at their Regent's Park home, The Priory, in a room adjacent to that in which Eliot wrote—as well as in the methodological debates around the meaning of consciousness to which Lewes's experiments directly pertained.[7] It is, therefore, no surprise that Eliot's descriptions of the mental processes of her characters continually revolve around new and varied formulations for what, following Palmer, we might call the nonconscious: the barely discernible background hum of biological homeostasis that is the neural root of all thought. In *Middlemarch* (1871–72), with characteristic irony, Eliot provides us with a physiological scientist, Tertius Lydgate, whose researches into the interrelations of different kinds of biological tissue leave him nonetheless incapable of self-comprehension. His work is thoroughly physiological: he strives in his laboratory toward a knowledge of "those minute processes which prepare human misery and joy . . . that delicate poise and transition which determine the growth of happy or unhappy consciousness" (Eliot 1988 [1872], 135). Yet he remains ignorant of the subtle, below-the-threshold roots of his infatuation with Rosamund Vincy.

Young love-making—that gossamer web! Even the points it clings to—the things whence its subtle interlacings are swung—are scarcely perceptible: momentary touches of finger-tips, meetings of rays from blue and dark orbs, unfinished phrases, lightest changes of cheek and lip, faintest tremors. The web itself is made of spontaneous beliefs and indefinable joys, yearnings of one life towards another, visions of completeness, indefinite trust. And Lydgate fell to spinning that web from his inward self with wonderful rapidity, in spite of experience supposed to be finished off with the drama of Laure—in spite too of medicine and biology. (Eliot 1988 [1872], 284)

The web is perhaps *Middlemarch*'s most famous metaphor, discussed in countless critical works. Yet its similarity to the web that most preoccupied Lewes—the network of human nerves—has gone unrecognized. Like that neural web, Lydgate's growing attachment to Rosamund is composed of minute sensations that obscurely, in some rapid and complex series of combinations, becomes not only an affect (desire) but a decision (to court her). The narrator is the only power in *Middlemarch* that can slow down mental time enough to be able to at least provisionally list some of the simple sensations out of which this combination is formed; Lydgate is conspicuously unable to perform this kind of self-analysis. The result in *Middlemarch*, as well as the later *Daniel Deronda* (1876), is the hallmark of Eliot's late work: a prolonged study of human behavior in dense social settings where real agency is never a possibility. Eliot's realism is thoroughly skeptical about individual agency, even the agency of introspection. Pivotal events—Lydgate's marriage to Rosamund, Dorothea's marriage to Casaubon, Bulstrode's role in the death of his blackmailer Raffles—are never quite *decisions*; they are instead simply *occurrences*, overdetermined confluences of numerous not-quite-perceptible causes, none of which has clear priority over the others.

When characters in Eliot's late realism attempt through introspection to sift through these causes, the result is usually either confusion or ethical failure. Nicholas Bulstrode prays after allowing his servant to administer to Raffles the liquor he suspects might kill him, but Eliot's narrator intervenes: "Does anyone suppose that private prayer is necessarily candid—necessarily goes to the roots of action? Private prayer is inaudible speech, and speech is representative; who can represent himself just as he is, even in his own reflections?" (Eliot 1988 [1872], 581). And when Bulstrode attempts to take a tour through his own memory, particularly the memory of the acts by which he separated Will Ladislaw from his legal inheritance, immersion in the past only excuses the actions of the past, makes them seem not only inevitable but even repeatable; as the narrator intones, "in the train of those images came their apology" (576). The physiological-psychological suspicion of the terminology of nonexperimental mental science, of such terms as "faculty," "association," the "unconscious," "imagination"—even the vexed term "consciousness"—lent itself to a general nominalist suspicion of language itself as opposed to the truths of biological experiment. Eliot's representations of conscious thought are similarly suspicious of linguistic representation. Unlike the confident terms of Elizabeth Bennet's self-castigating introspection, Bulstrode's self-analyses are necessarily second-order re-presentations, inherently false or misleading. The process whereby sensations are bonded into ideas is both too swift and too complex for language to encapsulate. The language of Eliot's narrators, a dense mixture of metaphor and guarded abstractions, is if more careful than the languages of her characters nonetheless not ontologically superior; the constitutively undescribable nature of consciousness renders any description a kind of approximation.[8]

Which is not to say that Eliot disowns ethical judgment; it is rather that the ethical and the psychological become in her realism discrete categories with nothing to say to each other. For Bulstrode to arrive at an ethically accurate sense of his past and present behavior, he must forgo introspection. For a reader to gain a thorough sense of the curiously accidental, contingent routes by which Raffles's death comes about, a complexly physiological psychology is necessary; but this complexity forestalls the judgment that Eliot nonetheless desires. In this sense physiological psychology, and the high realism of the nineteenth century that emerged from it, is decisively post-Kantian: the ethical cannot be in any way rooted in an account of mental processes. The necessary categories of ethics are in no way reflected in the findings of psychological science, which make relations of cause and effect, the basic causality necessary to assign blame and praise, almost impossible to decisively identify.

Eliot's narration thus faces an intellectually daunting task: to keep in productive tension both the psychological and the ethical without reducing the one to the other at any point. One result of this challenge is the highly abstract, even opaque quality of her narrators' discourse. Another result is her increasing interest in nervous, febrile psychologies—psychological types prone to erratic actions with no good causal lineage to explain them—and the ethically problematic events that befall them. In turn, a magnificent result of this interest is *Daniel Deronda*'s Gwendolen Harleth, the intensely nervous young woman prone to fits of terror. Her periodic moments of "hysterical violence"—occasioned by events both accidental and very much intentional—can be read as her body's acting out of its self-problematic state, as a way of asking: what am I? (Eliot 1967 [1876], 407). How am I related to the acts I have done, to events that can be judged? Insofar as the nervous body is both the site of psychological processes and also the subject of ethical judgment, it is confused, riven, fundamentally troubled. Gwendolen, that is, continually faces the impossible task of judging herself for actions that seem to have arisen from beyond the realm of personal responsibility, from some below-the-threshold realm of sensation.

It is only at the end of *Deronda* that a language adequate to address this problem is found, and it arises after the most clearly problematic of Eliot's scandal scenes: the drowning death of Henleigh Grandcourt, Gwendolen's despotic husband, during a boat ride taken with his wife. Gwendolen's subsequent account to Deronda is starkly different than the complexly subordinated syntax of Eliot's narration, but what it expresses is a similar effort: to hold psychology and ethics, the world of desire and the world of obligation, in some tension:

I remember then letting go the tiller and saying "God help me!" But then I was forced to take it again and go on; and the evil longings, the evil prayers came again and blotted everything else dim, till, in the midst of them—I don't know how it was—he was turning the sail—there was a gust—he was struck—I know nothing—I only know that I saw my wish outside me. (Eliot 1967 [1876], 761)

"I saw my wish outside me": this is the only possible form of self-alienation possible for consciousness in Eliot. Unlike the alienation of retrospection in Austen, which can be offset by a free indirect discourse confident in its relation to agency and judgment, Gwendolen can only recognize the foundational split between a desire and its actualization, without knowing how, or in what ways, inner springs created the outer reality. One can recognize one's wish, and one can recognize its presence in the world alongside other competing wishes and facts, and that is the best one can do. For the faculty psychologies that preceded physiological psychology, and also for the psychoanalytic paradigm that followed it, the relation between desire and action could be ascertained. But the physiological approach requires skepticism about the correlation between bodily and mental processes.

The Rise of Mass Selfhood

Even if, as I have been arguing, physiological psychology insisted on the logical fallacy of a notion of the unconscious, various other versions of the nonconscious flourished in the period, particularly as the century's end neared. Alongside the below-the-threshold sensations of physiology, there persisted the unconscious of mesmerism, which provided a model for the interpersonal dimensions of mental experience, and the newly emergent psychologies of evolutionary science, which offered behavioral explanations for the unconscious rooted in a more or less distant genetic past. Each model offered a distinct, even competing, version of what Dallas had posited as the key to aesthetics and the horizon of contemporary theory: the "secret flow of thought which is not less energetic than the conscious flow, an absent mind which haunts us like a ghost or a dream and is an essential part of our lives" (Dallas 1866, 1:199). Dallas was particularly talented at syncretizing disparate cultural or theoretical realms, and in the second volume of *The Gay Science* he noted the primary fact of these psychologies and the fiction written within their episteme: their erasure of personal, individual distinctiveness.

As Dallas described it, the lesson of contemporary fiction was "the withering of the individual as an exceptional hero, and his growth as a multiplicand unit" (Dallas 1866, 2:287). In this sense the novel of his time was true to the psychologies Dallas had studied: they were based in biological roots, roots which differed either not at all or in minor ways from organism to organism. A healthy, functioning nervous system works largely like every other; physiology was incapable, and uninterested, in difference—it sought to establish a *normative functioning of the mind*. Dallas saw this emphasis vividly presented not only in sensation fiction, where it might be expected to appear, but even in the most celebrated of multiplot realist fictions, Thackeray's *Vanity*

Fair, whose procedures Dallas ventriloquized as follows: "Let any two characters be as dissimilar as possible; let the circumstances in which they are placed be as opposite as the poles, I will prove that their natures are the same, and I do not doubt that, spite of our censures, we in their places would have acted precisely as they did" (Dallas 1866, 2:289). Individuality, for Dallas, was not the motive force of the contemporary novel; instead, its motive force was plot, a formal analogue for the intersubjectivity, or mass consciousness, that physiological psychology was devoted to describing. Read carefully, Dallas insisted, Victorian fiction reduced vividness and heroic agency to an average mass.

This is not, it bears remarking, the usual lesson historians of the novel have gleaned from Victorian fiction, which has instead been more typically described as producing increasingly vivid, three-dimensional, memorable, and sympathetic characters meant to encourage surrogate intimacies with readers. Attention to the links between physiological psychology and fictional representations of mental experience, however, might suggest otherwise. It might suggest a genre in which narrative voice was finally more distinctive than character; in which agency is dispersed into, or translated onto, plot rather than the decisions of characters, whereby *accident* becomes a category of considerable importance; in which somatic shocks take the place of language as an instrument of communication; in which deluded selves can only find understanding in an ontological frame—narration—to which they have no access. If canonical structuralist accounts of plot, from Vladimir Propp to the present, place an Aristotelian emphasis on character as agent (as defined by agency), Victorian fiction suggests the importance of a category—narrative voice—that narratologists have struggled to fit into these Aristotelian frames. Put another way, nervousness—the life of the nerves rather than, or even *as*, the life of the mind—suggests a new way to understand the stresses and complexities of the Victorian narration of consciousness.

Notes

1. See Taylor (1988) and Winter (1998, 320–31) for the most detailed treatments of sensation fiction's relation to the mental sciences.

2. For a fuller history of the links between literary theory and physiological psychology, see Dames (2007). Useful sources for the primary texts of Victorian physiology can be found in Taylor and Shuttleworth (1998), while Boring (1957), Ellenberger (1970), Danzinger (1982), Clarke and Jacyna (1987), and Reed (1997) provide ample contextualization of physiological psychology within the wider history of European theories of mind.

3. For a compelling argument against such neurophysiological reductivism, see Varela, Thompson, and Rosch (1991), whose alternative, enactivist approach David Herman discusses in his contribution to this volume.

4. Rick Rylance's study of Victorian mental theories offers a thorough account of Lewes's many metaphorical attempts to marry the indivisible units of consciousness with some larger synthesis (Rylance 2000, 309).

5. Ferguson (2000) offers the most recent defense of the idea that free indirect style is the primary formal innovation of the novel, and that the formal analysis of fiction is therefore essentially based on the relation between narration and character. Dames (2007) challenges this notion by arguing that the criticism written by Victorian physiologists suggests alternate ways of conceptualizing novelistic form.

6. Brontë was notable for her interest in Victorian mental theories that were less officially sanctioned than physiology, such as phrenology and physiognomy; Shuttleworth (1996) and Dames (2001, 76–124) each offer contextualizations of her work in the light of these so-called pseudosciences.

7. See Shuttleworth (1984) for the fullest account of Eliot's engagement with Victorian theories of mind, particularly the nascent biological sciences such as physiology.

8. I am indebted here to Logan (1997, 166–96) for his account of nervousness, or hysteria, and representation in *Middlemarch*.

References

Austen, Jane. 1982 [1813]. *Pride and Prejudice*. Ed. R. W. Chapman. Oxford: Oxford University Press.

Bain, Alexander. 1865. *The Emotions and the Will*. London: Longmans, Green.

Boring, Edwin. 1957. *A History of Experimental Psychology*. New York: Appleton-Century-Crofts.

Brontë, Charlotte. 1979 [1853]. *Villette*. Ed. Mark Lilly. Harmondsworth: Penguin.

Clarke, Edwin, and L. S. Jacyna. 1987. *Nineteenth-Century Origins of Neuroscientific Concepts*. Berkeley: University of California Press.

Collins, Wilkie. 1973 [1860]. *The Woman in White*. Ed. Harvey Peter Sucksmith. Oxford: Oxford University Press.

Dallas, E. S. 1866. *The Gay Science*. London: Chapman and Hall.

Damasio, Antonio. 2000. *The Feeling of What Happens: Body and Emotion in the Making of Consciousness*. New York: Harcourt.

Dames, Nicholas. 2001. *Amnesiac Selves: Nostalgia, Forgetting, and British Fiction, 1810–1870*. Oxford: Oxford University Press.

———. 2007. *The Physiology of the Novel: Reading, Neural Science, and the Form of Victorian Fiction*. Oxford: Oxford University Press.

Danzinger, Kurt. 1982. "Mid-Nineteenth-Century British Psycho-Physiology: A Neglected Chapter in the History of Psychology." In *The Problematic Science: Psychology in Nineteenth-Century Thought*, ed. W. R. Woodward and M. G. Gash, 119–46. New York: Praeger.

Eliot, George. 1967 [1876]. *Daniel Deronda*. Ed. Barbara Hardy. Harmondsworth: Penguin.

———. 1988 [1872]. *Middlemarch: A Study of Provincial Life*. Ed. David Carroll. Oxford: Oxford University Press.

Ellenberger, Henri. 1970. *The Discovery of the Unconscious: The History and Evolution of Dynamic Psychiatry*. New York: Basic Books.

Ferguson, Frances. 2000. "Jane Austen, *Emma*, and the Impact of Form." *Modern Language Quarterly* 61:157–80.

Lewes, G. H. 1860. *The Physiology of Common Life*. 2 vols. London: Blackwood.

———. 1872. "Dickens in Relation to Criticism." *Fortnightly Review* 17:143–51.

Logan, Peter Melville. 1997. *Nerves and Narratives: A Cultural History of Hysteria in Nineteenth-Century British Prose*. Berkeley: University of California Press.

Mansel, H. L. 1863. "Sensation Novels." *Quarterly Review* 113:482–514.

Meredith, George. 1968 [1879]. *The Egoist*. Ed. George Woodcock. Harmondsworth: Penguin.

Oliphant, Margaret. 1862. "Sensation Novels." *Blackwood's Edinburgh Magazine* 91:565–74.

Palmer, Alan. 2004. *Fictional Minds*. Lincoln: University of Nebraska Press.

Reed, Edward. 1997. *From Soul to Mind: The Emergence of Psychology, from Erasmus Darwin to William James*. New Haven: Yale University Press.

Rylance, Rick. 2000. *Victorian Psychology and British Culture, 1850–1880*. Oxford: Oxford University Press.

Shuttleworth, Sally. 1984. *George Eliot and Nineteenth-Century Science: The Make Believe of a Beginning*. Cambridge: Cambridge University Press.

———. 1996. *Charlotte Brontë and Victorian Psychology*. Cambridge: Cambridge University Press.

Taylor, Jenny Bourne. 1988. *In the Secret Theatre of Home: Wilkie Collins, Sensation Narrative, and Nineteenth-Century Psychology*. London: Routledge.

Taylor, Jenny Bourne, and Sally Shuttleworth, eds. 1998. *Embodied Selves: An Anthology of Psychological Texts, 1830–1890*. Oxford: Clarendon Press.

Trollope, Anthony. 1980 [1864]. *The Small House at Allington*. Ed. James Kincaid. Oxford: Oxford University Press.

Varela, Francisco, Evan Thompson, and Eleanor Rosch. 1991. *The Embodied Mind: Cognitive Science and Human Experience*. Cambridge MA: MIT Press.

Winter, Alison. 1998. *Mesmerized: Powers of Mind in Victorian Fiction*. Chicago: University of Chicago Press.

Part IV

Remodeling the Mind in
Modernist and Postmodernist Narrative

8. 1880–1945
Re-minding Modernism
DAVID HERMAN

> But she [Clarissa Dalloway] said, sitting on the bus
> going up Shaftesbury Avenue, she felt herself every-
> where; not 'here, here, here'; and she tapped the back
> of the seat; but everywhere. . . . Odd affinities she had
> with people she had never spoken to, some woman in
> the street, some man behind a counter—even trees,
> or barns.—Virginia Woolf, *Mrs Dalloway*

For many historians and theorists of the novel, the modernist
novel marked (for better or worse) a turning point in the development of methods for representing fictional minds. For these
commentators, despite their surface differences modernist authors
shared a common project: the project of foregrounding, whether
formally or thematically (or both), the nature and scope of the
experiences falling within the domain of the mental, including
sense impressions, emotions, memories, associative thought patterns, and so on. Thus, according to analysts ranging from Leon
Edel to F. K. Stanzel, from Ian Watt to Georg Lukács, modernist writers, departing from the course taken by their nineteenth-
century predecessors, shifted their emphasis from the detailed
profiling and authentication of the fictional worlds in which characters' experiences unfold to capturing the mental or psychological texture of those lived experiences themselves.[1] Or, to put the
same claim another way, the modernist accent falls less on fictional worlds than on fictional-worlds-as-experienced.

The later Henry James set a key precedent by using what he
called reflectors, or centers of consciousness providing vantage
points on the storyworld, to dramatize how events are experienced by fictional minds.[2] Stephen Dedalus famously functions

as a reflector in the opening paragraphs of James Joyce's *A Portrait of the Artist as a Young Man*; this 1916 *Künstlerroman* traces the development of the protagonist and the emergence of his desire to fly by the nets of "nationality, language, religion" so as to be able to "forge in the smithy of my soul the uncreated conscience of my race" (Joyce 1964 [1916], 203, 253). The beginning of the novel represents not only Simon Dedalus telling his very young son a story but also the quality of Stephen's experience as he engages with that narrative; the father's storytelling act is refracted through the perceptions of a child still in the process of acquiring basic linguistic competence:

> *Once upon a time and a very good time it was there was a moocow coming down along the road and this moocow that was coming down along the road met a nicens little boy named baby tuckoo. . . .*
>
> *His father told him that story: his father looked at him through a glass: he had a hairy face.* (Joyce 1964 [1916], 7)

Similarly, in her 1925 novel *Mrs Dalloway* Virginia Woolf developed a distinctive "mind-style" (Fowler 1977; Shen 2005) for Septimus Smith, a shell-shocked veteran of the First World War who suffers from hallucinations and eventually commits suicide.[3] In the following passage, Woolf uses Septimus not just to thematize mental disability but moreover to enact how the world is experienced by someone suffering from psychotic delusions:

> *But he would not go mad [sitting with his wife, Rezia, in Regent's Park in London]. He would shut his eyes; he would see no more.*
>
> *But they beckoned; leaves were alive; trees were alive. And the leaves being connected by millions of fibres with his own body, there on the seat, fanned it up and down; when the branch stretched he, too, made that statement. The sparrows fluttering, rising, and falling in jagged fountains were part of the pattern; the white and blue, barred with black branches. Sounds made harmonies with premeditation; the spaces between them were as significant as the sounds. A child cried. Rightly far away a horn sounded. All taken together meant the birth of a new religion—*
>
> *"Septimus!" said Rezia. He started violently.* (Woolf 1953 [1925], 22)

In the novel as a whole, Woolf adapts the method that Joyce used in his follow-up to *Portrait*, *Ulysses* (1922), which likewise deploys a constellation of minds (and mind-styles) to explore, from multiple perspectives, the multifaceted texture of lived experience on a single day.

As the previous excerpts suggest, by employing Jamesian reflectors writers such as Joyce and Woolf were also able to build on Gustave Flaubert's pioneering experiments with free indirect discourse, suffusing third-person narrative reports with the subjectivity and sometimes the language of the characters whose actions are being recounted. The discourse of narration can thus embed, more or less overtly, characters' own construal of events. For example, in a scene in *Portrait* in which Stephen walks near the sea after he has chosen to become an artist rather than pursue a career as a Jesuit priest, Joyce's third-person narration moves along a spectrum that ranges from relatively distanced reports of Stephen's actions—"He turned seaward from the road at Dollymount and as he passed on to the thin wooden bridge he felt the planks shaking with the tramp of heavily shod feet" (Joyce 1964 [1916], 165)—to passages in which the narration becomes a proxy for Stephen's thought processes, even as the broader context ironically undercuts Stephen's rather breathless (self-) assessments—"Did he then love [phrases like "A day of dappled seaborne clouds" because,] being as weak of sight as he was shy of mind, he drew less pleasure from the reflection of the glowing sensible world through the prism of a language manycoloured and richly storied than from the contemplation of an inner world of individual emotions mirrored perfectly in a lucid supple periodic prose?" (Joyce 1964 [1916], 166–67).[4]

To be sure, earlier instances of third-person or heterodiegetic narration likewise run the gamut from giving relatively distanced accounts of characters' situations and actions, thereby aligning themselves with what Stanzel (1984 [1979]) characterized as the authorial narrative situation, to providing reports colored by characters' own sense of what is going on, thereby exemplifying the figural narrative situation.[5] Take May Sinclair's 1907 novel *The Helpmate*, which focuses on the experiences of Anne

Majendie, who, shortly after being married, discovers that her husband, Walter, was involved in a two-year affair with another woman. This text predates Sinclair's more self-consciously experimental works like *Mary Olivier* (1919), which was patterned after the novels of Dorothy Richardson, among others. In *The Helpmate*, the narrative features fairly extensive passages reporting aspects of the characters' situations of which they are not even aware; it also includes scenes in which characters' perceptions and inferences merge with the discourse of narration. The less subjectivized style of recounting can be found in the following excerpt, which authoritatively reports what Anne does not recognize about herself when she forms the resolution to leave her home every time her husband invites for dinner a friend of whom she does not approve: "There were moments, Anne might have owned, when he [Walter] did not fail in sympathy and comprehension. Had she been capable of self-criticism, she would have found that her attitude of protest was a moral luxury, and that moral luxuries were a necessity to natures such as hers. But Anne had a secret, cherishing eye on martyrdom, and it was intolerable to her to be reminded in this way that, after all, she was only a spiritual voluptuary" (Sinclair 1907, 185). By contrast, after Anne hears one of Canon Wharton's sermons, about the need to be charitable toward others, the narration is refracted through Anne's thought processes as she reflects on her own treatment of Walter's dinner guest: "The problem it had raised remained with her [Anne], oppressed, tormented her. What she had done had seemed to her so good. But if, after all, she had done wrong? If she had failed in charity?" (201).

Overall, however, Sinclair's text features a more "distanced" narrative style than *Portrait* or *Mrs Dalloway*. More precisely, there is in Sinclair's novel both a greater preponderance of reports that comment on situations outside the characters' ken (cf. pages 5, 16–17, 63, 86–87, 123, 135, 183, 191) and a tendency for the narration to present itself as a more authoritative (or authenticated) account of the fictional world than does Joyce's or Woolf's. These claims provide support for interpretations of Sinclair as a protomodernist author (Kunka and Troy 2006; Raitt 2000), whose earlier works remain grounded in the realist techniques against which a later generation of writers began by reacting. At the same time, comparing Sinclair with Joyce and Woolf bolsters Stanzel's (1984 [1979]) suggestion that the figural method, where hetero-diegetic narration recounts events filtered through the focalizing perceptions of a reflector figure, is a distinctively modernist technique, beginning to appear in high concentrations only as the late nineteenth gave way to the early twentieth century (see also Cohn 1978, 26).

But beyond shifting from the authorial to the figural narrative situation as their preferred method of narration, and thus interweaving with reports of events characters' spoken or unspoken perceptions, inferences, memories, and evaluations, modernist writers also sought to develop an even finer-grained representation of the form and flow of mental activities as they unfolded in time. To this end, they used a technique that Sinclair, borrowing a term from the psychologist William James in her 1918 review of Dorothy Richardson's fiction, dubbed "stream of consciousness."[6] As Gerald Prince (2003) suggests, stream-of-consciousness technique can be viewed as a specific kind or modality of interior monologue. In this usage, "interior monologue" is a cover term that applies to more or less extended passages of free direct discourse; at issue is discourse that, though stripped of quotation marks and tag phrases such as "she reflected" or "he wondered," can be assumed to correspond to or quote the unexpressed thoughts of a character. But stream of consciousness does not just quote thoughts; more than that it "focus[es] on the random flow of thought and stress[es] its illogical, 'ungrammatical,' associative nature" (Prince 2003, 94). Thus when Stephen's conscience is tormented by Father Arnall's sermon during the retreat at Belvedere College, the emphasized material in the following passage can be characterized as interior monologue, but not of the stream-of-consciousness variety: "His soul sickened at the thought of a torpid snaky life feeding itself out of the tender marrow of his life and fattening upon the slime of lust. *O why was that so? O why?*" (Joyce 1964 [1916], 139–40; emphasis added). By contrast, in the final episode of Joyce's *Ulysses*, the narration purports to capture not just the contents but also the associative patterns of Molly's thoughts, with Joyce omitting punctuation to suggest a raw, unfiltered presentation of the movements of Molly's mind:

well theyre not going to get my husband again into their clutches if I can help it making fun of him then behind his back I know well when he goes on with his idiotics because he has sense enough not to squander every penny piece he earns down their gullets and looks after his wife and family goodfornothings poor Paddy Dignam all the same Im sorry in a way for him what are his wife and 5 children going to do unless he was insured comical little teetotum always stuck up in some pub corner. (Joyce 1986 [1922], 636)

In sum, the claim that modernist writers shifted the accent from fictional worlds to fictional-worlds-as-experienced finds support in their frequent use of reflectors, each with a more or less distinctive mind-style, to interweave the discourse of narration with characters' construal of events (whether verbalized or not), and to underscore thereby how any narrative report is anchored in a particular perspective on what is reported. The claim finds backing, too, in the modernists' thematization of mental (in)capacities through the experiences of characters such as Septimus Smith and their quotation of mental contents via interior monologue, some of it purporting to capture the moment-by-moment flow of consciousness itself. But how much of a shift in accent, a departure from the practices of nineteenth-century realism (as characterized for example by Nicholas Dames in the preceding chapter in this volume), did these modernist methods actually entail? Further, to the extent that the modernists did innovate on previous narrative practices, how might the general tenor of their innovations best be described—as a movement inward, an exploration of the mind viewed as an interior space, or in some other way? Is a concern with worlds-as-experienced in fact tantamount to an "inward turn"? More generally, what is the relation between modernist representations of the mind and frameworks developed by analysts investigating, across a number of fields, the nature and scope of the mental?

In what follows I sketch out strategies for addressing these issues. My next section reviews motivations for—and manifestations of—what has become something of a critical commonplace about modernist narratives: namely, that they participate in an inward turn, innovating on previous narratives by developing new means to probe psychological depths. I then suggest grounds for rethinking (and rejecting) this commonplace, arguing instead that modernist narratives can both be illuminated by and help illuminate postcognitivist accounts of the mind as inextricably embedded in contexts for action and interaction. Particularly relevant, in this connection, are enactivist frameworks (Thompson 2007; Torrance 2005; Varela, Thompson, and Rosch 1991) that move away from older, Cartesian geographies of the mental as an interior, immaterial domain; enactivists instead characterize the mind in terms of sensorimotor coupling between intelligent agents and the social and material environments that they must negotiate. Drawing on this research, I develop a critique of the continuum or scale that has organized prior research on techniques of consciousness representation in modernist narratives—namely, the scale stretching from the mind inside to the world outside. In critiquing the Cartesian premises of this scale, I do not dispute the assumption that the sorts of techniques just cataloged (the use of reflectors or centers of consciousness to narrate events, extended representations of characters' thought patterns, and so forth) appear in higher concentrations in modernist texts like Joyce's than in earlier narratives. Rather, my chapter proposes a different way of contextualizing those techniques and interpreting their functions.

Specifically, I seek to replace the internal-external scale with a continuum stretching between, at one pole, a tight coupling between an intelligent agent and that agent's surrounding environment, and, at the other pole, a looser coupling between agent and environment. From this perspective, rather than being interpreted as signs of an inward turn or a probing of psychological depths segregated from the material world, modernist techniques for representing consciousness can be seen as an attempt to highlight how minds at once shape and are shaped by larger experiential environments, via the particular affordances or opportunities for action that those environments provide. Modernist narratives, in other words, stage the moment-by-moment construction of worlds-as-experienced through an interplay between agent and environment. In this way, the study of modernist texts can contribute to and not just be informed by postcognitivist approaches to mind, underscoring the relevance of traditions of narrative analysis for research on human intelligence.

Beyond the Inward Turn

In their critical writing, twentieth-century authors like James and Woolf themselves helped establish a precedent for viewing modernism as contributing to what Erich Kahler described as the "inward turn" of narrative, a movement away from characters' environments for acting and interacting to the domain of the mental or psychological, characterized as an interior space separated from external, material reality. Although the historical trajectory traced in Kahler's study ends before the modernist period, his emphasis on a "progressive internalization [*Verinnerung*] of events" resonates with (and may have been influenced by) accounts of early twentieth-century fiction—both the programmatic accounts offered by modernist writers themselves and also the accounts developed by critics of modernism ex post facto. Thus in Kahler's characterization the inward turn involves "an increasing displacement of outer space by what Rilke has called inner space, a stretching of consciousness" that "brings with it an incorporation, an internalization, of more and more of the objective world" (1973 [1970], 5). Similarly, in her 1919 essay on "Modern Fiction" Woolf rejected the "materialism" of H. G. Wells, Arnold Bennett, and John Galsworthy, who "write of unimportant things" and rely on traditional plot mechanisms to create "an air of probability embalming the whole" (Woolf 1984 [1919], 148, 149). With these custom-bound methods Woolf contrasted those used by Joyce, who is "spiritual" rather than materialist and who seeks to "record the atoms as they fall upon the mind in the order in which they fall [and to] trace the pattern, however disconnected and incoherent in appearance, which each sight or incident scores upon the consciousness" (150). In other words, Joyce "is concerned at all costs to reveal the flickerings of that innermost flame which flashes its messages through the brain, and in order to preserve it he disregards with complete courage whatever seems to him adventitious, whether it be probability, or coherence, or any other of these signposts which for generations have served to support the imagination of a reader" (151). To extrapolate: "for the moderns . . . the point of interest . . . lies very likely in the dark places of psychology" (152).

This account of modernist narrative as an exploration of psychological depths, an attempt to move away from the external world to map out an interior, mental domain, has functioned for many commentators as a literary-historical given. Thus, quoting from early twentieth-century critics such as R. A. Scott-James and Elizabeth Drew, who noted then-contemporary writers' concern with psychology and psychological analysis, Randall Stevenson (1992) points up the "heightened concern with individual, subjective consciousness" as a defining trait of modernist fiction (2). Similarly, Jesse Matz (2006) suggests that "the modern novel's close attention to individual human psychology" entailed a "'movement inward' that was perhaps its most symptomatic feature" (220; cf. Matz 2004, 15–19). Kaplan (1975), focusing on twentieth-century female authors, argues that like their male counterparts women writers "found it necessary to break with tradition by shifting their focus from the outer world to the inner, from the confident omniscient narrator to the limited point of view, from plot to patterning, and from action to thinking and dreaming" (1–2). The question, for these analysts, is not whether modernism involved an inward turn but rather how to assess that turn's scope and significance.

For Leon Edel, who in his influential 1955 study of *The Psychological Novel* suggests that "the most characteristic aspect of twentieth-century fiction [is] its inward turning to convey the flow of mental experience" (7), the modernist break with nineteenth-century novelistic methods is a radical but productive one. Edel argues that "subjective novels" such as Joyce's invite the reader to enter into a new contract with the author, saying (in so many words): "'Here is the artistic record of a mind, at the very moment that it is thinking. Try to penetrate within it. You will still know only as much as this mind may reveal. It is you, not I, who will piece together any "story" there may be. Of course I have arranged his illusion for you. But it is you who must experience it'" (34). For Georg Lukács, by contrast, the inward turn of modernist narrative, its foregrounding of subjective awareness, is a symptom of its reactionary disengagement from the web of social forces and circumstances of which the great realist writers of the nineteenth century at least tried to take stock. In Lukács's view, modernist fiction, by failing to situate events within a larger chain of occurrences in a richly social context, replaced narration with description (1971 [1936]). In turn, this modernist refusal to narrate resulted in the "attenuation of reality" and, relatedly, the "dissolution of personality," whereby fictional characters are "reduced to a sequence of unrelated experiential fragments," becoming "as inexplicable to others as to [themselves]" (26). Notwithstanding the technical brilliance of Joyce, Proust, and other modernist writers, for Lukács their emphasis on individual consciousness bears the stigmata of alienation, substituting randomly triggered sense data for the purposeful, richly *inter*subjective world of the nineteenth-century realist novel.

Accounts of modernist representations of mind thus raise several, cross-cutting issues, including (1) the extent to which modernism marks a genuine break with realism and, if so, (2) whether to characterize that development in positive or negative terms. Also in question is whether (3) a focus on worlds-as-experienced should indeed be described as an inward turn. Part of the project of "re-minding modernism," as it is conceived in this chapter, entails separating out these different issues and exploring the logical configurations into which they can enter. As already indicated, the view that modernism marks a break from realism is consistent with both positive, negative, and neutral assessments of that break; such assessments are offered by commentators like Edel, Lukács, and Stanzel, respectively. But it is also possible to hold that modernist narratives move from external reality to an inner mental domain without viewing modernism as being fundamentally discontinuous with realism, pace Lukács. For example, Matz (2006) suggests that "the modern novel searches for a new realism in the actual incoherence of the human mind" (220). Along similar lines, Lewis (2007) writes that the modernists do not reject "realism in the broad sense defined by [Ian] Watt. Rather, they [tilt] the balance toward what Watt called a 'realism of presentation,' trying to show not necessarily how things really are, but how things are experienced, what it feels like to be alive" (158). And for her part, Fernighough (2007) argues that whereas Woolf's stated goal was to rid the novel of physical and material clutter bequeathed to her by the Edwardians, "there is a sense in which the stream-of-consciousness writer transmutes physical into psychological clutter, into a superabundancy of impressions and memories" (71–72).

As the list of issues included in my previous paragraph suggests, there is another, underexplored approach to modernist methods of representing minds. In this permutation, the claim would be that, though modernist narratives did in fact depart from realist protocols, this departure involved not an inward turning but rather a foregrounding of the inextricable interconnection between "inner" and "outer" domains—with the scare quotes indicating the extent to which the narratives in question undermine the classical, Cartesian dichotomy between mind and body, the mental and the material. Arguably, instead of moving inward, or shifting their focus from public environments for action to a private, interior domain of cognition and contemplation, modernist writers pointed to the inseparability of perceiving and thinking from acting and interacting. What modernist narratives suggest, on this reading, is that mental states have the character they do because of the world in which they arise, as a way of responding to possibilities (and exigencies) for acting afforded by that world. Narratives written during this period can thus be placed in productive dialogue with recent models of the mind as distributed across brain, body, and world (Clark and Chalmers 1998; Clark 1997, 1998, 2008; Rowlands 2009); rather than giving support to the notion of an inward turn, such models call into question the internal-external axis as a principle for mapping the relation be-tween mind and world. To put the same point another way, the upshot of modernist experimentation was not to plumb psycho-logical depths, but to spread the mind abroad—to suggest that human psychology has the profile it does because of the extent to which it is interwoven with worldly circumstances. The mind does not reside within; instead, it emerges through humans' dy-namic interdependencies with the social and material environ-ments they seek to navigate.

Remapping Modernism/Modernist Remappings: New Geographies of Mind

As some of the comments quoted in my previous section suggest, a prominent conception of mental phenomena is buttressed by a Cartesian geography of the mental, whereby the mind consti-tutes an interior space separated off from the world at large. In turn, frameworks for studying narrative representations of mind have inherited this Cartesian geography of mind. Analysts typi-cally identify an array of positions or increments along an inter-nal-external scale to which various methods of narration can be assigned—with some more proximal to the internal domain of the mind being represented, others closer to the characters' out-ward actions and thus more distally related to mind. For example, Stanzel (1984 [1979]) sought to mark off the authorial narrative situation from both the first-person and figural narrative situ-ations by proposing a continuum that stretches from noniden-tity to identity between the narrator and the protagonist—that is, from a position external to the protagonist's experiences to one that is internal to those experiences. Similarly, Leech and Short (2007 [1981], 276–77) suggest that methods of thought rep-resentation can be mapped out along a cline or scale stretching from relatively externalized views of characters' minds, which they term "narrative reports of thought acts" (e.g., *Leah sat and thought about home*), to progressively more internalized views, ranging from indirect thought (*Leah sat and thought how far away home seemed*), to free indirect thought (*Leah sat there quietly; home seemed so far away now*), to direct thought (*Leah sat there quietly* and thought, "Home is so far away"), to free direct thought (*Leah sat there quietly. Home is so far away*). Leech and Short argue furthermore that the norm for or default mode of thought representation moved rightward along this scale, from indirect thought to free indirect thought, as the nineteenth-century novel gave way to the twentieth-century novel. In other words, because of their interest in the "internal drama of the minds of their characters [writers such as Woolf and Joyce] moved the narrative focus of their *stories* into those minds" (277).[7]

By contrast, my argument is that modernist narratives figure a different geography of mind; in place of Cartesian mappings of the mental as a bracketed-off interior space, these texts allow the mind to be imagined as a kind of distributional flow, interwoven with rather than separated from situations, events, and processes in the world. The main business of this section is to consider how modernist modes of narration, when placed in dialogue with recent research in the sciences of mind, suggest the need to rethink the scope and validity of the scalar models of consciousness representation mentioned in my previous paragraph — models linked to an internalist conception of mind that is arguably called into question, rather than reinforced, by early twentieth-century narratives. But note that a post-Cartesian remapping of the mind also emerges as a theme in the passage from *Mrs Dalloway* that I have used as my epigraph. Though Woolf herself, in her essay on "Modern Fiction," had emphasized the need to capture the "innermost flame [flashing] its messages through the brain" with "as little mixture of the alien and external as possible" (1984 [1919], 150, 151), Woolf's protagonist resists situating self and other, mind and world, along an internal-external polarity. Instead, in accordance with a remark once made by Clarissa that is filtered through the memory of Peter Walsh some thirty years later, and that thus exemplifies its own semantic content, "to know her, or any one, one must seek out the people who completed them; even the places" (1953 [1925], 153).[8]

When the convergence of research in psychology, neuroscience, linguistics, computer science, and other fields led to the birth of first-wave cognitive science in the mid-twentieth century

(Gardner 1985), the Cartesian geography repudiated by Clarissa Dalloway (and mocked in Beckett's *Murphy*) lent support to an understanding of the mental sometimes characterized as *cognitivism*. As Varela, Thompson, and Rosch (1991) put it, in a study that has become a touchstone for postcognitivist research on mind, "cognitivism consists in the hypothesis that cognition . . . is the manipulation of symbols after the fashion of digital computers. In other words, cognition is mental representation: the mind is thought to operate by manipulating symbols that represent features of the world or represent the world as being a certain way. According to this cognitivist hypothesis, the study of cognition qua mental representation provides the proper domain of cognitive science" (8). Cognitivism thus reinstitutes a conception of mind rejected by the behaviorists, who considered the domain of the mental to be epiphenomenal rather than genuinely explanatory of human conduct, but redefines the mind as an information-processing device—the dominant metaphor of cognitivism being the mind as a software program that runs on the hardware of the physical brain (Harré and Gillett 1994, 17–34).

In contrast with this cognitivist approach, Varela, Thompson, and Rosch themselves influentially proposed an alternative orientation for the study of mind, using the term *"enactive* [or *enactivism*] to emphasize the growing conviction that cognition is not the representation of a pregiven world by a pregiven mind but is rather the enactment of a world and a mind on the basis of a history of the variety of actions that a being in the world performs" (9). Enactivism can be viewed as part of a constellation of postcognitivist approaches that also includes work on the extended mind, or how intelligence is distributed across social groups as well as physical structures (as with crews in airplane cockpits) (Clark 1997, 1998, 2008; Clark and Chalmers 1998; Hutchins 1995a, 1995b; Vygotsky 1978)[9]; research on the physical embodiment of minds, whether individually or in contexts of social interaction (Gallagher 2005; Johnson 1987); and discursive-psychological accounts of the mind as oriented to and accounted for in systematic, norm-governed ways by participants in multiperson episodes of talk (Harré and Gillett 1994; Herman

2007).[10] In parallel with these other approaches, enactivists seek to steer a course between the Scylla of viewing mental activities as recovering a pregiven outer world and the Charybdis of seeing those activities as projecting a pregiven inner world. Indeed, Varela, Thompson, and Rosch's "intention is to bypass entirely the logical geography of inner versus outer by studying cognition not as recovery or projection but as embodied action. . . . Thus the overall concern of an enactive approach to perception is not to determine how some perceiver-independent world is to be recovered; it is, rather, to determine the common principles and lawful linkages between sensory and motor systems that explain how action can be perceptually guided in a perceiver-dependent world" (172, 173).

The enactivist approach shares with other postcognitivist work a rejection of internalist, sandwich models of cognition as an interior buffer space between, on the one hand, perceptual inputs and, on the other, output that takes the form of behaviors or actions (Hurley 1998a, 1998b). Instead, mental states can be viewed as both shaped by and contributing to action possibilities, or what Gibson (1979) characterized as *affordances*, more or less tightly imbricated with local environments for acting.[11] The mind is "action-centered," such that "perception is tangled up with specific possibilities of action—so tangled up, in fact, that the job of central cognition often ceases to exist," and the intuitive divisions between perception, action, and cognition no longer hold (Clark 1997, 36, 50; Gangopadhyay and Kiverstein 2009). Accordingly, enactivists and others developing postcognitivist models maintain that intelligent agents "do not operate on the basis of internal representations in the subjectivist/objectivist sense. Instead of internally representing an external world in some Cartesian sense, they enact an environment inseparable from their own structure and actions. . . . In phenomenological language, they constitute (disclose) a world that bears the stamp of their own structure" (Thompson 2007, 59).

Modernist writers, rather than making an "inward turn," likewise foreground how intelligent agents navigate a world in which perception and cognition are guided by possibilities for acting, or affordances that arise from their own evolving interactions with surrounding physical and sociocultural environments. Modernist narratives figure this post-Cartesian geography of the mental not only by thematizing the extended or distributed nature of mind but also by developing techniques for emulating the mind's moment-by-moment experiences of and engagement with the world. Through these techniques, modernists put characters' mental states and dispositions into circulation with the possibilities for action and interaction that, from a postcognitivist perspective, help constitute the mind in the first place.

Consider, for example, this scene in Joyce's *Portrait*, which takes place when Stephen goes to the chapel across town to confess after hearing Father Arnall's sermon about hell:

> *The slide was shot back. A penitent emerged from the farther side of the box. The near slide was drawn. A penitent entered when the other penitent came out. . . . A soft whispering noise floated in vaporous cloudlets out of the box. It was the woman: soft whispering cloudlets, soft whispering vapour, whispering and vanishing.*
>
> *He beat his breast with his fist humbly, secretly under cover of the wooden armrest. He would be at one with others and with God. He would love his neighbor. . . . It was a terrible and a sad thing to sin. But God was merciful to poor sinners who were truly sorry. How true that was! That was indeed goodness.*
>
> *The slide was shot to suddenly. The penitent came out. He was next. He stood up in terror and walked blindly into the box.*
>
> *At last it had come. He knelt in the silent gloom and raised his eyes to the white crucifix suspended above him. God could see that he was sorry.*
> (Joyce 1964 [1916], 142–43)

This passage can be read against the grain of received traditions for studying early twentieth-century techniques for representing minds, whereby textual elements are arranged along a scale stretching from inner to outer domains and the preponderance of internal elements is taken to be the signature of modernist methods. Figuring a tight coupling of intelligent agent and broader environment, Joyce's text suggests how the history of Stephen's interactions with his material and social surroundings give rise to the world that he experiences or enacts. Thus, thanks in part to Stephen's past interactions with similar built environments and his familiarity with protocols for inhabiting and using them, the interior layout of the chapel affords opportunities for performing actions in a particular sequence. These actions include opening or closing the sliding door of a confessional booth, entering or exiting the booth, kneeling or rising from a kneeling position, and initiating, continuing, or concluding the process of confession through structured verbal interchanges with the officiating priest. Reciprocally, Stephen's action-oriented perception of his environment is shot through with his cognitive grasp of the behavioral protocols associated with confessional practices inside churches. Further, when the language of narration suggests that Stephen is aestheticizing or poeticizing the sound of woman's confession—"It was the woman: soft whispering cloudlets, soft whispering vapour, whispering and vanishing"—another aspect of his cultural situation, knowledge of poetic practices, is interwoven with Stephen's action-oriented perception and his understanding of the institutional protocols governing acts of confession. The passage in fact reflects a tension between two systems of understanding, religious and poetic/aesthetic, and suggests the extent to which Stephen oscillates between them, switching back and forth between two ways of orienting himself within his environment via two competing sets of action possibilities. But my broader point is that the passage points up the way any time slice of experience involves construing the world in terms of action possibilities that are understood to be afforded by a given environment—with different construal systems yielding different kinds of affordances and hence different perceptions of what is going on.

Joyce's text thus militates against the styles of analysis that have been brought to bear on narratives like *Portrait*. Instead of categorizing the elements of experience in terms of an internal-external polarity, the passage suggests how embodied actions are entailed by construals of the environment, which for their part entail perceptions, inferences, and other mental states that reciprocally regulate a cognitive agent's navigation of his or her environment, or enactment of a world. When Stephen beats his fist against his breast *humbly*, the adverb indexes, to be sure, Stephen's own construal of this action; but that construal itself emerges from the combined operation of factors that cut across any assumed internal-external divide: familiarity with institutional protocols, knowledge of practical routines prescribed (and proscribed) by those protocols, (self-)perceptions guided by the possibilities for action nested, in turn, in the practical routines, and a conception of the attitudinal or dispositional traits bound up with the quality of humility. This passage suggests that what is distinctive about modernist methods is not an inward turn, an unprecedented drilling down into the core of some mental interior; rather, what is distinctive is the explicitness with which modernist writers like Joyce anchored worlds-as-experienced in what Clark (1997) terms "action loops" that "criss-cross the organism and its environment" (35), thereby calling into question Cartesian geographies of the mind. By means of such action loops, intelligent agents take cognizance of the possibilities for action afforded by their environment, as when one develops strategies for navigating a city one has never visited before or for interacting with strangers on the basis of their demeanor—with the pathway thus chosen leading to new construals, by means of which further environmental contingencies can be made sense of and accommodated.

Similar action loops can be found in *Mrs Dalloway*. Take, for example, this short passage, which recounts part of what happens when the prime minister puts in an appearance at Clarissa Dalloway's party at the end of the novel:

"The Prime Minister," said Peter Walsh.

The Prime Minister? Was it really? Ellie Henderson marvelled. What a thing to tell Edith!

One couldn't laugh at him. He looked so ordinary. You might have stood him behind a counter and bought biscuits—poor chap, all rigged up in gold lace. (Woolf 1953 [1925], 172)

Is it really possible, or profitable, to locate in an interior domain of the mind Ellie Henderson's (unvocalized) response to Peter Walsh's announcement of the Prime Minister's arrival, or for that matter Peter's own, contrasting assessment of the prime minister's presence and demeanor? And if the text calls into question the internal-external polarity in terms of which analysts have approached passages like this one, what of attempts to align different techniques for mind representation—indirect thought for Ellie versus interior monologue (or free direct thought) for Peter—with different increments along a scale stretching from the world outside to the mind inside? Arguably, instead of highlighting the more or less private, interiorized nature of the characters' responses, the text reveals how those responses involve a similar anchoring of sense-making procedures in action-guided perception. Thus, both Ellie and Peter construe the prime minister's arrival, like the party as a whole, as a situation affording action possibilities of a specific sort: namely, those associated with framing, for a particular interlocutor, an ex post facto account of events.

In Ellie's case, the target interlocutor is her friend Edith, for whom Ellie resolves to "remember everything" (169). Here the process of remembering involves less an internalization of events than a procedure whereby what happens can be structured— understood—in ways that optimize the performance of subsequent acts of narration. In other words, Ellie experiences events in the way she does because she perceives them as more or less relevant for a particular course of action—namely, that of telling Edith about what happened at the party. In Peter's case, Clarissa can be identified as the target interlocutor, given that ever since Clarissa rejected him as a suitor some thirty years prior Peter had "felt . . . unable to get away from the thought of her; she kept coming back and back like a sleeper jolting against him in a railway carriage" (76). For Peter, events at the party afford opportunities for performances of satiric critique by means of which he might conceivably prove Clarissa wrong in having chosen Richard Dalloway over him—and thereby putting herself in the position of having to host parties that expose the pitiable ordinariness of public officials like the prime minister. Accordingly, rather than locating Ellie's and Peter's responses in an internal domain of the mental, the passage situates their perceptions and inferences in an action loop that criss-crosses between these characters and their environment; what they take to be happening emerges from their understanding of the requirements not only for navigating the material and social spaces of the party, but also for performing subsequent acts of telling, critiquing, and disputing. Those acts provide a raison d'être and orienting frame for more localized feats of sense-making.

Or consider this scene, where the strenuously religious Doris Kilman has tea with Clarissa's daughter, Elizabeth, after shopping for petticoats in the Army and Navy stores:

> *Like some dumb creature who has been brought up to a gate for an unknown purpose, and stands there longing to gallop away, Elizabeth Dalloway sat silent. Was Miss Kilman going to say anything more?*
>
> *"Don't quite forget me," said Doris Kilman; her voice quivered. Right away to the end of the field the dumb creature galloped in terror. . . .*
>
> *Elizabeth turned her head. The waitress came. One had to pay at the desk, Elizabeth said, and went off, drawing out, so Miss Kilman felt, the very entrails in her body, stretching them as she crossed the room, and then, with a final twist, bowing her head very politely, she went.*
>
> *She had gone. Miss Kilman sat at the marble table among the éclairs, stricken once, twice, thrice by shocks of suffering.* (Woolf 1953 [1925], 132–33)

By means of what Stanzel would call figural narration, the text shifts between Miss Kilman's and Elizabeth's very different takes on their encounter, with Elizabeth wondering how soon she will able to terminate the interaction without seeming rude and Miss Kilman suffering visceral agony when she realizes that her attraction to Elizabeth is not reciprocated ("to see Elizabeth turning against her; to be felt repulsive even by her—it was too much" [132]). At the same time, a third construal of events, emanating from what Stanzel would characterize as the authorial narrative situation, is interwoven with the two reflectors' divergent interpretations; this construal is the source of the simile comparing Elizabeth with a voiceless creature brought up to a gate for a purpose unknown to her, longing to bolt, and finally galloping away in terror. The structure of the passage thus underscores how making sense of the tea-time encounter, understanding the motivations for and implications of the characters' actions, requires factoring in all these construals and shuttling back and forth between the wider and narrower scope views that they afford. In the process, the text reorients the geography of mind, replacing the Cartesian coordinate system based on an inner-outer polarity with a dynamic, two-way coupling between intelligent agents and their environments—a dialectical interplay between experiencers and the environments whose negotiation confers on their experiences the specific quality that they have. Elizabeth's experience of the tea-time encounter emerges from how, in an action loop that both derives from and feeds back into her negative assessment of the interaction, Elizabeth scans the environment for an opportunity to break free from Miss Kilman. The similes contextualize Elizabeth's scanning activities, constrained by the dictates of politeness, as comparable to the actions of a language-less creature longing to escape. Miss Kilman's far-different evaluation of and response to her and Elizabeth's conversation emerges from her divergent goals (prolonging the interaction, deepening the connection with Elizabeth), which in turn give rise to very different action-oriented perceptions. In other words, as with Ellie Henderson's and Peter Walsh's divergent reactions to Clarissa's party, the text points to a common basis for Miss Kilman's and Elizabeth's experiences, even as it indicates the contrast between them. Specifically, the passage anchors intentions, desires, inferences, and emotional responses in possibilities for action that are shaped by—and also shape—the characters' sense of what is going on.

Storyworlds/*Umwelten*:
Exploring Worlds-as-Experienced

In this chapter, I have argued for the need to rethink standard accounts of modernism as engaging in (or deepening and radicalizing an already-unfolding) inward turn, a movement away from external, material, and social realities into the interiority of characters' psychologies. In suggesting that modernist narratives be read in dialogue with postcognitivist models of mental experience, I do not seek to deny or minimize the innovativeness of modernist methods for representing minds. What I wish to dispute, rather, is that those methods entail the geography of mind assumed by advocates as well as detractors of modernism—and, for that matter, by critics who more neutrally define modernism's break with nineteenth-century realism as a shift inward along this same internal-external polarity. Instead of reinforcing internalist or sandwich models of mind as a buffer zone between perceptual inputs and output in the form of actions (Hurley 1998a, 1998b), modernist narratives suggest the degree to which perceiving, acting, and thinking are inextricably interlinked, with the constant cross-circulation among these activities accounting for intelligent agents' enactment of a world. Thus, contrary to standard literary-historical accounts, modernist techniques were not centered on, or geared toward, an inner, mental domain. Rather, in using figural narration to interweave the discourse of narration with characters' construal of events, and developing techniques for representing, with more or less detail or granularity, characters' inferences about or emotional responses to events, the modernists emphasized the tight coupling between mind and world, the nexus between intelligent agents and the environments they seek to navigate. Indeed, these narrative methods can be compared to experimental methods that aspire to what researchers in the cognitive sciences have come to call ecological validity (Cole 1999), a trait shared by research models that allow the analyst to approximate how intelligence operates in the wild (cf. Hutchins 1995a). Any ecologically valid model of mind will need to take into account, as modernist writers tried to take into account, the action loops by virtue of which humans recognize, exploit, and reinterpret the affordances that arise from their modes of being-in-the-world.

For reasons of space and strategy, I have focused mainly on how postcognitivist frameworks can illuminate what is genuinely distinctive about modernist methods for representing minds. But as my previous paragraph suggests, the direction of the argument can be reversed: modernist narratives can be viewed as concretizing the lived, phenomenal worlds that postcognitive theorists have subsequently tried to describe in more abstract terms. And here modernist narratives point a way back to the future. By demonstrating what it is like to live out situations and events with which the mind is indissolubly linked via action loops, which vary in turn with the agent's structure, cultural equipment, and surrounding environment, modernist texts in effect flesh out a concept developed one hundred years ago by the German-Estonian biologist Jakob von Uexküll, namely, the concept of the *Umwelt*. As Thompson (2007) notes, enactivist accounts "of a sensorimotor world—a body-oriented world of perception and action—is none other than von Uexküll's original notion of an *Umwelt*. An *Umwelt* is an animal's environment in the sense of its lived, phenomenal world, the world as it presents itself to that animal thanks to its sensorimotor repertoire" (Thompson 2007, 59; cf. Clark 1997, 24–25). Or, in von Uexküll's own words:

The Umwelt *of any animal that we wish to investigate is only a section carved out of the environment [*Umgebung*] which we see spread around it—and this environment is nothing but our own human world. The first task of* Umwelt *research is to identify each animal's perceptual cues among all the [potential] stimuli in its environment and to build up the animal's specific world with them. . . . As the number of an animal's performances grows, the number of objects that populate its* Umwelt *increases. It grows within the individual life span of every animal that is able to gather experiences. (1957 [1934], 13, 48)*

In addition to studying how *Umwelten* vary across species, von Uexküll also stressed intraspecies variation: "The best way to find out that no two human *Umwelten* are the same is to have yourself led through unknown territory by someone familiar with it. Your guide unerringly follows a path that you cannot see" (50).[12] Modernist writers can be viewed as *Umwelt* researchers in von Uexküll's sense—explorers of the lived, phenomenal worlds that emerge from, or are enacted through, the interplay between intelligent agents and their cultural as well as material circumstances. The storyworlds through which modernist texts guide readers constitute a staging ground for procedures of *Umwelt* construction; these procedures, deployed by modernist authors and characters alike, are at odds with Cartesian models of phenomenal experience that are premised on the polarization of mind and world.[13] Furthermore, the modernist texts discussed in my chapter suggest how narrative itself forms part of the cultural equipment by means of which humans seek, with more or less success, to transform unknown territories into negotiable places—to adapt von Uexküll's phrase. Early twentieth-century authors demonstrate through their practice how narrative furnishes crucial resources for such world construction and negotiation. In doing so, they open up early twenty-first-century possibilities for exploring how research on stories can contribute to—and not just benefit from—postcognitivist approaches to the mind.

Notes

I am grateful to Porter Abbott for his careful reading of an earlier draft of this chapter and his invaluable comments and questions about the argument outlined here. I also thank Stephen Kern for even earlier discussions about how to approach the chapter. I gratefully acknowledge, as well, the invaluable insights of the Modernism Reading Group, hosted by Steve Kern of Ohio State University. Members Morris Beja, Sarah Copland, Kate Elkins, Marty Hipsky, Ellen Carol Jones, Jesse Matz, Brian McHale, and Jim Phelan kindly read and commented on the penultimate draft of the chapter.

1. Doležel (1980) argues that fictional facts reported by third-person narrators have more authority or mark a higher degree of certainty—that is, are more strongly *authenticated*—than first-person reports given by characters or character-narrators occupying specific positions in a storyworld.

2. Thus in his preface to *The Golden Bowl* for the New York edition of his works, James writes: "[The works that] I have gathered into this Series have ranged themselves not as my own impersonal account of the affair in hand, but as my account of somebody's impression of it—the terms of this person's access to it and estimate of it contributing thus by some fine little law to insensification of interest" (665).

3. As Shen (2005) notes, "mind-style is typically a matter of the narrator's use of language to imitate in an implicit way the structure of the character's mental self" (311).

4. In this paragraph and the next I emulate previous commentators by invoking an internal-external scale along which various methods of narration can be located—some closer to the internal end, and thus more proximal to the mind being represented, others closer to the external end, and thus more distally related to mind. Below, however, I argue that modernist narratives, when put into dialogue with postcognitivist research (Potter 2000), provide grounds for rejecting this internal-external polarity and the Cartesian geography of the mental with which it is associated.

5. In Jahn's (2005) synopsis, whereas "the authorial narrative situation is characterised by a highly audible and visible narrator who tells a story cast in the third-person," and who "sees the story from the ontological position of an outsider, that is, a position of absolute authority which allows her/him to know everything about events and characters, including their thoughts and unconscious motives" (364), the "figural narrative situation presents the story's events as seen through the eyes of a 'reflector' character (also called 'internal focalizer' or 'figural medium'). The narrator is . . . a largely inconspicuous presenter, silent arranger, and recorder" (365).

6. Nicholas Dames, in his contribution to this volume, notes that G. H. Lewes seems to have been the first to use the term "stream of consciousness," in his 1860 book *The Physiology of Common Life*. For further discussion of Sinclair's review of Richardson, see Kaplan (1975, 9–10), Raitt (2000, 2–3), and Trotter (1999, 91). Lewis (2007, 158) notes that, for his part, Joyce credited the French novelist Edouard Dujardin with pioneering the use of stream-of-consciousness technique in his 1888 novel, *Les Lauriers sont coupés* (cf. Edel 1955, 43–44). Stevenson (1992) suggests that "even if the stream of consciousness was not the wholly original invention of Dorothy Richardson or James Joyce, it had not been employed previously in English on the scale, or with the flexibility, which those authors had established for it by the mid-1920s" (5).

7. For Matz (2004, 55–58) the modern novel is distinctive not only for its attempts to create psychological immediacy but also for the way it runs the gamut from "the most inward narration to the most outward" (58).

8. Meanwhile, for an overt parody of Cartesian geographies of mind, see Beckett's late-modernist or proto-postmodernist novel *Murphy* (1938). At the Magdalen Mental Mercyseat, where Beckett's antihero gets a job as an orderly, Murphy realizes that the pure Cartesianism to which he had aspired is tantamount to a debilitating solipsism. Further, after Murphy dies

in what was likely an act of suicide, the person entrusted with his ashes hurls them at his antagonist during an angry dispute in a pub, such that Murphy's fate enacts, in a lower, Swiftean register, Clarissa Dalloway's anti-Cartesian model of mind: "By closing time the body, mind and soul of Murphy were freely distributed over the floor of the saloon; and before another dayspring greyened the earth had been swept away with the sand, the beer, the butts, the glass, the matches, the spits, the vomit" (275).

9. Herman (2006) and Palmer (2004, 130–31, 162–65; 2005) explore how research on the extended mind or distributed intelligence can inform the study of fictional narratives.

10. See Potter (2000) for a general account of the notion of postcognitivism and an overview of postcognitivist approaches to mind. For Potter, what unites these approaches is their shared focus on people's situated practices (33–36), which postcognitivists view not just as reflecting but also helping to constitute the mind.

11. Varela, Thompson, and Rosch (1991) suggest that "stated in precise terms, affordances consist in opportunities for interaction that things in the environment possess relative to the sensorimotor capacities of the animal. For example, relative to certain animals, some things, such as trees, are climbable or afford climbing. Thus affordances are distinctly ecological features of the world" (203).

12. Von Uexküll (1957 [1934]) notes that the Umwelt-based concept of the familiar path also calls into question the ecological validity of experiments involving animals' navigation of mazes (51). Tolman (1948) conducted experiments of this sort in developing his influential idea of cognitive maps. Meanwhile, see Botar (2001) and Herwig (2001) for discussion of how von Uexküll's ideas may have influenced early twentieth-century writers and artists, particularly in the German-language tradition.

13. The conflict between Cartesian dualism and the modernists' emphasis on situated minds can be compared with the clash between dualistic and monistic models of mind discussed by Leslie Lockett in her contribution to this volume. Although modernist and Old English narratives are separated by a millennium and more, in both contexts dominant, recessive, and emergent intuitions about (and imagery for) the character of phenomenal experience are at stake. A task for future research, in the domain of inquiry that this volume only begins to map out, will be to establish a more precise time line for the emergence and recession of more or less dominant models of the mental across epochs, genres, and broader narrative traditions. For this purpose, methods of interpretation aligned with what Moretti (2005)

calls distant reading, in which the microanalysis of individual texts gives way to the study of how those texts are imbricated in larger cultural patterns or trends, may be required.

References

Beckett, Samuel. 1957 [1938]. *Murphy*. New York: Grove Press.

Botar, Oliver A. I. 2001. "Notes towards a Study of Jakob von Uexküll's Reception in Early Twentieth-Century Artistic and Architectural Circles." *Semiotica* 134 (1/4): 593–97.

Clark, Andy. 1997. *Being There: Putting Brain, Body, and World Together Again*. Cambridge MA: MIT Press.

———. 1998. "Embodied, Situated, and Distributed Cognition." In *A Companion to Cognitive Science*, ed. William Bechtel and George Graham, 506–17. Oxford: Blackwell.

———. 2008. *Supersizing the Mind: Embodiment, Action, and Cognitive Extension*. Oxford: Oxford University Press.

Clark, Andy, and David J. Chalmers. 1998. "The Extended Mind." *Analysis* 58 (1): 7–19.

Cohn, Dorrit. 1978. *Transparent Minds: Narrative Modes for Presenting Consciousness in Fiction*. Princeton: Princeton University Press.

Cole, Michael. 1999. "Ecological Validity." In *The MIT Encyclopedia of the Cognitive Sciences*, ed. Robert A. Wilson and Frank C. Keil, 257–59. Cambridge MA: MIT Press.

Doležel, Lubomír. 1980. "Truth and Authenticity in Narrative." *Poetics Today* 1 (3): 7–25.

Edel, Leon. 1955. *The Psychological Novel, 1900–1950*. New York: J. B. Lippincott.

Fernighough, Anne. 2007. "Consciousness as a Stream." In *The Cambridge Companion to the Modernist Novel*, ed. Morag Shiach, 65–81. Cambridge: Cambridge University Press.

Fowler, Roger. 1977. *Linguistics and the Novel*. London: Methuen.

Gallagher, Shaun. 2005. *How the Body Shapes the Mind*. Oxford: Oxford University Press.

Gangopadhyay, Nivedita, and Julian Kiverstein. 2009. "Enactivism and the Unity of Perception and Action." *Topoi* 28:69–73.

Gardner, Howard. 1985. *The Mind's New Science: A History of the Cognitive Revolution*. Boston: Basic Books.

Gibson, J. J. 1979. *An Ecological Approach to Visual Perception*. Boston: Houghton-Mifflin.

Harré, Rom, and Grant Gillett. 1994. *The Discursive Mind*. London: Sage.

Herman, David. 2006. "Genette Meets Vygotsky: Narrative Embedding and Distributed Intelligence." *Language and Literature* 15 (4): 375–98.

———. 2007. "Storytelling and the Sciences of Mind: Cognitive Narratology, Discursive Psychology, and Narratives in Face-to-Face Interaction." *Narrative* 15 (3): 306–34.

Herwig, Malte. 2001. "The Unwitting Muse: Jakob von Uexküll's Theory of *Umwelt* and Twentieth-Century Literature." *Semiotica* 134 (1/4): 553–92.

Hurley, Susan. 1998a. *Consciousness in Action*. Cambridge MA: Harvard University Press.

———. 1998b. "Vehicles, Contents, Conceptual Structure, and Externalism." *Analysis* 58 (1): 1–6.

Hutchins, Edwin. 1995a. *Cognition in the Wild*. Cambridge MA: MIT Press.

———. 1995b. "How a Cockpit Remembers Its Speeds." *Cognitive Science* 19:265–88.

Jahn, Manfred. 2005. "Narrative Situations." In *Routledge Encyclopedia of Narrative Theory*, ed. David Herman, Manfred Jahn, and Marie-Laure Ryan, 364–66. London: Routledge.

James, Henry. 2000 [1909]. "Preface to *The Golden Bowl*." In *Theory of the Novel: A Historical Approach*, ed. Michael McKeon, 665–72. Baltimore: Johns Hopkins University Press.

Johnson, Mark. 1987. *The Body in the Mind: The Bodily Basis of Meaning, Imagination, and Reason*. Chicago: University of Chicago Press.

Joyce, James. 1964 [1916]. *A Portrait of the Artist as a Young Man*. New York: Penguin.

———. 1986 [1922]. *Ulysses*. Ed. Hans Walter Gabler. New York: Vintage.

Kahler, Erich. 1973 [1970]. *The Inward Turn of Narrative*. Trans. Richard Winston and Clara Winston. Princeton: Princeton University Press.

Kaplan, Sydney Janet. 1975. *Feminine Consciousness in the Modern British Novel*. Urbana: University of Illinois Press.

Kunka, Andrew J., and Michele K. Troy, eds. 2006. *May Sinclair: Moving Towards the Modern*. Aldershot: Ashgate.

Leech, Geoffrey, and Michael Short. 2007 [1981]. *Style in Fiction: A Linguistic Introduction to English Fictional Prose*. 2nd ed. Harlow: Pearson/Longman.

Lewis, Pericles. 2007. *The Cambridge Introduction to Modernism*. Cambridge: Cambridge University Press.

Lukács, Georg. 1971 [1936]. "Narrate or Describe?" In *Writer and Critic and Other Essays*, ed. and trans. Arthur D. Kahn, 110–48. New York: Grosset and Dunlap.

Matz, Jesse. 2004. *The Modern Novel: A Short Introduction*. Oxford: Blackwell.

———. 2006. "The Novel." In *A Companion to Modernist Literature and Culture*, ed. David Bradshaw and Kevin J. H. Dettmar, 215–26. Oxford: Blackwell.

Moretti, Franco. 2005. *Graphs, Maps, Trees: Abstract Models for a Literary History*. New York: Verso.

Palmer, Alan. 2004. *Fictional Minds*. Lincoln: University of Nebraska Press.

———. 2005. "Intermental Thought in the Novel: The Middlemarch Mind." *Style* 39 (4): 427–39.

Potter, Jonathan. 2000. "Post-cognitive Psychology." *Theory and Psychology* 10:31–37.

Prince, Gerald. 2003. *A Dictionary of Narratology*. 2nd ed. Lincoln: University of Nebraska Press.

Raitt, Suzanne. 2000. *May Sinclair: A Modern Victorian*. Oxford: Oxford University Press.

Rowlands, Mark. 2009. "Enactivism and the Extended Mind." *Topoi* 28:53–62.

Shen, Dan. 2005. "Mind-Style." In *Routledge Encyclopedia of Narrative Theory*, ed. David Herman, Manfred Jahn, and Marie-Laure Ryan, 311–12. London: Routledge.

Sinclair, May. 1907. *The Helpmate*. New York: Holt.

———. 1918. "The Novels of Dorothy Richardson." *Egoist* 5:57–59.

Stanzel, F. K. 1984 [1979]. *A Theory of Narrative*. Trans. Charlotte Goedsche. Cambridge: Cambridge University Press.

Stevenson, Randall. 1992. *Modernist Fiction*. Lexington: University Press of Kentucky.

Thompson, Evan. 2007. *Mind in Life: Biology, Phenomenology, and the Sciences of Mind*. Cambridge MA: Harvard University Press.

Tolman, Edward. 1948. "Cognitive Maps in Rats and Men." *Psychological Review* 55 (4): 189–208.

Trotter, David. 1999. "The Modernist Novel." In *The Cambridge Companion to Modernism*, ed. Michael Levenson, 70–99. Cambridge: Cambridge University Press.

Varela, Francisco J., Evan Thompson, and Eleanor Rosch. 1991. *The Embodied Mind: Cognitive Science and Human Experience*. Cambridge MA: MIT Press.

von Uexküll, Jakob. 1957 [1934]. "A Stroll through the Worlds of Animals and Men: A Picture Book of Invisible Worlds." Illustrated by George Krisat. In *Instinctive Behavior: The Development of a Modern Concept*, ed. and trans. Claire H. Schiller, 5–80. New York: International Universities Press.

Vygotsky, Lev S. 1978. *Mind in Society: The Development of Higher Psychological*

Processes. Ed. Michael Cole, Vera John-Steiner, Sylvia Scribner, and Ellen Souberman. Cambridge MA: Harvard University Press.

Watt, Ian. 1957. *The Rise of the Novel.* Berkeley: University of California Press.

Woolf, Virginia. 1953 [1925]. *Mrs Dalloway.* San Diego: Harcourt Brace Jovanovich.

———. 1984 [1919]. "Modern Fiction." In *The Common Reader: First Series,* ed. Andrew McNeillie, 146–54. San Diego: Harcourt Brace Jovanovich.

9. 1945–
Ontologies of Consciousness

ALAN PALMER

This chapter draws on four case studies in order to examine some of the techniques of consciousness representation present in fiction in the British Isles from 1940 to the present day. They are Evelyn Waugh's *Men at Arms* (1952), Martin Amis's *Success* (1978), Flann O'Brien's *The Third Policeman* (written in 1940 but not published until 1967), and Ian McEwan's *Atonement* (2001). The four novels can be considered as a spectrum or continuum, starting with what I will describe below as the neorealism or antimodernism of *Men at Arms*, continuing with the modernism (with postmodern tendencies) of *Success*, and ending with the postmodernism of *The Third Policeman* and *Atonement*.

A brief contextualizing statement on modernism and postmodernism generally will contain a more specific discussion of Brian McHale's work (1987, 1992, 2005) on the epistemological and ontological dominants in modernist and postmodernist fiction respectively. This section will trace, in broad outline, the shift from modern to postmodern minds. Subsequent discussion will use the analytical tool that I call *attribution theory* (that is, how narrators, characters, and readers attribute states of mind to others and to themselves) to consider the implications of epistemological and ontological instabilities for the fictional minds operating within the storyworlds of the four texts. This discussion will attempt to recontextualize McHale's account by showing how the domain of consciousness representation forces us to come to terms with the complex, dynamic relationship between mind and world. Processes of attribution provide an especially fruitful way to study the various stages in the emergence of the mind in narrative fiction because they allow us to hold constant a particular parameter or heuristic for investigation to use as a kind of lens that can expose both commonalities and contrasts among texts written in different periods or in different styles. In using attribution theory as a parameter for cross-comparing the four case studies, I will consider, in particular, whether texts with an ontological dominant present particular challenges to attribution theory since processes of attribution operate in fundamentally different ways for texts that foreground the making and unmaking of worlds. The analysis will involve ranging the four texts along a scale in terms of how they relate to standard or default mechanisms of attribution, and I will suggest that their positions on this scale correlate exactly with their positions on the neorealist/modernist/postmodernist continuum referred to above.

The discussion that follows will consider two separate but related issues. One is the story-level issue of the mind treated as a theme in narrative, the nature of the fictional minds that are constructed by texts, the *what* that is the content of those minds. The other is the discourse-level issue of the techniques used to represent consciousness in narrative, *how* minds are presented in the discourse. It will, however, soon become apparent that it is difficult in practice to maintain a distinction between the two issues. Although, in the treatments of the four novels, I will be focusing primarily on the second issue, the *how*, it is impossible to talk about the *how* without also talking in detail about the *what*. You have to describe the contents of fictional minds when you are considering how those minds are presented in the text. Also, the techniques for fictional mind presentation will determine, to a certain extent, what thoughts are described. The repellent preoccupations of Gregory and Terry in *Success* are more appropriately presented in their deeply unreliable homodiegetic (or first-person) narrative streams than they would be by the calm, measured, heterodiegetic (or third-person) narration of *Men at Arms*. The mind is treated as a theme in *Atonement*, and the choice of this theme strongly influences the means by which the minds of its characters are presented in its discourse.

Modernism and
Postmodernism, Epistemology and Ontology

The modernist novel is characterized by a move away from the omniscient third-person narration that is typical of the realist novel and toward an experimental and impressionistic emphasis on subjectivity, inner states of consciousness, and fragmentary and discontinuous character construction.[1] However, the modernist novel is still based on a belief in truth and reality. Modernist writers' use of the techniques of stream of consciousness and interior monologue reflects their interest in the problems raised by the attempt to record as faithfully as possible the workings of fictional minds. Postmodern narratives, on the other hand, are often arbitrary and indeterminate. They reveal a delight in disorder, discontinuity, and ambiguity and a correspondingly cavalier attitude toward the conventions of coherent plot, realistic characterization, and clearly identifiable settings. Both time and space in the postmodern novel can be unstable and incomprehensible. There is a self-reflexive interest in the processes of narrative and a frequent use of metafictional devices that draw attention to the fictional status of the text. The notion of subjectivity is problematical because the self is viewed as a construct and a fiction. However, arguments that certain features are characteristic of, or, worse, specific to, a particular type of fiction are vulnerable to counterarguments that these features can also be found elsewhere. "So novels in the second half of the twentieth century are ontologically destabilizing? So what! So is *Don Quixote*." This does not leave much room for maneuver. I will not, therefore, be claiming that the characteristics of modernist or postmodern fiction are *exclusive* to such fiction.

It is tempting to regard the terms "modernism" and "postmodernism" as labels for discrete historical periods. But, as McHale (1992) remarks, modernism and postmodernism "are not successive stages in some inevitable evolution from less advanced to more advanced aesthetic forms, but rather alternative contemporary practices, equally 'advanced' or 'progressive,' equally available, between which writers are free to choose" (207). Part of the purpose of this chapter is to support his argument. The postmodern reaction to modernism that occurred in the British and Irish novel of the second half of the twentieth century is clearly evident in the work of two of the four writers under discussion: Flann O'Brien and Ian McEwan. However, the Martin Amis novel, which is more modernist in tone, seems to me to be equally characteristic of this period. In addition, another reaction to modernism that is very different from postmodernism is the movement that I will call neorealism or antimodernism (Lodge 1981): the traditional, formally conservative work of such writers as the later Evelyn Waugh and Kingsley Amis who doubted the value of the modernist attempt to record in detail the minute workings of fictional minds. Obviously, these movements are not mutually exclusive, and writers such as David Lodge have incorporated elements of all of them into their novels.

A good deal of insightful work has been done on the narratology of postmodernism by such scholars as Monika Fludernik (1996), H. Porter Abbott (1996), Brian McHale, and Brian Richardson (2006). Within this field, I will focus for the remainder of this chapter on McHale's suggestion that the shift from modernism to postmodernism marks a change from an epistemological to an ontological dominant. I am doing so because the combination of this perspective with the attribution theory approach described in the next section is particularly illuminating when applied to the fictional minds contained in modernist and postmodernist novels.

McHale argues that the epistemological question posed by the modernist novel is, How can we *know* reality? The ontological question raised by the postmodern novel is, What *is* reality? Modernist narrative is oriented toward the investigation of such issues as perception and cognition, perspective, the subjective experience of time, and the circulation and reliability of knowledge. It is preoccupied with such questions as, What is there to know about the world? Who knows it, and how reliably? How is knowledge transmitted, to whom, and how reliably? Postmodern narrative is oriented differently, toward issues of fictionality, modes of being and the differences among them, the nature and plurality of worlds, and how such worlds are made and un-made. It is preoccupied with such questions as, What is a world? How is a world constituted? Are there alternative worlds? If so, how are they constituted? How do different worlds, and different kinds of world, differ, and what happens when someone passes from one world to another? (McHale 1992, 247; 2005, 457). The two dominants result in differing constructions of self and sub-jectivity, the subject matter of this volume. "Modernist perspec-tivism . . . multiplied points of view on the world, but without, for the most part, undermining the underlying unity of the self. . . . Each perspective is lodged in a subjectivity which is itself relatively coherent, relatively centred and stable" (McHale 1992, 254). By contrast, "postmodernism's shift of focus to ontologi-cal issues and themes has radical consequences for literary mod-els of the self. A poetics in which the category 'world' is plural, unstable and problematic would seem to entail a model of the self which is correspondingly plural, unstable and problematic" (McHale 1992, 253).

In making his distinction, McHale (1987) quite rightly stresses that epistemological questions cannot be raised without imme-diately raising ontological questions and vice versa. However, the dominant "specifies the *order* in which different aspects are attended to, so that, although it would be perfectly possible to interrogate a postmodernist text about its epistemological im-plications, it is more *urgent* to interrogate it about its ontologi-cal implications" (11). My perspective will, I think, reinforce the argument that ontological and epistemological concerns are so intertwined that it is difficult to keep them apart for long and that any differences are of emphasis only. Though a particular text's dominant determines which concern is more urgent, in practice, questions of knowledge are necessarily intimately en-tangled with questions of being and vice versa.

Attribution Theory

I will be considering the making and unmaking of the fictional worlds in all four novels in turn, attempting to show how the in-sights contained in the framework described above can be illuminatingly reinterpreted in terms of the minds functioning within these worlds. I will be focusing in particular on how the last three novels are concerned with the instability and fragmentation of their fictional minds. But, before doing so, I will briefly describe attribution theory in very general terms in order to show how it may fruitfully be combined with McHale's ideas.

Attribution theory (Palmer 2010) is concerned with how narrators, characters, and readers attribute states of mind to characters and, where appropriate, also to themselves. How do heterodiegetic narrators attribute states of mind such as emotions, dispositions, and reasons for action to their characters? By what means do homodiegetic narrators make attributions of states of mind to themselves and also to other characters? And, with regard to the issue of characterization, how does an attribution of a mental state by a narrator help to build up in the reader a sense of the whole personality of the character who is the subject of that attribution? Attribution theory rests on the concept of *theory of mind*. This is the term used by philosophers and psychologists to describe our awareness of the existence of other minds, our knowledge of how to interpret our own and other people's thought processes, our mind-reading abilities in the real world. Readers of novels have to use their theory of mind in order to try to follow the workings of characters' minds. Otherwise, they will lose the plot. The only way in which the reader can understand novels is by trying to follow the workings of characters' minds—that is, by attributing states of mind to them. This mind reading also involves trying to follow characters' attempts to read other characters' minds.[2] An important element in the application of attribution theory to fictional texts is what I call the *continuing consciousness frame* (Palmer 2004, 175–83). This term describes the ability of readers to take a reference to a character in the text and attach to it a presumed consciousness that exists continuously within the storyworld of the novel between the various, more or less intermittent references to that character.

Attributions of mental states to individuals are *discursive* in the sense that the descriptions arising from these attributions are performative speech acts that occur within complex language games and are always embedded in specific social contexts. Attributions tend to be discursively constructed as apparently factual and objective, but they often contain self-interested attributions of motives. Pure mental descriptions are rare. A mental state or event will be described in a certain way and not in other ways for particular purposes, and these alternatives can vary greatly as to how they ascribe agency, impose responsibility, justify behavior, explain motivations, assign praise, deflect criticism and blame, and so on. This approach has obvious relevance to the novel, where mental functioning can only exist within the words of a fictional discourse.

An analysis of the nature of the attribution of mental states to characters in the four novels within McHale's framework raises a number of questions. How reliable or secure can these attributions be in view of the disruptions to be discussed below? How can attributions be used by the reader to build up a picture of a character's whole mind when narratives typically foreground the world-creating power of narrative itself, generating multiple ontologies within any given fictional domain and hence ontologically plural minds? In particular, how can attributions of specific states of mind be used to build up a picture of the whole mind when, as I will suggest in the case of the narrator-character in *The Third Policeman* and the main characters in *Atonement*, there are doubts over whether or not there *is* one whole mind? In summary, different sorts of attributional unreliability are in operation in the three nonrealist novels. The unreliability in *Success* is obvious to the reader, as the two narrators provide wildly different accounts of the same events for obviously self-justificatory purposes. The third-person attributions in *The Third Policeman* are extremely odd and, as the narrator does not know he is dead, his first-person attributions are unreliable in the sense that he thinks they are taking place in one ontological plane when they are in fact taking place in another. Many of the attributions in *Atonement* are sensible and plausible, and so appear at first to be reliable. It is only later that these apparently authoritative judgments are shown not to be so or, even worse, to be simply false.

Men at Arms

The antimodernist/neorealist *Men at Arms* raises neither epistemological nor ontological concerns. The story concerns Guy Crouchback, who, at the outbreak of the Second World War, leaves his family's villa in Italy to go to London to enlist as an officer in the army. He finds this difficult due to his age (he is thirty-five) but eventually finds an old and unfashionable regiment, the Halberdiers, that is willing to take him. There he meets another officer, the eccentric Apthorpe, who is also older than the others. The novel then follows the development of his relationships with his fellow officers and with the regiment. It is a heterodiegetic narrative told by an omniscient narrator and focalized through Crouchback. Throughout, mental causation conforms to the models of the workings of the mind that were in general circulation in his world. To adapt Marie-Laure Ryan's (1991) phrase, there is minimal departure from the real world. Within this single, stable storyworld, perception and cognition are generally reliable. There are no ontological or epistemological surprises that compel the reader to reconstruct the storyworld, as in the other three novels. The application of the continuing consciousness frame is unproblematic. The consciousness of the main character, Guy Crouchback, like that of all the other characters in the book, exists from the beginning to the end of the narrative just as real minds do. As the storyworld is stable, so are the selves contained in it. Guy is seen in different roles: as husband, son, soldier, and Catholic. But they certainly do not conflict with each other to the extent that the self fragments in any way. The cognitive frames put in place by the reader at the beginning of the novel remain in place by the end.

In *Men at Arms* the standard or default mechanisms for the attribution of states of mind apply. Explanations of motivations for actions are confident and secure, and are generally complete, satisfying, genuine, and logical. No doubts are ever raised about the nature of characters' mental functioning. There are frequent panoramic sweeps across the whole range of a character's mind. Background information is given, for example, on dispositions: "He was not a sensitive man" (19) and "He was not an imaginative man" (21). The sections of the narrative relating explicitly to fictional minds satisfy Grice's four conversational maxims of quantity (being just informative enough), quality (not saying what you do not know to be true), relevance, and manner (being clear, brief, and orderly). The humor in this extremely funny novel is beautifully controlled by means of the flow of attribution and often arises from the mismatch between a particular situation and the response to it that is attributed to a particular character. Guy finds that "any firm passage between Apthorpe's dreamlike universe and the world of common experience was a thing to cherish" (107–8). However, the dislocations between the solipsistic "dreamlike universe" of Apthorpe's mind and the "world of common experience" shared by everyone else's minds are clear to everyone but Apthorpe himself.

The nature of the attribution in the novel can be illustrated by a description of the development of Guy's relationship with his regiment. At first, Guy has difficulty in adjusting to being part of this intermental unit. (Intermental thought [Palmer 2010] is joint, group, shared, or collective thought.) Initially, he feels isolated and separate and is aware that he is setting himself apart from the other officers. Eventually, though, he comes for a while to feel much closer to the group:

> Those days of lameness, he realized much later, were his honeymoon, the full consummation of his love of the Royal Corps of Halberdiers. After them came domestic routine, much loyalty and affection, many good things shared, but intervening and overlaying them all the multitudinous, sad little discoveries of marriage, familiarity, annoyance, imperfections noted, discord. (78)

Later, there are various crises during which he feels close to the regiment, then alienated from it again, and so on. This ebb and flow in his relationship with the intermental unit continues throughout the novel. These developments are organic and comprehensible. Such intermental/intramental relationships are only possible against a stable background, and within an understandable storyworld.

Evelyn Waugh once said, "I regard writing not as investigation of character but as an exercise in the use of language, and with this I am obsessed. I have no technical psychological interest. It is drama, speech and events that interest me." This disclaimer of any interest in psychology should be treated with care. Drama, speech, and events only make sense, and only have any interest, as indications and expressions of psychological processes. Waugh *was* deeply interested in character and psychology; otherwise, his books would not be so funny and so painful to read. To put his remark another way: he was interested in character and psychology only insofar as they are revealed in drama, speech, and events, and he did not see that any serious epistemological or ontological concerns are raised by fictional attributions of states of mind. In particular, he was not interested in the modernist attempt to find revolutionary means to represent consciousness such as the techniques of stream of consciousness and interior monologue. And I suspect that he would have been even less impressed by postmodern explorations of ontological instabilities.

Success

In contrast to *Men at Arms*, *Success* is preoccupied with the unreliability of perception and cognition, but, unlike *The Third Policeman* and *Atonement*, the unreliability occurs within a single storyworld. Set in London in the late 1970s, it concerns the relationship between two foster brothers, Gregory and Terry. Terry is of working class origin and was adopted as a small boy by Gregory's upper middle class family. The two young men live together in a London flat but lead apparently very contrasting lives. Gregory is an extraordinarily arrogant success. Wealthy and cruel, he is immensely sexually attractive to both sexes and has many friends, a fast sports car, and a glamorous job in a West End art gallery. Terry is a failure: poor, physically ugly, and sexually unsuccessful, with no friends and a dreary job. The balance of the relationship then changes. It becomes clear (although some readers may guess sooner than I did!) that it is Gregory who is the failure: he is a pathetic fantasist, his job is humiliatingly menial, he has no money, and his "friends" exploit him. Terry, on the other hand, turns into a ruthlessly Thatcherite success as he becomes more attractive and earns more money. The novel ends with Terry as the dominant figure in his adopted family. The homodiegetic narration is shared between Gregory and Terry. All of the twelve chapters, titled "January" through to "December," are divided into two parts, with Terry always narrating the first part. There is minimal departure from the real world. The book is very uncomfortable to read because both main characters' motives and intentions are generally extremely sordid, scatological, misanthropic, and misogynist. A deeply Swiftian disgust and rage is expressed in a curiously arch, Baroque prose style.

The following is a heavily edited version of the long passage in which the true nature of Gregory's mental functioning is made clear (the background is that Gregory has admitted to having panic attacks on the Underground):

I turned and looked into the pit of harm from which I had triumphantly climbed. Well, I thought, that's put paid to that.

Recognize the style (I suppose I'd better change that too now)?

If you believed it, you'll believe anything. It was a lie. The very entrance to the Underground makes me want to pee with dread. . . .

It was a lie. I tell lies. I'm a liar. I always have been. I'm sorry. Here come the secrets.

My job, for instance, is, and always has been, fucking awful. . . .

I expect, too, that you think that my sexual life is as gleaming and ripe as Terence's is joyless and jejune. . . . But then all that's gone bad on me too, bad and sad, bad and sad and mad. . . .

Why? Is it part of the same thing? (Suddenly I keep needing to ask all these questions. Why? Tell me, someone, why won't someone tell me?) I know there are other bits of my life just waiting to go next; they have no other function but to snuff out when it will do me most harm. I wander into the kitchen first thing, and it looks intensely familiar and yet intensely irritating, as if all night I had wearily dreamt of forks and spoons; and the lies of the past are already queuing up to point their fingers. . . .

I am going to try to tell the truth from now on. It has all become too serious for lying, and I must protect myself as best I can. I'll try. But will you listen? No, I suppose you'll trust Terence's voice now, with its dour fidelity to the actual, rather than mine, which liked to play upon the surface of things. (180–84)

Both Terry's and Gregory's narrative streams in *Success* consist of a torrent of attribution of motives and intentions. There is hardly a sentence in the novel that does not consist of first-person or third-person attribution. As the passage shows, Gregory self-consciously attributes a variety of states of mind to himself, first untruthfully and then, at this climax, more honestly. The two young men are locked together in a frenzied attributional embrace. This truly is a Bakhtinian novel "with a sideways glance" at the other. Both characters have highly developed images of themselves and also of the other. They obsess about what the other is thinking. Notice how, in the final paragraph of the quotation, Gregory's sideways glance is directed toward Terry via the very prominent narratee: "But will you listen? No, I suppose you'll trust Terence's voice now." This sort of appeal to the narratee occurs throughout the novel: "Has Terence said anything about my sexual dispositions? No doubt he has" (18). Both frequently use this narratee to try to make the other's narration seem as unreliable as possible: "Or does he still tell you lies?" (156); "For Christ's sake don't listen to a word Greg says: he's totally unreliable on this point" (54); and "Gregory is a liar. Don't believe a word he says. He is the author of lies" (88). Both attempt by these means to try to destabilize the reader's reliance on the other in arriving at a sense of the true nature of the novel's storyworld.

The perspectivism or presentation of multiple viewpoints that is a characteristic of modernist fiction is clearly the most notable feature of the novel. We do not experience the storyworld directly, in the sense that events are presented to the reader through the consciousnesses of two very different minds with very different results. Indeed, their accounts conflict substantially until very late in the novel when, principally because Gregory becomes more honest, they are much more consistent with each other. Nevertheless, these epistemological difficulties take place against a stable ontological background. There is only one London that the two minds are experiencing, albeit in completely different ways. Terry refers, in fact, to "the distance between how [Ursula, his stepsister,] sees things and how things actually are" (148). The importance of this remark is that the existence of an objective "how things actually are" is acknowledged. Gregory finally admits in the quoted passage that it is undeniably true to say of the storyworld that he is having panic attacks.

There certainly is what may be called an epistemological shock that transforms the two main characters into very different people by the end of the novel. The balance of power between them is wrenched so violently that it becomes clear that the actual storyworld is nothing like the one presented in most of the text. The continuing consciousness frames remain in place, but with major adjustments: pathetic fantasist instead of arrogant young toff, and Thatcherite success story instead of embarrassing oik. There is one "objective" storyworld only, but the reader is profoundly misled about its nature until the end. Readers are obliged to reconstruct their storyworld (although, as mentioned earlier, the point at which this happens will vary from reader to reader). The postmodern edge to this predominantly modernist novel arises from the disintegration of Gregory's self due to his inability to cope with the world that he inhabits. There is a certain continuity to Terry's development but not to Gregory's far more discontinuous transformation. Terry's may be the relatively coherent and stable self of the modernist novel, but Gregory's selves are different. As he says above, "I know there are other bits of my life just waiting to go next," and, elsewhere, "all the bits that were me have been re-shuffled yet again" (213). Once the arrogant fop is recognized as an invention, and once the fantasies have ended, Gregory does not know what is left. He does not know which bits of the self to attribute beliefs, motives, and feelings to. In the nightmarish scene quoted above, Gregory is in the kitchen seeing the lies of the past queuing up to point their fingers at him. At the end of the novel he is standing alone in the garden of his mother's house where he has gone to hide, suffering a devastating breakdown. He has nothing left and nowhere to go.

The Third Policeman

The Third Policeman fits squarely into the postmodern category. Its unnamed narrator commits a robbery and a violent murder. After a long delay his accomplice, John Divney, tells him where the box containing the proceeds is hidden. From the point at which the narrator reaches for this box, the setting, the Irish countryside during an unspecified period, becomes increasingly unfamiliar. After several bizarre adventures involving discussions of very peculiar concepts and nonsensical artifacts and including a brief but passionate love affair with a bicycle, he goes to Divney's house to find his accomplice twenty years older. When Divney sees the narrator, he has a heart attack. Before he dies, he shouts that the narrator died twenty years ago, blown up by a bomb contained in the box. As the narrator runs off, it becomes clear that he has been in hell since his death, and he will go through the same series of events again and again without retaining any memory of them.

This is the passage in which, as the reader discovers at the end of the novel, the narrator is killed:

Without stopping to light another match I thrust my hand bodily into the opening and just when it should be closing about the box, something happened.

I cannot hope to describe what it was but it had frightened me very much long before I had understood it even slightly. It was some change which came upon me or upon the room, indescribably subtle, yet momentous, ineffable . . . I heard a cough behind me, soft and natural yet more disturbing than any sound that could ever come upon the human ear. That I did not die of fright was due, I think, to two things, the fact that my senses were already disarranged and able to interpret to me only gradually what they had perceived and also the fact that the utterance of the cough seemed to bring with it some more awful alteration in everything, just as if it had held the universe standstill for an instant, suspending the planets in their courses, halting the sun and holding in mid-air any falling thing the earth was pulling towards it. (24–25)

The Third Policeman is a homodiegetic narrative in which the narrator-character's attempts to attribute motivation to himself and others are humorously unsatisfactory. Mental causation is plentiful but idiosyncratic, tending eccentrically to give undue weight to such matters as bicycles. There are no obvious departures from the real world until the above passage, when there is a complete departure as the narration becomes steadily more and more fantastical and nightmarish. Third-person attribution is beguilingly nonsensical and becomes more and more so after the death of the narrator: "'He is a melody man,' the Sergeant added, 'and very temporary, a menace to the mind'" (78); "'A constituent man,' said the Sergeant, 'largely instrumental but volubly fervous'" (84); and "'He is as crazy as bedamned, an incontestable character and a man of ungovernable inexactitudes'" (158).

The first-person attribution is no better. Following his death, the narrator's self steadily disintegrates over the course of the narrative into a stream of highly self-conscious but increasingly incoherent self-attribution. The disarranged senses described in the quoted passage never recover. "When I awoke again two thoughts came into my head so closely together that they seemed to be stuck to one another; I could not be sure which came first and it was hard to separate them and examine them singly" (156). "I felt my brains struggle on bravely . . . I knew that I would be dead if I lost consciousness for one second. I knew that I could never awaken again or hope to understand afresh the terrible way in which I was if I lost the chain of the bitter day I had had" (189–90). "I felt my brain cluttered and stuffed with questions and blind perplexity and I also felt the sadness of my position coming back into my throat" (115). "Perhaps I was dreaming or in the grip of some horrible hallucination. There was much that I did not understand and possibly could never understand to my dying day" (191). "I know that I would go mad unless I got up from the floor and moved and talked and behaved in as ordinary a way as possible" (27). As these quotations show, the narrator is literally disoriented. Revealingly, he hears a voice in his head, decides that it is the voice of his soul, and names it "Joe." He also realizes that he does not know his own name. These attributional difficulties are vividly expressive of a mind that cannot engage successfully with the ontology of its storyworld. When the revelation that he is in hell occurs, it feels appropriate.

In contrast to *Success* and especially *Men at Arms*, the two postmodern novels, *The Third Policeman* and *Atonement*, end with *ontological* shocks that fundamentally disrupt the continuing consciousness frame and cause doubt over the status of characters' consciousnesses. In the case of *The Third Policeman*, although readers are aware for most of the novel that the storyworld of the novel differs substantially from the real world, it is a shock when the true nature of the storyworld is revealed. Also, the boundary between two worlds (life before death and life after death) is unstable: in the climax of the novel, the narrator briefly and unknowingly visits the real world when he appears as a ghost to his former accomplice. The continuing consciousness frame is necessarily severely disrupted when worlds are made and unmade in this way. The key question is this: Is it possible to say that there is one single continuing consciousness that belongs both to the character when alive and also to that character when dead and unaware of it? The self-attribution difficulties discussed above would suggest not.

Atonement

Within the modernist/postmodernist continuum, *Atonement* can be placed a stage further along from *The Third Policeman*, despite first impressions to the contrary. In part 1 of the novel, a 1930s country house party includes Briony Tallis, an imaginative thirteen-year-old, her older sister Cecilia, and Robbie, a working class young man whose university education has been paid for by the Tallis family. (The positions occupied by Terry in *Success* and Robbie in *Atonement* are curiously similar: both are working class boys who are fully or semi-adopted by an upper middle class family.) When Briony discovers Robbie and Cecilia making love in the library, she misinterprets it as an assault. Then Briony's cousin, Lola, really is raped, and Briony wrongly claims that she saw Robbie do it. Part 2 follows Robbie, now a soldier after his imprisonment, in northern France in 1940 during the retreat to Dunkirk. In part 3, Briony, now a nurse in London, visits Cecilia and Robbie to ask for their forgiveness. They are not quite able to give it. However, in a short epilogue titled "London 1999," written by Briony when she is an old woman who has just been diagnosed with progressive dementia, it becomes clear that the previous three parts comprise a novel within a novel written by Briony herself as an act of atonement. The scene in which she asks for forgiveness never happened because Robbie died at Dunkirk and Cecilia was killed by a bomb soon after.

Until the homodiegetic epilogue, *Atonement* appears at first reading to be a traditional heterodiegetic narrative in which there is minimal departure from the real world. Brian Richardson (2006) has very perceptively drawn attention to the use by a large number of writers of this device of replacing one fundamental cognitive frame, that of the omniscient heterodiegetic narrator, with another, the unreliable homodiegetic narrator. Examples include Camus's *La Peste*, Robbe-Grille's *Dans le Labyrinthe*, and Borges's "The Shape of the Sword" (10–11). When compared with *The Third Policeman*, *Atonement* is even more explicitly concerned with the structure and dynamics of world creation; as McEwan's text unfolds, it foregrounds the relationship between the storyworld of Briony's novel and the larger storyworld in which it turns out to be embedded. In fact, Briony's epilogue, by frequently drawing attention to the constructed and contingent nature of her novel storyworld, goes some way to unmaking that world. In addition, *Atonement* is also deeply and seriously concerned with the *purposes* of world construction: that is, not just *how* alternative worlds are made and unmade but *why* they are. The clue is given in the title of the novel; Briony's purpose is atonement. Again, the text raises a number of epistemological issues related to fictional minds, such as, How can Briony attribute states of mind to Cecilia and Robbie? And, How does the reader know what really happened in the whole storyworld of the novel when most of the evidence is contained in Briony's unreliably narrated novel? These profound and complex problems related to the coherence and unity of the various selves arise directly from the ontological instabilities introduced by the way in which the selves are revealed to be constructs of Briony the novelist.

The mental states experienced by Briony, Cecilia, Robbie, and the others as presented in the heterodiegetic section of the novel are simply Briony's *descriptions* of those mental states. These attributions are clearly performative speech acts that are designed by Briony to fulfill certain purposes. Behind the apparently objective purpose of explaining motivations, there lies Briony's overriding goal of deflecting blame wherever possible. Her novel is a hugely tendentious document because it is an exercise in blame management. This may sound unfair to Briony, bearing in mind that she does accept a certain amount of responsibility for her actions and does not try too obviously to find excuses for herself. But bear in mind that the novel within a novel presents a fairly sympathetic portrait, both of Briony as a young girl acting under the pressures of her overactive imagination and of Briony as a young nurse doing everything she can to atone for her mistake. Remember also the point made above that descriptions can always be worded in different ways to achieve different ends. Then consider how the presentation of Briony as a young girl and as a nurse in her own novel would differ from how you might imagine Cecilia's novel or Robbie's novel would have presented her, had those novels been written, had the dead spoken. My guess is that you would envisage that Robbie's and Cecilia's versions would be a good deal harsher on Briony than she is on herself. And that gap is precisely the discursive work that is done by Briony's novel. Alternatively, forget Briony's novel for a moment and look at the whole storyworld. Once you strip away the fantasy near-reconciliation in the Balham flat, what does the real Briony actually *do* to make atonement? She writes a novel, eventually, that will be published only after her death and after the death of the real rapist. That is all. Is that enough?

In any event, how reliable is her novel? Part 1 is explicitly about theory of mind and first- and third-person attribution. Specifically, it is about the development of the thirteen-year-old Briony's theory of mind and her growing ability to attribute mental states to others. There are many explicit references to this issue:

Was everyone else really as alive as she was? . . . If the answer was yes, then the world, the social world, was unbearably complicated, with two billion voices, and everyone's thoughts striving in equal importance and everyone's claim on life as intense, and everyone thinking they were unique, when no one was. (36)

Within two paragraphs, Briony's novel refers to "three points of view" (40), "separate minds" (40), "other minds" (40), "different minds" (40), and again to "other minds" (40). Unfortunately, though, the catastrophe results from a misattribution by Briony to Robbie. She thinks that Robbie wants to attack Cecilia when in fact he loves her.

It is therefore deeply ironic that, despite Briony's novel being in part about this issue, its narration is based on an illicit use of theory of mind and attribution. There is no way in which the adult Briony, many years later, can know in such detail what was going on in the consciousnesses of Robbie and Cecilia. Simply put, Briony makes it up. Obviously, Briony is entitled, and even required, to speculate about the minds of others and to try to understand the consequences of her actions within their minds. Such attempted mind reading is commendable. But what makes these attributions illicit is her presentation of them in her novel as the world-creating and therefore unchallengeable statements of an omniscient narrator of a heterodiegetic novel. It was Briony's decision to write a heterodiegetic rather than a homodiegetic novel. To consider the force of this argument, imagine how different Briony's novel would have been if it had been a homodiegetic one explicitly narrated by Briony as a character-narrator. Significantly, the novelist Briony acknowledges in the text of her novel the fallibility of her adult first-person attribution of states of mind to her younger self. She admits that her account will "refine itself over the years. She was to concede that she may have attributed more deliberation than was feasible to her thirteen-year-old self" (40). "She knew . . . that it was not the long-ago morning she was recalling so much as her subsequent accounts of it" (41). However, the novelist Briony pointedly refuses to draw attention to the unreality of her third-person attribution to Robbie and Cecilia.

The central question posed by the novel is, What is the relationship between the storyworld created by Briony's novel and the whole storyworld? A series of events took place in the latter, but the relationship between these events and the accounts of them in Briony's novel remains unclear. Some elements in the Briony text we discover to be untrue, but what about the others? It does not help that the epilogue, the only glimpse of the whole storyworld apart from her novel, is written by Briony as well and not by a genuinely disinterested heterodiegetic narrator. So we never get an unmediated view of the whole storyworld. Of course, this is true of *all* first-person narratives. The difference is that we usually know this; we do not know it during a first reading of Briony's novel. So, the concealment of the unreliability in Briony's novel causes a kind of *double* unreliability. In any event, like all storyworlds, the Briony novel is an aspectual world. That is, the events in it are viewed under certain aspects and not others. As the storyworld is aspectual, then Briony's novel, even if it was generally factually accurate, would be an accurate transcription of *Briony's* storyworld only.

In fact, a close reading of the text of her novel reveals that it contains several indicators of unreliability and pointed reminders to take epistemological and ontological care when drawing conclusions from it. I referred above to her misrepresentation of young Briony's thought processes. In the context of the most obvious indicator, the fabricated climax, Briony makes it explicit that she is not writing a realistic novel. She asks, in explanation of her fantasy ending: "Who would want to believe that [that is, the early deaths of the lovers] except in the service of the bleakest realism?" (371). It is easy to lose sight of the importance of her question in the understandable desire of readers to recuperate Briony's narrative as a realistic and generally reliable account of the events in the whole storyworld. But it is worth underscoring the point that Briony is admitting that she has not written her novel in the service of realism.

In addition, it is revealed in the epilogue that the Briony novel has gone through many drafts. This hardly suggests that the final draft is a transparent and unmediated view of events. While Briony is musing on the various drafts of her novel, she refers to the one that we read (dated March 1999) as the *latest* draft (369). She then states: "It is only in this *last version* that my lovers end well" (370). Generally, the use of the words *draft* and *version* does not give much confidence that the novel that we read is a definitive and unproblematically accurate account. Would there have been further drafts if she had been well enough to complete them? More specifically, she is explicitly saying that this latest version is *less* accurate than previous drafts. And there are other indicators of the provisional, contingent, and arbitrary nature of Briony's storyworld, its *constructedness*. The "Robbie" of part 1 becomes "Turner" in part 2. The difference in perspective is significant. It draws attention to the fact that, like all individuals, Robbie is aspectually presented. He differs depending on the perspective from which he is viewed and so a complete picture is never possible. Finally, the epilogue draws attention to the various, admittedly minor, errors of fact in the draft of the novel that are corrected by a retired soldier. If she gets the small things wrong, why should we believe that she gets the larger things right?

James Phelan has pointed out that the following passage can be seen as "marking the seam between history and fiction":

She left the café, and as she walked along the Common she felt the distance widen between her and another self, no less real, who was walking back towards the hospital. Perhaps the Briony who was walking in the direction of Balham was the imagined or ghostly persona. This unreal feeling was heightened when, after half an hour, she reached another High Street, more or less the same as the one she had left behind. (329)

As Phelan (2005) says, "The historical Briony returns to the hospital while her ghostly persona continues her wish-fulfilling journey to Cecilia and Robbie" (334). The passage is reminiscent of the one in *The Third Policemen* quoted earlier when the narrator is killed by an exploding bomb and does not realize it. Both resemble those fantasy film sequences in which characters split in two and one character image remains while the other floats off in a ghostlike way. Both passages mark the boundary between what Phelan (2005) calls "different ontological levels" (333): in this case between the representation of events in Briony's novel that are based on events in the whole storyworld and those that are simply based on Briony's wish fulfillment. However, it is significant that Phelan refers to the latter boundary as marking the seam between *history* and fiction. As I hope to have shown, to refer to Briony's novel up until the fantasy meeting as *history* is to underestimate the epistemological, ontological, and discursive difficulties that are present in the *whole* text of Briony's novel.

As an example of these epistemological and ontological difficulties, it is worth bearing in mind, when attributing mental states to the character of Robbie, that there are in fact several Robbies:

Robbie 1 is the Robbie of the country house section. Here, Briony had some contact with him during the events described in that section and so her account of his actions, thoughts, and feelings has a reasonable basis. The attributions of mental states to Robbie 1 by Briony the narrator are superficially plausible and coherent and are apparently realistic. However, they are still colored by her aspectual storyworld view, and should be treated carefully. Ultimately, Briony does not know about his mental functioning at anything like the level of detail contained in part 1.

Robbie 2 is the "Turner" of the Dunkirk section. Here, assuming that all the events described actually occurred, Briony will have had no direct experience of them, so her presentation of Robbie's mind will be even more speculative than for Robbie 1. But, in any event, how would Briony know about the events in part 2? True, she has the letters that Robbie sent to Cecilia, and she can use these for general background, but the events in part 2 take place after Robbie sent his last letter. And, as I said,

Briony explicitly draws attention to the factual errors contained in this section.

Robbie 3 is the one we meet in the Balham flat. This Robbie never existed. He was dead before this scene could ever take place.

Robbie 4 is the real Robbie: the one who exists outside of Briony's novel and who the reader never has direct access to. This is the one who, we are told in the epilogue, died at Dunkirk.

And there are others. As Briony states that the novel that we read has gone through several drafts, this means that there will have been a Robbie 5 (for example, the one who is described in Briony's novella—the first draft of the novel), a Robbie 6, and so on.

To reinforce the point, let us look at the number of Brionys who are present specifically at the point when we are reading Cyril Connolly's comments on Briony's novella (311–15):

1. The narrator of Briony's novel;
2. The nurse who is the character within Briony's novel and who is reading Connelly's commentary;
3. The narrator of Briony's novella;
4. The child 1 who is the character in Briony's novella;
5. The child 2 who is the character in part 1 of Briony's novel and who readers will have in mind while they read about the novella; and
6. The child 3 who exists outside of Briony's novel and the novella.

The complex entanglement of both epistemological and ontological concerns raised by the various relationships between all of the Robbies and all of the Brionys bears out the view that epistemology and ontology cannot be separated from each other. For epistemological and also for ontological reasons, the reader can, in most cases, never know for sure the true relationship between the various Robbies and the various Brionys. We know that Robbie 3 lives longer than Robbie 4, but not whether Robbie 4 actually had the thoughts that are attributed to Robbies

1, 2, and 3. The same is true of the relationships between the real Brionys (1 and 6) and the fictionalized Brionys (2 to 5). So the challenge for the reader is to find a way of reconciling all of the Robbie selves and all the Briony selves. In the light of these dilemmas, I doubt that it can be said that the umbrella terms *Robbie* or *Briony* represent single continuing consciousnesses, or stable, coherent selves.

When I read critical commentary on McEwan's novel that involves generalizations about Robbie's or Briony's characterization, I find myself asking, Which Robbie, which Briony are you talking about? Perhaps the most postmodern aspect of the novel is the way that it appears so successfully to seduce its commentators into forgetting its postmodernity. It is easy, when not taking care, to drift into a view of the epilogue as simply a postmodern add-on and to forget that its purpose is to transform completely our reading of parts 1–3 of McEwan's novel. I have consistently referred to the bulk of the novel as *Briony's novel* in order to remind readers that it is only a *version* of events, and an admittedly unreliable one at that. The epilogue fundamentally destabilizes what appears to be an epistemologically and ontologically secure foundation. However, it is tempting, even when rereading the novel, not to maintain the vigilance required to keep these instabilities in mind.

The first part of *Atonement* describes how Briony's mind is opening up. Her mind is shown acquiring some knowledge of the existence of other minds, although what knowledge she has does not prevent her from fatally misreading Cecilia's and Robbie's minds. Many years later, in the epilogue, she realizes that, because of her progressive dementia, "my brain, my mind, is closing down" (354). The deeply disturbing final scene of *Success* contains Gregory's description of how his mind is also closing down. In *The Third Policeman*, the narrator's mind shuts down too as he starts to reexperience the same events over and over again without realizing it. This is a depressingly Beckettian end to the chronological review of the history of narrative in the British Isles that is contained in this volume. But, given the nature of the last period to be reviewed, from the Second World War to the present day, it was hardly to be expected, I suppose, that a discussion of some of the ontologies of consciousness contained in it would end on an exhilarating, life-affirming high note.

Notes

1. But see David Herman's contribution to this volume for a contrasting account of modernist narratives.

2. For more on theory of mind and the novel, see Zunshine (2006).

References

Abbott, H. Porter. 1996. *Beckett Writing Beckett: The Author in the Autograph.* Ithaca: Cornell University Press.

Amis, Martin. 2004 [1978]. *Success.* London: Vintage.

Fludernik, Monika. 1996. *Towards a "Natural" Narratology.* London: Routledge.

Lodge, David. 1981. "Modernism, Antimodernism, Postmodernism." In *Working with Structuralism*, 3–16. London: Routledge.

McEwan, Ian. 2001. *Atonement.* London: Vintage.

McHale, Brian. 1987. *Postmodernist Fiction.* New York: Methuen.

———. 1992. *Constructing Postmodernism.* London: Routledge.

———. 2005. "Postmodern Narrative." In *Routledge Encyclopedia of Narrative Theory*, ed. David Herman, Manfred Jahn, and Marie-Laure Ryan, 456–60. London: Routledge.

O'Brien, Flann. 1988 [1967]. *The Third Policeman.* London: Paladin.

Palmer, Alan. 2004. *Fictional Minds.* Lincoln: University of Nebraska Press.

———. 2010. *Social Minds in the Novel.* Columbus: Ohio State University Press.

Phelan, James. 2005. "Narrative Judgments and the Rhetorical Theory of Narrative: Ian McEwan's *Atonement*." In *A Companion to Narrative Theory*, ed. James Phelan and Peter J. Rabinowitz, 322–36. Oxford: Blackwell.

Richardson, Brian. 2006. *Unnatural Voices: Extreme Narration in Modern and Contemporary Fiction.* Columbus: Ohio State University Press.

Ryan, Marie-Laure. 1991. *Possible Worlds, Artificial Intelligence, and Narrative Theory.* Bloomington: Indiana University Press.

Waugh, Evelyn. 1964 [1952]. *Men at Arms.* Harmondsworth: Penguin.

Zunshine, Lisa. 2006. *Why We Read Fiction: Theory of Mind and the Novel.* Columbus: Ohio State University Press.

Contributors

Elizabeth Bradburn is associate professor of English at Western Michigan University, specializing in seventeenth-century British literature. She has published articles on cognitive theory, John Milton, and George Meredith. Her essay on Shakespeare and Cognition will appear in the forthcoming *Oxford Handbook to Shakespeare*.

Nicholas Dames is Theodore Kahan Associate Professor in the Humanities at Columbia University. He is the author of *Amnesiac Selves: Nostalgia, Forgetting, and British Fiction, 1810–1870* (2001) and *The Physiology of the Novel: Reading, Neural Science, and the Form of Victorian Fiction* (2007). He is currently working on a history of the chapter, from manuscript bibles to the modern novel.

Monika Fludernik is professor of English at the University of Freiburg in Germany. Her publications include *The Fictions of Language and the Languages of Fiction* (1993), *Towards a "Natural" Narratology* (1996), and *An Introduction to Narratology* (2009). She has edited several special issues of journals as well as a number of collections of essays, including *Postclassical Narratology: Approaches and Analyses* (2010, with Jan Alber); *In the Grip of the Law: Prisons, Trials, and the Space Between* (2004, with Greta Olson); *Diaspora and Multiculturalism* (2003); and *Hybridity and Postcolonialism* (1998).

F. Elizabeth Hart is associate professor of English at the University of Connecticut, Storrs. She has authored essays on cognitive approaches to literature and culture in *Mosaic, Philosophy and Literature,* and *Configurations* and recently coedited (with theater historian Bruce McConachie) a volume on *Performance and Cognition: Theatre Studies and the Cognitive Turn* (2006). Her essays on

Shakespeare have appeared in *Shakespeare Quarterly* and *Studies in English Literature*, and she is currently working on a book about the character sketch in seventeenth-century English literature.

David Herman teaches in the Department of English at Ohio State University. The editor of the Frontiers of Narrative book series as well as the new journal *Storyworlds* (also published by the University of Nebraska Press), he is the author, editor, or co-editor of a number of studies in the field, including *Story Logic* (2002), *Narrative Theory and the Cognitive Sciences* (2003), the *Routledge Encyclopedia of Narrative Theory* (coedited with Manfred Jahn and Marie-Laure Ryan, 2005), *The Cambridge Companion to Narrative* (2007), and *Basic Elements of Narrative* (2009).

Leslie Lockett is an assistant professor in the Department of English at Ohio State University, where she specializes in Old English and Medieval Latin literature. Her forthcoming book, *Anglo-Saxon Psychologies in the Vernacular and Latin Traditions*, explores the relationships among conflicting concepts of mind that coexisted in Anglo-Saxon England. She is currently working on a book that traces the history of Latin retrograde verse (that is, poems that can be read both backward and forward) from the classical era through the early modern period.

Alan Palmer is an independent scholar living in London. His first book, *Fictional Minds* (2004), was a cowinner of the MLA Prize for Independent Scholars and also a cowinner of the Perkins Prize (awarded by the Society for the Study of Narrative Literature). His second book, *Social Minds in the Novel*, was published by the Ohio State University Press in 2010. His articles have been published in the journals *Narrative*, *Semiotica*, and *Style*, and he has contributed chapters to a number of edited volumes. He is an honorary research fellow at the Department of Linguistics and English Language, Lancaster University.

David Vallins is a professor in the Graduate School of Letters at Hiroshima University and has taught at universities in Britain and Hong Kong. He is the author of *Coleridge and the Psychology of Romanticism* (2000) and the editor of *Coleridge's Writings: On the Sublime* (2003). His essays on Akenside, Coleridge, Mary Shelley, Emerson, Virginia Woolf, and other authors have appeared in a number of books and journals, including *Journal of the History of Ideas*, ELH, *Modern Philology*, *Prose Studies*, and *Symbiosis*.

Lisa Zunshine is Bush-Holbrook Professor of English at the University of Kentucky, Lexington. She is the author and editor of nine books, including *Bastards and Foundlings: Illegitimacy in Eighteenth-Century England* (2005), *Why We Read Fiction: Theory of Mind and the Novel* (2006), *Strange Concepts and the Stories They Make Possible: Cognition, Culture, Narrative* (2008), *Acting Theory and the English Stage, 1700–1830* (2009), and *Introduction to Cognitive Cultural Studies* (2010).

Index

Abbott, H. Porter, 4, 266, 276
Addison, Joseph: *The Spectator*, 162
Aers, David, 97n11
affect. *See* Austen, Jane; emotion;
  empathy; Radcliffe, Ann; sublime; Wordsworth, William
affordances, 253–54, 256–66,
  268n11. *See also* consciousness;
  consciousness representation;
  post-Cartesian models of mind;
  postcognitivism
Alber, Jan, 11, 30
allegory, 107, 137, 139–43. *See also*
  landscapes; metaphor
Amis, Kingsley, 276
Amis, Martin: *Success*, 273, 282–86,
  288, 296
Amodio, Mark C., 97n11
Andrew, Donna T., 176
Anna Karenina (Tolstoi), 174
antimodernism. *See* postmodern
  fiction; Waugh, Evelyn
Aristotle, 236
associationist psychology, 196–97,
  211n12, 220, 227
Atonement (McEwan), 273, 274, 279,
  288–97
attention. *See* consciousness
attribution theory. *See* consciousness representation
Austen, Jane: *Emma*, 227; and
  emotion, 189–90, 210n5; introspection in work of, 226; and
  landscapes, 187, 209, 209n3;
  Mansfield Park, 209n3; *Northanger
  Abbey*, 189–90, 210n6, 227; *Persuasion*, 189, 209n3, 210nn4–5;
  Pride and Prejudice, 226, 227, 228–
  29, 233

authentication. *See* consciousness
  representation
authorial narrative situation. *See*
  consciousness representation
autobiographical self. *See*
  consciousness
autobiography, 230

Bachelard, Gaston, 187, 192, 209n2,
  211n9
Bain, Alexander, 219, 221, 222
Baisch, Martin, 97n11
Bakhtin, M. M., 284
Banfield, Ann, 3, 7, 31n7, 71
Barbauld, Anna Laetitia: *Hymns in
  Prose for Children*, 171–72, 175, 184
Baron-Cohen, Simon, 121, 165
Bartsch, Anne, 79, 96n6
Beckett, Samuel: *Murphy*, 256,
  267n8
The Beggar Girl and Her Benefactors
  (Bennett), 161–62
behaviorism, 22, 35n20, 256
Behn, Aphra: *Oroonoko*, 133, 145–
  50, 156
Beja, Morris, 266
Bender, John, 183
Bennett, Anna Maria: *The Beggar
  Girl and Her Benefactors*, 161–62
Benveniste, Emile, 32n7
Beowulf, 49, 52–53, 63–64
Bering, Jesse M., 165
The Blazing World (Cavendish), 104,
  133, 137, 143–45, 146, 149
blending theory. *See* conceptual
  blends; conceptual metaphor
  theory
Boethius, 51, 64, 103, 126n2
Boring, Edwin, 237n2

Botar, Oliver A. I., 268n12
Boyd, Brian, 12
Bradburn, Elizabeth, 20, 21, 209n1
brain. *See* consciousness
Bridget Jones (Fielding), 174
Brockmeier, Jens, 32n9
Brontë, Charlotte, 237n6; *Villette*, 229–30
Bruner, Jerome, 17, 35n18
Bunyan, John: *Pilgrim's Progress*, 133, 137, 139–43
Burke, Edmund, 188, 210n8
Burney, Frances: *Cecilia*, 179
Butte, George, 4, 15, 168

Capgrave, John: *The Life of Saint Katharine*, 90–92
cardiocentric models of mind. *See* consciousness
Cartesianism. *See* consciousness representation; Exceptionality Thesis; post-Cartesian models of mind
Cavallo, Guglielmo, 112
Cavendish, Margaret: *The Blazing World*, 104, 133, 137, 143–45, 146, 149
Caygill, Howard, 211n9
Cecilia (Burney), 179
cephalocentric models of mind. *See* consciousness; emotion
Chafe, Wallace, 72, 128n20
Chalmers, David J., 253, 256
characterization. *See* consciousness representation
Charlton, Kenneth, 108–9, 128nn13–14
Chartier, Roger, 111–12, 128n19
Chaucer, Geoffrey, 81–83, 85–86, 96n7, 97n9
children's narratives (stories written for children), 170, 171–72, 178
The Citizen of the World (Goldsmith), 161, 180
Clarissa (Richardson), 162, 167, 174
Clark, Andy, 22, 35n19, 253, 256, 257, 260, 265
Clark, Edwin, 237n2

cognitive approaches to literature: and evolved cognitive adaptations, 167–68, 175; relation of, to historicist approaches, 163–64, 175–80, 181, 183; and unidirectional borrowing from cognitive science, 34n12. *See also* conceptual metaphor theory; consciousness; consciousness representation; Exceptionality Thesis; mind as theme
cognitive linguistics. *See* conceptual blends; conceptual metaphor theory; mental spaces; text worlds
cognitive maps, 268n12
cognitive psychology, 8, 114, 176, 255
cognitive science, 255–56. *See also* cognitive approaches to literature; consciousness
cognitivism, 256. *See also* post-Cartesian models of mind; postcognitivism
Cohn, Dorrit, 1, 3, 4, 5–6, 7–8, 9, 23, 33n10, 35n21, 69, 247
Cole, Michael, 264
Coleridge, Samuel Taylor, 191, 192, 195–96, 198, 211n10
collective consciousness. *See* consciousness representation; intermental thought
Collins, Wilkie: *The Woman in White*, 215–17, 219, 222
conceptual blends, 44, 54–55, 56, 128n21. *See also* conceptual metaphor theory
conceptual metaphor theory: and a community's standards of literalness, 55–59; and embodied experience, 133–34, 145; and embodied realism, 44, 53–59, 63–64, 66n10; and folk psychology, 134; and genre, 137–38; limits of, vis-à-vis Old English narratives, 19, 43–44, 53–59, 64n2, 65n10; and literary metaphors, 135–37, 154–55; and modes

of narration, 138–39, 147–50; and narrative structure, 137–39; and seventeenth-century narratives, 20, 133, 135–38, 139–56. *See also* conceptual blends; consciousness representation; metaphor; metonymy; transcultural psychiatry

consciousness: and attention, 222, 224–25; and the autobiographical self, 218–19, 224–25, 226, 230; and the brain, 47, 103, 109–11, 126n1, 218; and cardiocentric models of mind, 46–52, 126n4; and cephalocentric models of mind, 58, 65n5, 103–4, 119–21, 126, 126nn3–4; changing conceptions of the scope of, 30n1, 73–74, 103, 126n1, 221–22; and culture, 109, 268n13; and evolved cognitive adaptations, 109, 164, 165, 167, 169, 175, 180; and individuality, 95, 103; and literacy skills, 108, 109–12, 115, 127n7, 128n17; materialist theories of, 220–21, 222, 225–26, 232–33; and mind-body dualism, 44, 45–46, 58, 59–62, 63–64, 253–54, 256–57, 268n13; of nonhuman animals, 144, 265; nonverbal elements of, 73, 74, 94; and perception, 257; and social experience, 15–18, 109, 112, 163–64, 165–84, 254; thematization of, in *Paradise Lost*, 153–55; theories of, and Victorian novelists, 225–26, 236n1, 237nn5–7. *See also* affordances; behaviorism; cognitive approaches to literature; cognitive psychology; cognitivism; consciousness representation; continuing-consciousness frame; core consciousness; distributed intelligence; ecological validity; emotion; empathy; landscapes; mass consciousness; memory; mental disability; mind

as theme; neuroscience; nonconscious; post-Cartesian models of mind; postcognitivism; self-consciousness; sensation novel; sensorimotor coupling; Shakespeare, William; silent reading; somatization; soul; unconscious; unreliability

consciousness representation: and action loops, 22, 260–63; and advent of the novel, 132, 147–150, 175; and attribution theory, 22–23, 34n15, 273–74, 277–97; and authentication (Doležel), 10, 33n10, 246, 266n1; and authorial vs. figural narrative situations, 245–47, 262–63, 267n5; and Cartesianism, 249, 253–56, 258, 261, 267n4; and characterization, 105–6, 122, 125–26, 177–80, 236; and collective or group minds, 90–92, 118; and counterfactual constructions, 28; diachronic approaches to, 2–3, 4, 7, 23–30, 35n23, 74, 95–96, 118–19, 132, 149, 170–71, 268n13; and direct thought (direct discourse), 5–6, 31n7, 69, 71–72, 77–79, 92–93, 94, 254–55; and drama, 75, 94, 104, 105–6, 121, 126n6, 157n7, 183, 185n8; and dream narratives, 141–42, 190–91; and embodied action, 11, 15–16, 19, 44, 75–76, 104, 118, 174, 233–34, 253–54, 258–66; and enactivist models of mind, 22, 237n3, 249–50, 253–54, 256–66; and ethical judgments, 233–34, 290; and false free indirect style, 228–29; and free indirect thought (free indirect discourse), 5–6, 31n7, 69, 87–89, 95, 227, 234, 237n5, 245, 254–55; and gesture, 75–76; as grounded in conceptions of the mind, 9–10, 30n3, 32n8, 103, 126nn3–4, 274; and heterodiegetic vs. homodiegetic narration, 147–48, 274, 275, 279, 287, 289; and hy-

evolutionary psychology, 4, 8, 168–69, 175

Exceptionality Thesis: Accessibility argument against, 15–23, 34n11, 35n18, 35n20; and accounts of folk psychology, 8, 11, 12–16, 17–18, 19–20, 21, 32n9, 34nn13–14, 34nn16–17; and "anti-mimetic" narratives, 11, 33n11; and Cartesian dualism, 8–11, 32n8; and the concept of "person," 11; definition of, 8; and the distinction between fiction and nonfiction, 9–10, 12, 15, 17, 18–23, 31n5, 31n7, 33n10; Mediation argument against, 12–15, 18–23, 33n10; and modernist narratives, 35n21; and potential trivialization of fiction, 12. *See also* consciousness representation; post-Cartesian models of mind; postcognitivism

experiencer, 156n5

extended mind. *See* distributed intelligence; post-Cartesian models of mind; postcognitivism

Fabrega, Horacio, Jr., 60–61

faculty psychology, 220, 227, 234

The Faerie Queene (Spenser), 105, 106–7, 123–25, 127n8

Fairchild, H. N., 211n12

false free indirect style. *See* consciousness representation

Fauconnier, Giles, 113, 128n21

Fechner, Gustav, 222

Ferguson, Frances, 237n5

Fernighough, Anne, 253

fictional autobiography, 230

fiction vs. nonfiction. *See* Exceptionality Thesis

Fielding, Helen: *Bridget Jones*, 174

Fielding, Henry: *Tom Jones*, 25–27, 29, 173

Fielding, Sarah: *The History of Ophelia*, 161

figural narrative situation. *See* consciousness representation

Flaubert, Gustave, 245

Fleischman, Suzanne, 97n10

Fludernik, Monika, 3, 19–20, 31n7, 36n23, 55, 69, 72, 89, 95n1, 97n9, 126n5, 149, 156n5, 157n7, 276

fMRI, 221. *See also* consciousness; neuroscience

focalization, 35n22, 247, 284

folk psychology. *See* conceptual metaphor theory; ethnopsychology; Exceptionality Thesis

Fowler, Roger, 244

Fox, Adam, 108, 128n14, 128n19

framed narrative, 107, 124–25

Frankenstein (Shelley), 187, 190–92, 201–8, 212nn17–19

free direct thought. *See* interior monologue

free indirect thought (narrated monologue). *See* consciousness representation; dual-voice hypothesis

Freeman, Donald C., 55

Freeman, Margaret H., 55

Freeman, Walter, 109

Freud, Sigmund, 184n3, 190, 209. *See also* psychoanalysis; unconscious

Gallagher, Shaun, 15, 16, 34n14, 256

Gallese, Vittorio, 121

Gangopadhay, Nivedita, 257

Gavins, Joanna, 113

Gerrig, Richard, 113

gestalt theory, 114, 128n21

gesture. *See* consciousness representation

Gevaert, Caroline, 47, 65n10

Gibson, J. J., 257

Gillett, Grant, 256

Godden, Malcolm, 45–46, 65n5

Goldsmith, Oliver: *The Citizen of the World*, 161, 180

Gorman, David, 8

Gothic novel, 69, 89, 188, 191, 209, 230

Grady, Hugh, 97n11

Greene, Robert: *Pandosto*, 105, 120, 123, 127n8

Grenby, Matthew O., 178, 184n7
Grice, Paul, 281
Grob, Alan, 211n13, 212n14
group mind. *See* consciousness
   representation; intermental
   thought; mass consciousness
Gurwitsch, Aaron, 15

Hamburger, Käte, 7–8, 9, 32n7
Hamilton, Paul, 211n13
Hamlet (Shakespeare), 123, 126n1,
   126n6
Hanson, Elizabeth, 97n11
Harré, Rom, 256
Harris, Paul L., 12
Hart, F. Elizabeth, 20, 31n6, 184n6
Hartley, David, 194, 196–97, 211n12
Haufe, Hendrikje, 97n11
Haywood, Eliza: *Jemmy and Jenny*
   Jessamy, 179–80
Hebb, Donald, 109
Heliodorus: *The Ethiopian Story*, 115–
   18, 119, 129n23, 172–75, 184n6
The Helpmate (Sinclair), 245–46
Herman, David, 14, 17, 22, 31n6,
   32n9, 35n20, 35n22, 36n24, 113,
   114–15, 184n2, 237n3, 256–57,
   268n9, 297n1
Herwig, Malte, 268n12
heterodiegetic narration. *See* con-
   sciousness representation
Hipsky, Marty, 266
historical pragmatics, 3, 30n2
The History of Ophelia (Fielding), 161
Hobson, Peter, 12, 16
Hogan, Patrick Colm, 3, 4, 55, 96n3
homodiegetic narration. *See* con-
   sciousness representation
Hunter, J. Paul, 175
Hurley, Susan, 257, 264
Hutchins, Edwin, 256, 264
Hutto, Daniel D., 16, 17, 34n14
hydraulic model of mind. *See* consciousness representation
Hymns in Prose for Children (Bar-
   bauld), 171–72, 175, 184

ideology. *See* consciousness
   representation

immersion, 114–15, 120–21. *See also*
   storyworlds
indirect thought (psychonarration). *See* consciousness
   representation
interior monologue (free direct
   thought), 7, 69, 73, 79, 247, 248,
   261, 275, 282. *See also* consciousness representation; stream of
   consciousness
intermental thought, 90, 118, 119,
   281. *See also* consciousness representation; mass consciousness
intersubjectivity. *See* consciousness representation; intermental thought
introspection. *See* Austen, Jane;
   consciousness representation
inward turn. *See* consciousness
   representation; Woolf, Virginia
Iversen, Stefan, 11

Jacyna, L. S., 237n2
Jäger, Christoph, 79, 96n6
Jahn, Manfred, 267n5
James, Henry, 243, 266n2
Jemmy and Jenny Jessamy (Haywood),
   179–80
Johnson, Mark, 44, 55, 56, 63, 133–
   34, 256
Johnstone, Barbara, 36n24
Jones, Ellen Carol, 266
Joyce, James: *A Portrait of the Artist*
   as a Young Man, 243–44, 245, 247,
   258–60; *Ulysses*, 73, 245, 247–48.
   See also Woolf, Virginia
Jucker, Andreas H., 3, 30n2

Kahler, Erich, 250
Kant, Immanuel, 175, 188, 192, 198,
   199, 201, 202, 204, 206, 210n8,
   211n13, 212n16, 233
Kaplan, Sydney Janet, 251, 267n6
Kaufmann, Walter, 185n8
Kay, Christian J., 58
Keen, Suzanne, 96
Kern, Stephen, 30n2, 266
Kirmayer, Laurence J., 60, 61, 62

Exceptionality Thesis; mind as theme

mind as theme, 9–10, 30n3, 32n8, 255, 267n8, 274. *See also* consciousness representation

mind-body dualism. *See* consciousness

mind reading. *See* consciousness representation; Theory of Mind

mindscape, 107

mind-style, 244–45, 248, 267n3

Mize, Britt, 43

"Modern Fiction" (Woolf), 250–51, 253, 255

modernist novel, 243–56, 257–66, 275–77, 282, 284, 297n1. *See also* Exceptionality Thesis; postmodern fiction; reflector; Sinclair, May; Woolf, Virginia

Moretti, Franco, 268n13

Mrs Dalloway (Woolf), 167, 243, 255, 260–63, 268n8

Murphy (Beckett), 256, 267n8

The Mysteries of Udolpho (Radcliffe), 210n8

narrated monologue (free indirect thought). *See* consciousness representation; dual-voice hypothesis

narratee, 84, 284

narration. *See* conceptual metaphor theory; consciousness representation

narrative understanding. *See* contextual frames; continuing-consciousness frame; immersion; mental spaces; possible worlds; storyworlds; text worlds

narrative universals, 3

narrative voice, 236

narrativity, 184

neorealism. *See* postmodern fiction; Waugh, Evelyn

Nettle, Daniel, 165–66, 167, 184n2, 184n4

neuroscience, 109, 110, 129n26, 218, 221, 255. *See also* consciousness; fMRI

New Arcadia (The Countess of Pembroke's Arcadia) (Sidney), 105, 106, 119–20, 122–23, 127n8

Newcomb, Lori Humphrey, 127n9

Nichols, Shaun, 34n14

Nielsen, Henrik Skov, 11, 30

nonconscious, 223, 231–35

nonhuman animals. *See* consciousness

non-Western psychologies. *See* somatization; transcultural psychiatry

Northanger Abbey (Austen), 189–90, 210n6, 227

novel. *See* consciousness representation; Gothic novel; modernist novel; postmodern fiction; sensation novel; sentimental novel

O'Brien, Flann: *The Third Policeman*, 273, 279, 286–88, 294, 296

Old French, 97n10

Oliphant, Margaret, 216–18

Olson, David, 110–11, 115

On Chesil Beach (McEwan), 25, 26, 28–29

Ong, Walter, 127n7

Oroonoko (Behn), 133, 145–50, 156

Othello (Shakespeare), 157n7

Owen, David, 176

Palmer, Alan, 3–4, 14, 19, 22–23, 30n1, 31n3, 34n15, 35n23, 69, 74, 117, 121, 170, 184n1, 223, 268n9, 278

Pandosto (Greene), 105, 120, 123, 127n8

Paradise Lost (Milton), 133, 135–37, 150–56, 156n1. *See also* consciousness

Pavel, Thomas, 33n10

Perner, Joseph, 35n17

person concept. *See* Exceptionality Thesis

Persuasion (Austen), 189, 209n3, 210nn4–5

Phelan, James, 266, 293–94

phenomenology, 15

philosophy of mind. *See* cognitivism; consciousness; consciousness representation; Exceptionality Thesis; phenomenology; post-Cartesian models of mind; postcognitivism

physiological psychology. *See* consciousness representation

Pilgrim's Progress (Bunyan), 133, 137, 139–43

plot. *See* consciousness representation; emotion

Poovey, Mary, 191

A Portrait of the Artist as a Young Man (Joyce), 243–44, 245, 247, 258–60

possible worlds, 3, 113, 276–77. *See also* contextual frames; mental spaces; storyworlds; text worlds

post-Cartesian models of mind, 249–50, 255–66. *See also* cognitivism; consciousness representation; Exceptionality Thesis; postcognitivism

postcognitivism, 250, 256–58, 264–65, 266, 267n4, 268n10. *See also* cognitivism

postmodern fiction, 237, 273, 275–77, 280–82, 285–86. *See also* modernist novel

Potter, Jonathan, 267n4, 268n10

The Prelude (Wordsworth), 188, 192–201, 211n13

Premack, David, 12–13, 34n13

Pride and Prejudice (Austen), 226, 227, 228–29, 233

Priestly, Joseph, 196, 197

Prince, Gerald, 247

print technology, 104–5, 106–7, 127n7. *See also* consciousness; consciousness representation; literary marketplace

Propp, Vladimir, 236

psychoanalysis, 223, 235

psychologization. *See* somatization

psychology. *See* associationist psychology; cognitive approaches to literature; cognitive psychology; cognitive science; consciousness; consciousness representation; developmental psychology; discursive psychology; ethnopsychology; evolutionary psychology; Exceptionality Thesis; faculty psychology; psychoanalysis; psychophysics

psychonarration (indirect thought). *See* consciousness representation

psychophysics, 222

Pye, Christopher, 97n11

quantitative methods of analysis. *See* consciousness representation; corpus-based approaches

quoted monologue (direct thought). *See* consciousness representation

Radcliffe, Ann: and affect, 191–92, 194, 198–99, 201; and landscapes, 187, 191–92, 194, 198–99, 201, 208; *The Mysteries of Udolpho*, 210n8; *A Sicilian Romance*, 210n8, 211n11

Raitt, Suzanne, 246, 267n6

Rappaport, Herman, 156n1

Ratcliffe, Matthew, 34n14

reading. *See* consciousness; consciousness representation

realist novel. *See* consciousness representation

Reed, Edward, 237n2

reflector, 243, 245, 247, 248, 266n2

Richardson, Brian, 11, 33n11, 276, 289

Richardson, Dorothy, 246, 247, 267n6

Richardson, Samuel, 216; *Clarissa*, 162, 167, 174

Ricks, Christopher, 135

Robinson, Jenefer, 96n2

romance. *See* consciousness representation

Rosch, Eleanor, 222–23, 237n3, 249, 256, 257, 268n11

Rowlands, Mark, 253

Royce, Josiah, 183
Ryan, Marie-Laure, 3, 33n10, 113
Rylance, Rick, 237n4

Said, Edward, 189, 209n3
Salway, Andrew, 36n24
Salzman, Paul, 127n9
Sanders, Eve Rachele, 128n14
Saussure, Ferdinand de, 23
Scheler, Max, 15
Schelling, F. W. J., 195, 199
scriptio continua, 111, 128n18
self-consciousness, 178. *See also*
   consciousness; consciousness
   representation
Semino, Elena, 36n24, 72, 95, 113
sensation novel, 216–18, 229, 235,
   236n1
sensorimotor coupling, 249–50,
   258–66. *See also* consciousness;
   consciousness representation
sentimental discourse, 162
*A Sentimental Journey through France
   and Italy* (Sterne), 161, 165, 168
sentimental novel, 167
Shakespeare, William, 104; *Hamlet*,
   123, 126n1, 126n6; *Othello*, 157n7
Shapiro, James, 126n6
Shelley, Mary: *Frankenstein*, 187,
   190–92, 201–8, 212nn17–19
Shelley, Percy Bysshe, 191
Shen, Dan, 244, 267n3
Short, Michael, 3, 6, 36n24, 71, 72,
   95, 254–55
Shuttleworth, Sally, 237n2, 237n7
A Sicilian Romance (Radcliffe),
   210n8, 211n11
Sidney, Sir Philip: *New Arcadia* (*The
   Countess of Pembroke's Arcadia*),
   105, 106, 119–20, 122–23, 127n8
Sieber, Andrea, 97n11
silent reading, 111–12, 113, 115,
   128n19. *See also* consciousness;
   consciousness representation
simulation theory. *See* consciousness representation; Exception-
   ality Thesis
Sinclair, May, 246–47, 267n6; *The
   Helpmate*, 245–46

Slors, Marc, 12–13, 14, 34n14
The Small House at Allington (Trollope), 228–29
Smith, Adam: *The Theory of Moral
   Sentiments*, 181–82, 183, 184
Smith, André, 60, 61
social class. *See* consciousness
   representation
Sodian, Beate, 34n13
soliloquy, 70, 77, 78, 83, 92–93,
   94, 157n7. *See also* consciousness
   representation
somatization, 59–62
Sorrell, Tom, 33n9
soul, 45–46, 103, 144–45, 224
space in narrative. *See* Austen,
   Jane; consciousness representation; landscapes; Radcliffe, Ann;
   Wordsworth, William
Spearing, Anthony C., 97n11
The Spectator (Addison and Steele),
   162
speech-category approach. *See* con-
   sciousness representation
speech representation. *See* con-
   sciousness representation
Spenser, Edmund: *The Faerie
   Queene*, 105, 106–7, 123–25, 127n8
Spinoza, Baruch, 193, 211n10
Spufford, Margaret, 108–9, 127n9,
   128nn13–14
Stanley, Eric G., 64n2
Stanzel, Franz Karl, 3, 4, 243, 245,
   247, 252, 254
Stawarska, Beata, 34n17
Steele, Richard: *The Spectator*, 162
Sternberg, Meir, 34n12
Sterne, Laurence: *A Sentimental
   Journey through France and Italy*,
   161, 165, 168
Stevens, Scott Manning, 103,
   126nn3–4
Stevenson, Randall, 251, 267n6
Stich, Stephen, 32n9, 34n14
Stiller, James, 184n2
storyworlds, 4, 5, 14, 31n6, 112–15,
   117, 124–26, 265–66, 273, 281, 284,
   289–90, 292. *See also* contextual

Wolf, Maryanne, 128n17
The Woman in White (Collins), 215–17, 219, 222
Wood, James, 36n25
Woodruff, Guy, 12–13, 34n13
Woolf, Virginia, 250–51, 253, 255; "Modern Fiction," 250–51, 253, 255; *Mrs Dalloway*, 167, 243, 255, 260–63, 268n8
Wordsworth, William: and affect, 188, 191, 192–201, 204–6, 207, 208; and landscapes, 188, 191, 192–201, 204–6, 207, 208, 211n10; *The Prelude*, 188, 192–201, 211n13
Wynne, Martin, 72

Zahavi, Dan, 15, 34n14
Zunshine, Lisa, 4, 13, 20–21, 118, 121, 167–68, 297n2
Zwicker, Steven N., 127n10

In the Frontiers of Narrative series:

Useful Fictions
Evolution, Anxiety, and the Origins of Literature
by Michael Austin

Telling Children's Stories
Narrative Theory and Children's Literature
Edited by Mike Cadden

Coincidence and Counterfactuality
Plotting Time and Space in Narrative Fiction
by Hilary P. Dannenberg

The Emergence of Mind
Representations of Consciousness in
Narrative Discourse in English
Edited by David Herman

Story Logic
Problems and Possibilities of Narrative
by David Herman

Handbook of Narrative Analysis
by Luc Herman and Bart Vervaeck

Spaces of the Mind
Narrative and Community in the American West
by Elaine A. Jahner

Talk Fiction
Literature and the Talk Explosion
by Irene Kacandes

The Imagined Moment
Time, Narrative, and Computation
by Inderjeet Mani

Storying Domestic Violence
Constructions and Stereotypes of Abuse
in the Discourse of General Practitioners
by Jarmila Mildorf

Fictional Minds
by Alan Palmer

Narrative Beginnings
Theories and Practices
Edited by Brian Richardson

Narrative across Media
The Languages of Storytelling
Edited by Marie-Laure Ryan

To order or obtain more information on these or other University of Nebraska Press titles, visit www.nebraskapress.unl.edu.

Breinigsville, PA USA
04 March 2011
256918BV00001B/2/P